Latin America–European Union relations in the twenty-first century

Manchester University Press

Latin America–European Union relations in the twenty-first century

Editors: María J. García and
Arantza Gómez Arana

MANCHESTER UNIVERSITY PRESS

Copyright © Manchester University Press 2022

While copyright in the volume as a whole is vested in Manchester University Press, copyright in individual chapters belongs to their respective authors, and no chapter may be reproduced wholly or in part without the express permission in writing of both author and publisher.

Published by Manchester University Press
Oxford Road, Manchester M13 9PL
www.manchesteruniversitypress.co.uk

British Library Cataloguing-in-Publication Data
A catalogue record for this book is available from the British Library

ISBN 978 1 5261 3647 9   hardback
ISBN 978 1 5261 9563 0   paperback

First published 2022
Paperback published 2026

The publisher has no responsibility for the persistence or accuracy of URLs for any external or third-party internet websites referred to in this book, and does not guarantee that any content on such websites is, or will remain, accurate or appropriate.

EU authorised representative for GPSR:
Easy Access System Europe – Mustamäe tee 50,
10621 Tallinn, Estonia
gpsr.requests@easproject.com

Typeset
by New Best-set Typesetters Ltd

Contents

List of tables and figures	*page* vi
Notes on contributors	vii
List of abbreviations	ix
Introduction – Arantza Gómez Arana and María J. García	1
1 Latin American and European Union relations in an interdependent world going through "deglobalisation" – Arantza Gómez Arana	7
2 EU–LAC: a relationship beyond trade: political dialogues between unequal partners – Susanne Gratius	24
3 Interlinkages in EU–Andean Community trade negotiations – Daniel Schade	44
4 The EU–Peru/Colombia Trade Agreement: balancing, accommodation or driver of change? – María J. García	66
5 EU–Mexican relations: adaptation to global trade relations – Roberto Domínguez	94
6 Twenty years of EU–MERCOSUR negotiations: inter-regionalism and the crisis of globalisation – José Antonio Sanahuja and Jorge Damián Rodríguez	117
7 Inter-regionalism beyond the executives: contemporary dynamics of EU–LAC inter-parliamentary relations – Bruno Theodoro Luciano	154
8 The impact of European political dialogue upon Chilean and Mexican domestic policies – Francis Espinoza-Figueroa	172
Conclusion: The more things change the more they stay the same? – María J. García and Arantza Gómez Arana	192
Index	200

List of tables and figures

Tables

2.1	EU–LAC political dialogues	*page* 28
2.2	Political dialogues as part of EU–LAC agreements	36
4.1	Comparison of US and EU trade agreements with Peru and Colombia	73–75
5.1	Negotiation of the modernisation of the GA EU–Mexico	107–108

Figure

2.1	Types of interregionalism by issue, form and partners	35

Notes on contributors

María J. García is a Senior Lecturer in international political economy in the Department of Politics, Languages and International Studies at the University of Bath (UK), and previously held a Marie Curie International Fellowship at the NCRE in New Zealand. Her research focuses on the politics of trade, international competition in trade agreements and the formation of EU trade policy, and has appeared in various journals including the *Journal of Common Market Studies*. She is co-editor of the *Handbook on EU and Trade Policy* (Edward Elgar, 2018). She also participates as a researcher in several Jean Monnet projects, including EUinLAC, which explores EU and members states' policies towards Latin America in the aftermath of Brexit.

Arantza Gómez Arana is a Senior Lecturer in International Relations at Northumbria University (UK). She has previously taught at several Universities and worked as a Research Associate at Glasgow University. She is currently a UACES elected Committee Member (2019–22) and also collaborates with Fundación Carolina. She received her PhD from Glasgow University and has previously published on European Union–Latin America relations, including a monograph on EU–MERCOSUR relations with Manchester University Press (2017).

Susanne Gratius is a full-time Lecturer at the Political Science and International Relations Department, Law Faculty of the Autonomous University of Madrid and an Associated Senior Researcher at CIDOB, Barcelona. In previous years (2005–13) she worked as a senior researcher at the private Spanish think-tank FRIDE and as an Associate Professor at the Department of International Relations at the Universidad Complutense de Madrid. Prior to these positions, Shea researcher at the German Institute for International and Security Affairs in Berlin, at GIGA's Latin American in Hamburg, and the European-Latin American Relations Institute, Madrid. She holds a PhD in Political Science (International Relations) from the University of Hamburg. Her research focuses on EU–Latin American relations, EU/Spain and Latin American foreign policy, Cuba, Venezuela, Brazil and emerging powers.

Roberto Domínguez is Professor of International Relations at Suffolk University in Boston, Massachusetts. He was Jean Monnet fellow at the European University Institute in Florence and Researcher at the European Union Center of Excellence of University of Miami. He holds a doctoral degree from University of Miami. His current research interest is on comparative regional security governance, security governance in Latin America and European Union–Latin American Relations. Currently he is Senior Editor of the upcoming *Encyclopedia of European Union Politics* (Oxford University Press). Professor Dominguez has also contributed as consultant for projects for the European Parliament, the European Commission, Transparency International, and the US Library of Congress.

Francis Espinoza-Figueroa is a faculty member in the School of Journalism, Universidad Católica del Norte.

Bruno Theodoro Luciano is Teaching Fellow in Public Policy and European Studies at the Department of Politics and International Studies, University of Warwick, UK. He has research experience in comparative regionalism, regional integration and inter-regionalism, with a particular focus on the European Union, South American and African regionalisms, as well as on regional parliaments in these regions.

Jorge Damián Rodríguez is assistant researcher and professor of the International Studies Program of the Faculty of Social Sciences at the University of the Republic, Uruguay. Phd student in the PhD Program in Political Sciences and International Relations of the Complutense University of Madrid, Spain. Doctoral fellow of the Carolina Foundation. Bachelor in Political Science (UDELAR) and Master in Political Science (University of Salamanca). Assistant to the Observatory of Regionalism in Latin America and the Caribbean.

José Antonio Sanahuja is PhD. in Political Sciences from the Complutense University, Madrid (Spain) and MA in International Relations by the United Nations University for Peace (Costa Rica). Full Professor of International Relations at the Complutense University of Madrid and the Spanish Diplomatic Academy. Director of the Carolina Foundation, and Special Advisor for Latin America and the Caribbean to the High Representative of the European Union for Foreign Affairs and Security Policy and vice-President of the European Commission, Josep Borrell (*ad honorem*).

Daniel Schade is a Visiting Assistant Professor in the Department of Government at Cornell University. He holds a PhD in International Relations from the London School of Economics and Political Science and has previously worked at the Vienna School of International Studies, Sciences Po Paris, and the Otto-von-Guericke University Magdeburg, Germany.

List of abbreviations

AA	Association Agreement
AC	Andean Community
ACP	Africa, Caribbean, Pacific
AIIB	Asian Infrastructure Investment Bank
ALBA	Alternativaa Bolivariana para las Américas – Bolivarian Alternative for the Americas
ALBA-TCP	Bolivarian Alternative for the Americas / Trade Treaty of the Peoples
ASEAN	Association of South East Asian Nations
BRI	Belt and Road Initiative
BRICs	Brazil, Russia, India, China
CAN	Comunidad Andina – Andean Community
CAP	Common Agricultural Policy
CARICOM	Caribbean Community
CBN	Comité Biregional de Negociaciones – Bi-regional Negotiations Committee
CELAC	Comunidad de Estados de Latinoamerica y Caribe – Latin America and Caribbean Community of States
CETA	Comprehensive Economic and Trade Agreement
CITES	Convention on the International Trade in Endangered Species
COP	Conference of the Parties
COREPER	Committee of Permanent Representatives
CPTPP	Comprehensive and Progressive Agreement for Trans-Pacific Partnership
CUMEX	Consorcio de Universidades Mexicanas – Consortium of Mexican Universities
DAG	Domestic Advisory Group
DG	Directorate-General
DG RELEX	Directorate-General for External Relations

EC	European Commission
EEAS	European External Action Service
EMIFCA	Inter-regional Framework Co-operation Agreement
EP	European Parliament
EU	European Union
FDI	Foreign Direct Investment
FTA	Free Trade Agreement
FTAA	Free Trade Area of the Americas
GA	Global Agreement
GATS	General Agreement on Trade in Services
GATT	General Agreement on Trade and Tariffs
GDP	Gross Domestic Product
GI	Geographic Indications
GPA	Government Procurement Agreement
GSP	Generalised System of Preferences
HE	Higher Education
HLD	High-Level Dialogue
IADB	Inter-American Development Bank
ILO	International Labour Organisation
IMF	International Monetary Fund
LA	Latin America
LAC	Latin America and Caribbean
MERCOSUR	Mercado Común del Sur – Southern Common Market
MGA	Modernised Global Agreement
NAFTA	North American Free Trade Agreement
NGO	Non-governmental Organisation
OAS	Organisation of American States
OECD	Organisation for Economic Cooperation and Development
OIDHACO	Oficina Internacional de Derechos Humanos Acción Colombia – International Office for Human Rights Colombia Action
PDCA	Political Dialogue and Cooperation Agreement
PP	Partido Popular – People's Party
PR	Public Relations
PRI	Partido Revolucionario Institucional – Institutional Revolutionary Party
PSOE	Partido Socialista Obrero Español – Spanish Socialist Workers' Party
SICA	Sistema de Integración Centroamérica – Central American System of Integration
SME	Small- and medium-sized enterprise

SP	Strategic Partnership
TiSA	Trade in Services Agreement
TNI	Transnational Institute
TPP	Trans-Pacific Partnership
TRIPS	Trade-Related Aspects of Intellectual Property Rights
TSD	Trade and Sustainable Development
TTIP	Transatlantic Trade and Investment Partnership
UN	United Nations
UNASUR	Union of South American Nations
UNGASS	United Nations General Assembly Special Session
US	United States
USMCA	US-Mexico-Canada (Free Trade Agreement)
WB	World Bank
WTO	World Trade Organisation

Introduction

Arantza Gómez Arana and María J. García

The international arena has changed dramatically since 2016, mainly due to the austerity measures that followed the financial crisis that materialised in the 2010s in addition to the increase in populism caused by the same measures. This is as well as the significant decrease in the quality of life. This has affected many countries including Europe and some countries in the Americas. Several countries have turned against different aspects of globalisation and multilateralism, returning to some extent to economic protectionism and political and social nationalism. Trump decided to break with the negotiations developed by Obama with the EU on the Transatlantic Trade and Investment Partnership (TTIP) and decided to leave the Trans-Pacific Partnership (TPP) as well as the Paris agreement. Biden has since re-entered the US in the agreement. And China took notice of these changes. Xi discussed, at Davos, the idea of continuing with free market policies with the help of China by filling in the leadership vacuum that the US had created through Trump's isolationism and the domestic problems in the European Union (Nordin and Weissmann 2018).

From a political point of view the impact of the financial crisis added fuel to populist right-wing arguments against migration. Since 2016 many countries have started to face the empowerment of populist parties, politicians or ideologies, either through referendums such as the one on Brexit (June 2016) or through elections as in the US (November 2016). These pro-nationalist and anti-globalisation movements have severely criticised the EU project and in particular the idea of an "Ever Closer Union". Within the EU there is an increase in the popularity of Europhobic parties, and the current political positions of the governments of Poland and Hungary brings in more uncertainty. In Latin America the election of Bolsonaro in 2018 also symbolises a move towards populism that could affect negotiations with other parties such as MERCOSUR or with the European Union. However, in the end agreement between the EU and MERCOSUR was achieved during the presidency of Bolsonaro.

There are other events that have affected Latin American and EU relations that are directly linked to the shift in the balance of power between the North and the South. The redistribution seems to come at the expense of Europe in favour of countries in the Global South with the help of the US (Wade 2011). It seems that Europe's relevance in the international arena as a partner has decreased, according to Washington (Peterson 2016). The rise of emerging economies in countries with large populations and with power projection in their regions became more noticeable at the beginning of the twenty-first century. The co-operation of these emerging economies soon materialised. Brazil, Russia, India and China (BRICs) since 2006 have started a process where they became politically closer as a group, counterbalancing to some extent the political alliances of Western countries. In 2011 South Africa joined them, which adds more validity to the argument of the South counterbalancing the North. But the rise of these leading economies actually surprised Western countries (Prashad 2013) even though, according to the IMF, from 2004 to 2008 developing market economies – mainly those in Asia – grew by a rate of 7.8 per cent. The countries considered to have a higher income grew at a rate of 2.7 per cent. This gap has never been this wide (McGrew 2008). Brazil became the tenth economy at international level by 2005, for example (McGrew 2008). In the case of China there are similarities with the experiences developed in Western countries when they joined multilateral institutions. In the same way that many countries had high levels of growth after the Second World War, China has engaged with globalisation through the Bretton-Woods rules and benefited from them for the last three decades (Rodrik 2011). China, however, has controlled the movement of capital and avoided foreign finance (Rodrik 2011).

At the same time the financial crisis lasted for almost a decade and affected other parts of the world, creating more opportunities for the redistribution of economic power from the North to the South. The rapid redistribution affected economically powerful countries in the world that use the G8 forum (G7 after 2014) including Japan, the US, Canada, Germany, the UK, France, Italy and Russia. According to the IMF, in 2000 the G8 accumulated 72 per cent of the global GDP whilst in 2011 it represented around 53 per cent (Wade 2011). This is a significant decline in power in the North. During the crisis the G20, a forum of 19 countries including Argentina, Brazil, Mexico, the US, Canada, South Africa, Italy, France, the UK, Germany, Russia, Turkey, Saudi Arabia, India, China, Indonesia, South Korea, Japan, Australia and the EU, became significant again. The first summit was in Washington at the end of the Bush administration in 2008 (Prashad 2013). G20 became the key forum where global responses to the financial crisis were discussed and co-ordinated, displacing the G8 forum and proving politically what was already in place at economic level regarding the redistribution of power (McGrew 2008). However, after the financial crisis, the idea of dismantling the G8 in favour of the G20 was put aside (Prashad 2013).

Still, it cannot be denied that, even after the decline of the G20, the redistribution of power in institutional terms has taken place after pressure from the South. The BRICs favoured the reform of the IMF, for example (Prashad 2013). In fact the redistribution of power can be seen in the IMF, where China is now the third country in terms of shareholders, and in Brazil, as well as in countries labelled under "Honorary BRICS" such as Mexico, which have also improved their position (Wade 2011). However, the outcome of the reform of the IMF did not have enough influence to have a candidate from the South as its Executive in 2011 (Prashad 2013).

The near future only brings in a bigger redistribution of power. The predictions for 2040 point to the overpassing of the economies of the G8 (G7 since 2014) by the economies of the BRICs together with the economy of Mexico, placing China at the top of the world's economies. This new scenario is challenging the conceptualisation of a unipolar world where US economic and military power has been unchallenged since the end of the Cold War. The BRICs defend multilateralism and are not in favour of the US hegemony (Prashad 2013). With Brazil and Russia providing natural resources to China and India for the creation of manufactured products, they could overcome the traditional traders at work level, as in the US, Europe and Japan (Prashad 2013). In fact China has become the most important trading partner for Brazil, taking the place that the US held for a long time (Wade 2011). Russia and China are in particular trying to question this vision of a unipolar world but the role of the latter in challenging the US is more significant. In fact it is debatable whether there is any other country other than China truly contesting the US (Peterson 2016). From a security point of view the military power of the US is still unchallenged, but the South China Sea could be an exception to the rule. It is an area where the US potentially cannot exercise its control due to China's resources and political position on the matter (Peterson 2016).

Latin America and the European Union

The EU and Latin America have developed over time a different degree of interdependence at both the political and economic levels. Over the years, and in particular since the membership of the Iberian countries in 1986, the EU has developed relations with Latin America, and the other way round, for both economic and political reasons using different approaches (Gómez Arana 2017). These relations are not even, as the special partnership with

Brazil demonstrates. The trade agreements have been developed with groups of countries, as in the case of MERCOSUR and the Central American Common Market, and with single countries as in the case of Peru and Colombia. The international environment has influenced these agreements, and in particular the role of the US has had an impact Gómez Arana 2015).

However, there are other countries that have engaged with Latin America both in the past and currently. The political influence of Russia during the twentieth century resulted in alliances with some of the countries in the region that still exist in the twenty-first century. The role of China is seen these days as a challenge to what could be interpreted as a decline in the power of the US, creating a new era in international politics (Brand et al. 2015). In 2004 China became a permanent observer of the OAS, and a few years later it became a member of the Inter-American Development Bank in which it invested $350 million (Brand et al. 2015). In 2018 China achieved the status of observer at the Summit of the Americas whereas for the first time the president of the US did not attend it, reflecting a change in the priorities of both countries (Farah and Babineau 2019).

There are also domestic politics in both Latin America and the EU that affect their relations, such as Brexit on one side and the presidency of Bolsonaro and the crisis in Venezuela on the other. However, since 2016 the possibility of further developing their interdependence could become a desired outcome for these countries in order to overcome the decline in multilateralism at the international level, and in response to the protectionist and isolationist stances of the US as well as the rise of China. The book was planned with the idea of capturing all of the recent changes at the international level and interpreting how they would affect Latin America and the EU. The book aims to discuss this interdependence in order to facilitate a discussion on how significant these regions have become for each other, as well as in relation to other international actors. With all of this in mind, the chapters discuss EU-Latin America relations and cover the following topics. Gómez Arana develops a discussion on the international context and redistribution of power that seems to be taking place between the South and the North, and the move towards protectionism from 2016 in some countries. Gratius follows this with an analysis of the political and economic relations over time between these regions. She also discusses in depth the type of inter-regionalism that has been developing, touching on economic, political and developmental aspects, concluding that there is a decline in trade flows despite the trade agreements that have developed over time. Schade develops a deep discussion on interlinkages in EU–Andean Community trade negotiations and explains the shift from inter-regionalism to bilateral agreements. His conclusion explains the importance of analysing the general context of EU–LA relations in order to understand the bilateral agreements. García follows up with a discussion of the EU–Peru/Colombia Trade Agreement and explains how the role of the US has had an impact on the agreement, showing again the importance of context in understanding the outcomes of EU–LA relations. Chapter 5 is a discussion of EU–Mexican relations by Domínguez and covers a historical overview of the first agreement with Mexico and how it was upgraded in 2018. Chapter 6 by Sanahuja and Rodríguez discusses in-depth the twenty years of EU–MERCOSUR negotiations within a context where globalisation is in crisis and inter-regionalism is increasing. They highlight how the barriers that prevented the agreement in the past are not fully resolved (as in the agricultural sector) as well as new barriers being added to the agreement such as environmental issues. The last two chapters move away from trade aspects towards political and educational ones. In Chapter 7 Luciano discusses inter-regionalism beyond the executives: contemporary dynamics of EU–LAC inter-parliamentary relations. He explains how the diplomatic aspect of EU–LA relations and in particular the role of inter-parliamentary relations tends to be overlooked, but how in the current circumstances, with the degree of populism in both regions, it might require focusing on again. Last but not least, Espinoza-Figueroa discusses the role of the educational sector and the role of European norms and values, considering domestic policies in Chile and Mexico. Overall this book offers the different points of views of academics using different approaches to the question of how Latin America and the EU have engaged with one another over time, considering the role of both domestic and international politics. It seems clear that the political aspect and economic aspect are interlinked. Since 2016 this has only become even more relevant.

References

All websites last visited 30 September 2021.

Brand, A., McEwen-Fial, S. and Muno, W. (2015). "An 'Authoritarian Nexus'? China's alleged special relationship with autocratic states in Latin America", *European Review of Latin American and Caribbean Studies / Revista Europea de Estudios Latinoamericanos y del Caribe*, 7–28. www.jstor.org/stable/43673489?seq=1#metadata_info_tab_contents.

Farah, D. and Babineau, K. (2019). "Extra-regional actors in Latin America", *PRISM* 8 (1), 96–113. https://cco.ndu.edu/News/Article/1767399/extra-regional-actors-in-latin-america-the-united-states-is-not-the-only-game-i/.

Gómez Arana, A. (2015). "The European Union and the Central American Common Market signs an association agreement: pragmatism versus values?". *European Foreign Affairs Review* 20 1 (2015), 43–64. www.kluwerlawonline.com/abstract.php?area=Journals&id=EERR2015004.

Gómez Arana, A. (2017). *The European Union's Policy towards Mercosur*. Manchester: Manchester University Press.

McGrew, A. (2008). "Globalization and Global Politics", in Baylis, J., Smith, S., and Owens, P. (eds), *The Globalization of World Politics: An Introduction to International Relations*. Oxford: Oxford University Press.

Nordin, A. H. and Weissmann, M. (2018). "Will Trump make China great again? The belt and road initiative and international order", *International Affairs* 94 (2), 231–49. https://academic.oup.com/ia/article/94/2/231/4851910.

Peterson. J. (2016). "Introduction: where things stand and what happens next", in Alcaro, R., Peterson, J. and Greco, E. (eds), *The West and the Global Power Shift: Transatlantic Relations and Global Governance*. London: Springer.

Prashad, V. (2013). "Neoliberalism with Southern characteristics". *The Rise of the BRICS*. Rosa Luxemburg Stiftung, New York Office. www. rosalux-nyc.org/wp-content/files_mf/prashad_brics.pdf.

Rodrik, D. (2011). *The Globalization Paradox: Democracy and the Future of the World Economy*. New York and London: W. W. Norton & Company.

Wade, R. H. (2011). "Emerging world order? From multipolarity to multilateralism in the G20, the World Bank, and the IMF", *Politics & Society* 39 (3), 347–78. https://journals.sagepub.com/doi/pdf/10.1177/0032329211415503.

1

Latin American and European Union relations in an interdependent world going through "deglobalisation"

Arantza Gómez Arana

Introduction

The first two decades of the twenty-first century have seen both significant high and low economic growth, as well as an increased degree of integration (World Trade Organisation and European Union) and de-integration (Brexit and the US–Paris agreement). Until 2007, after the significant negative economic impact of 9/11, the growth in Europe was one of the highest in decades, in particular in countries that traditionally have not been considered the wealthiest, such as Spain and Ireland. However, the Eurocrisis that followed the financial crisis brought about bailouts and austerity measures for many EU countries, including Spain and Ireland. The austerity measures affecting public services among other aspects of the economy, together with the high level of unemployment, created enough discontent among Europeans to attract populist parties. The political discourse of these parties favours a return to the type of nationalistic ideologies that make them incompatible with globalisation and regional integration. In particular they are against the nature of the EU and the goal of an ever-closer union. Large numbers in society point to the already existing and future degree of European integration as the reason for their decline in quality of life in both economic and social terms. This is capitalised on by the populist parties. However, this pro-nationalistic anti-integration agenda is implemented differently at the economic and social levels when the populist parties become electorally successful. Limitations to migration are implemented but economic protectionism is not always fully developed. Even countries with no successful extreme right-wing parties since returning to democracy, such as Spain and Portugal, have recently seen limited success of Vox and Gente respectively. The pandemic seems to have allowed more room for populist ideas. Conspiracy theories around the existence of the virus and anti-vaccine groups became moderately successful during 2020, and extreme right-wing groups have questioned the lockdown measures.

The increase in populist ideas since 2016 in particular has materialised in different ways with the UK voting to leave the EU, Donald Trump becoming the president of the US, and Bolsonaro becoming the president of Brazil. The way that some of these populist governments have interacted with each other is also relevant. Trump seemed to have a confrontational attitude against several actors such as Latin America, the EU and China. This increased the already existent lack of trust, and consequently they are more inclined to diversify their external relations agenda (Santander 2020). According to Santander, both the US and China are trying to take advantage of each other's position in relation to LA countries where politically some of them are naturally closer to one of them. The relations between the EU and Latin America are being affected by all of these events.

Brazil is also part of another relevant trend. The rise of emerging economies in countries with large populations and with power projection in their regions became more noticeable at the beginning of the twenty-first century. The increase of these emerging economies surprised Western countries (Prashad 2013). Brazil became the world's tenth largest economy in 2005 (McGrew 2008). Brazil, Russia, India and China (BRICs) since 2006 have started to discuss political matters as a group. In 2011 South Africa joined them, with the acronym changing to BRICs. Having representation from Africa gave more validity to the aim of the South counterbalancing the North. The prediction was that by 2040 the economies of the BRICs and Mexico together will be superior to those of the G8 economies, with China at the top. This new scenario is challenging, in particular due to the conceptualisation of a unipolar world as the US's economic and military power have been unchallenged since the end of the Cold War. But, the role of China in challenging this unipolarism is significant. There is a debate in which the only one competing against US hegemony is China (Peterson 2016). However, from a security point of view, the military power of the US is still unchallenged, with the exception of the South China Sea (Peterson 2016).

The first two decades of the twenty-first century have seen a redistribution of power at the expense of mainly the EU and the US, favouring new powers which have become international players (Santander 2020). Apart from the US and the EU, in the last two decades other countries, including China, Japan, Iran and India, are investing in Latin America in sectors such as trade and transport and, of course, energy (Santander 2020). If a zero-sum game approach is taken, this means that Europe and the US are losing their power and presence in the region.

Russia has also invested in the region in terms of military alliances, through loans or investments and by selling weapons to countries such as Venezuela. This has had an impact on both the EU and the US (Santander

2020). Even Turkey has increased its presence through trade and with diplomatic links, increasing the number of embassies in the region from six to thirteen (Santander 2020).

In Latin America the election of Bolsonaro in 2018 with an individualistic agenda was expected to affect the negotiations with the other countries within MERCOSUR or with the EU. However, the agreement between the EU and MERCOSUR was achieved in 2019 during the presidency of Bolsonaro. Bolsonaro seemed to take the side of Trump in relation to China. According to Bolsonaro, China is "buying" Brazil (Santander 2020). Therefore Brazil could look at the agreement with the EU as a way of counterbalancing China. Although the EU and LA had intended for years to review their links, Trump's unilateral and conflictive measures against them actually accelerated their agendas (Santander 2020). Therefore, the counterbalancing exercise took place for some of them against Trump, potentially against China for others, or even against both.

This chapter argues that the shift in world politics that commenced in 2016 has created the best momentum to further develop Latin American and EU relations for political and economic reasons. For political reasons the shift is intended to reinforce an international arena where multilateralism and respect for international forums and international law continue to exist. For economic reasons it is a way of creating growth and redistributing economic power away from the two largest economies (the US and China) which have clear foreign policy goals regarding the projection of power in both Latin America and the EU. The remainder of this chapter discusses the economic balance of power that has developed over time between the North and the South with a discussion of the BRICs as well as a discussion of the potential outcomes of those struggles, followed by the development of mega-regional agreements until 2016.

The BRICs

It is becoming more noticeable how the US and the EU are no longer the only main actors in the international arena. Latin America is affected by this redistribution of power. In 2006 the BRICs decided to create a forum where they would engage as a way of counterbalancing the power projection of the North and to pursue multipolar regionalism (Prashad 2013). In 2011 South Africa joined them. Together they cover around 40 per cent of the population and around 25 per cent of both the land and GDP in the entire world (Prashad 2013). Economically speaking, the financial crisis of 2007 also debilitated the position of the US and the EU in comparison to other countries. However, for some, the only real competition for the US is China and India, as a consequence of the economic slowdown in Brazil and the contraction of the economy in Russia due to the decline in oil prices together with the impact of the economic sanctions after the Crimea crisis (Peterson 2016). The creation of the New Development Bank by the BRICS with a budget of $100 billion was intended to create pressure on the type of representation within both the World Bank (WB) and the IMF (Peterson 2016). The development of the Asian Infrastructure Investment Bank (AIIB) in 2015, which attracted EU countries, created a potential division with the US. It could be interpreted as a way of resisting the conditions of the WB and the IMF (Peterson 2016). However, there is no direct confrontation with the North or neoliberal agendas per se. Instead the focus is on trade relations among themselves (Prashad 2013). The appearance and increased presence of the BRICs shows how economic growth is uneven and the power that they are accumulating puts the US in a difficult position (Schaefer and Poffenbarger 2014). The rise of these countries can be interpreted as a response of a unilateral nature to US foreign policy but it does not mean that the BRICS will develop an agenda of balancing power because they would suffer economically if they did (Schaefer and Poffenbarger 2014). In other words the degree of interdependence is enough to avoid a direct confrontation. The following subsections will elaborate on the impact that some of the BRICs have on South American foreign policy.

Russia

During the Cold War the role of Russia in Latin America was associated with counterbalancing the influence of the US. These countries' projection of power over Central and South America has been studied in academia at length. Since the end of the Cold War, and with the disappearance of the Soviet Union, the US has been considered the most important country influencing Latin America (and the world). However, Russia has become relevant to some extent in the region again. Russian's new policy towards Latin America can be considered another sign of a further move towards a multipolar world (Jeifets 2015).

Since 2008 the presence of Russia in Latin America has increased as part of Putin's foreign policy to counterbalance the US (Farah and Reyes 2016). This presence has covered both economic and military goals (Farah and Reyes 2016). From 2000 to 2013 the increase in trade between both regions was tripled with an increase of $5.8 billion (Ciccarillo 2016). In addition Putin is attempting to project Russian's power over Latin America to compete against the US using the Gerasimov Doctrine. This includes the selling of weapons and military training as well as donations, among other activities (Farah and Babineau 2019). In fact several Latin American countries including Brazil have increased their arms imports from Russia (Ciccarillo 2016). Russia is prioritising some countries over others. Since 2008 Brazil has been perceived as a strategic partner, whilst there is interest in developing political as well as economic co-operation with other relevant countries including Argentina, Venezuela, Mexico and Cuba, followed later by Nicaragua. This is because Russia considers the region to be increasing its influence at the international level (Jeifets 2015). In relation to Peru there have been discussions on a potential Russian investment into infrastructure in the rail and maritime sector (ports) (Jeifets 2015). Therefore it can be understood that Russia is trying to increase its international presence through Latin America with a view to the benefits of having a significant partner at the international level. Since 2014 this has been of importance for Putin due to the Crimea crisis and the way that the West reacted. In fact Russia requested the status of observer from the UNASUR and at Alcopaz (Latin American Association training centres for peacekeeping operations) (Jeifets 2015).

Russia has also taken advantage of its position at the United Nations Security Council to avoid international sanctions against Venezuela and Nicaragua (Farah and Babineau 2019). Russia has helped them to avoid accountability at the United Nations in relation to sensitive issues such as violations of human rights and problems over questionable actions related to the general elections. In return these countries help with the isolationism suffered by Russia by supporting it diplomatically (Farah and Reyes 2016). This is of particular importance after the G8 expelled Russia (becoming G7) as a consequence of Russia–Crimea relations. It is important to highlight that several Latin America countries did not automatically condemn the referendum of Crimea in 2014. In fact the Bolivarian Alliance supported the position of Russia on the matter (Ciccarillo 2016). In addition several MERCOSUR countries decided to abstain from a vote held at the UN in relation to Crimea (Ciccarillo 2016).

The return to Latin America can be seen also as a part of a PR campaign at the international level as well as at the domestic level where there is a sort of nostalgic sentiment over the Soviet Union era (Jeifets 2015). In fact the visit of the Minister of Defence of Russia in early 2015 reinforced the military links that wanted to be developed with Latin America. As a consequence of this visit, several technical agreements were implemented (Jeifets 2015).

The Gerasimov Doctrine also includes engagement with the region through soft power measures, and from 2015 to 2017 many – around forty-four – visits took place from senior Russian officials to Latin America and the other way around (Farah and Babineau 2019). On one of these trips that involved Cuba there was an attempt to reclaim some of Russia's previous influence on the island against the competition of the EU and China (Jeifets 2015). The visit of the Argentinian president to Moscow in 2015 resulted in a co-operation agreement on atomic energy and on the broadcasting in Spanish of "Russia Today" (Jeifets 2015). Other changes incorporated by Russian foreign policy include the facilitation of travel from some Latin American countries to Russia. The country now allows citizens from Argentina, Cuba, Venezuela and Brazil to travel to Russia without a visa, which demonstrates good diplomatic relations (Ciccarillo 2016).

There is also a shift in pragmatism in relation to the countries that traditionally would not have relations with Russia. From an economic point of view countries that are closer to US politics, such as Mexico, Colombia and Peru, also have economic links with Russia that cover different sectors, including the exploration of natural gas and oil (Ciccarillo 2016). In 2016 Paraguay and Russia made public their partnership on nuclear energy, and the Russian oil company Rosneft is still investing in Venezuela (Farah and Babineau 2019). This shows the type of involvement that Russia is providing. Overall, the most strategic of all visits was the one to Brazil, where co-operation was sought in relation to bilateralism as well as multilateralism in different forums including the G20 and, of course, the BRICs (Jeifets 2015).

Overall, Russia under Putin is a country that needs to be taken into consideration when analysing Latin America's foreign affairs, in particular in relation to competing against other actors such as China, the US and the EU. China had the first ministerial forum between CELAC and China in 2015 and it is expected to increase the trade between theregions by up to $500 billion in less than ten years, while in contrast Russia is in need of trade partners as a consequence of the new Cold War (Jeifets 2015).

China

Although the Chinese interest in Latin America can be interpreted as mainly economic, there is also the argument that explains Chinese policy in the region as part of a drive towards multipolarity with the aim of counterbalancing the US hegemonic role (Jenkins 2018). In particular, since 9/11 North America seems to have diluted its presence in Latin America, which has been helpful for China to step in. This can be interpreted as a counterbalancing exercise against the US presence in East Asia (Jenkins 2018).

China has named several LA countries as comprehensive partners, including the biggest from an economic point of view such as Brazil, Argentina and Mexico. This symbolises different levels of relevance (Brand et al. 2015:

17). It has also signed FTAs with some of them (Chile 2006, Peru and Costa Rica 2010) (Brand et al. 2015). The first FTA between China and a Latin America country was with Chile, and this South American country is now the supplier of 25 per cent of Chinese copper imports (Brand et al. 2015).

By 2017 the amount of trade between China and the region of Latin America and the Caribbean reached $266 billion, and the investment of the ASEAN countries in the region reached $250 billion between 2007 and 2017 (Farah and Babineau 2019). China's economic interest in Latin America is linked to the immense amount of natural resources, to access to a market of six hundred million consumers and to diplomatic recognition (Brand et al. 2015). However, there are three countries in Latin America – Brazil, Ecuador and Venezuela – that receive most of the funding (around 95 per cent) from China. Their production of raw materials is of interest (Long 2018). The current Chinese foreign policy supports Chinese companies investing abroad as a way of gaining access to natural resources such as those principally found in Latin America (Brand et al. 2015). The mining projects in Latin America developed by China are located in two Andean countries, Peru and Ecuador, and also in Chile (Brand et al. 2015).

China tends to bring together security and commercial matters in Latin America (Brand et al. 2015). Russia and China have attempted to develop training programmes, and it seems that in 2015 "China for the first time trained more Latin American military officers than the United States, and the difference has grown every year since" (Farah and Babineau 2019: 3). "However, defence analysts such as Evan Ellis argue that China will refrain from overtly provocative military activities such as establishing bases in Latin America in order not to appear threatening to the United States (Ellis, 2014, p. 10)" (Brand et al. 2015: 4). In the China–Latin America High Level Defence Forum of 2012 in China, six countries participated including Cuba, Colombia, Bolivia and Uruguay (Brand et al. 2015). China has sold military equipment to Venezuela for many years but, since the arms embargo of 2006 by the US on the Caribbean country, China has become one of the main vendors in this sector (Brand et al. 2015). In relation to Venezuela, China, as well as Russia and other countries, supports Maduro, the president of Venezuela, for political reasons (anti-Americanism) and economic ones (oil). Other countries in the region, as well as in the US and Europe, support the other political candidate, Juan Gaido (Santander 2020).

There is also a very particular issue linked to Chinese politics and that is its foreign policy. China's increased presence in Latin America is linked to trade and to the diplomatic matter of Taiwan (Farah and Babineau 2019). Panama, El Salvador and the Dominican Republic changed their diplomatic position on Taiwan and received large amount of aid as well as some promises of investment from China (Farah and Babineau 2019). Costa Rica changed its recognition of Taiwan in 2007, and the trade between the countries increased significantly since the trade agreement was enforced in 2011 (Brand et al. 2015). In 2013 Costa Rica reached an agreement of nearly $2 billion during the visit of Xi Jinping, the president of China (Brand et al. 2015).

In 2013 Xi Jinping launched what it is known as the BRI (Belt and Road Initiative), which is focused on creating more interdependence between Asia and Europe through the creation of traditional links such as land routes and railways. This is in addition to less traditional ones such as pipelines for natural gas and oil (Nordin and Weissman 2018). The Belt aspect of the BRI evokes the Silk Road and the Road refers to a Maritime Silk network of communications that will connect China and Europe through the Indian Ocean (Nordin and Weissmann 2018). The president of China explained in 2017, when hosting the president of Argentina, that Latin America is considered to be a natural extension of the BRI (Farah and Babineau 2019). It is unclear where the US is placed in the official narrative (Nordin and Weissmann 2018). Through the Maritime Road created through the BRI, China has access to key channels of communication. Through those ports Beijing can develop its political influence abroad such as in relation to naval operations (Farah and Babineau 2019). Panama, due to its strategic position, is becoming the entrance of the Silk Road in the region. When Panama changed its stance on Taiwanese politics likr other Central American countries, it caused a negative impact on the US (Santander 2020).

China has become the main trade partner for Brazil, leaving the US in second position in part as a consequence of soy production in the South American country. This is significant considering the role that Brazil might want to play counterbalancing the US due to geopolitical matters in the Americas (Schaefer and Poffenbarger 2014). Latin America provides most of China's soybean imports but in particular it is Brazil and Argentina that produce most of this agricultural product. This helps to avoid overdependence on the US and it also helps with food security matters (Jenkins 2018). China in general aims to reduce its reliance on Europe and the US after experiencing the impact of the financial crisis. Latin America represents 10 per cent of the increase in Chinese exports during the 2007 to 2012 crisis (Jenkins 2018).

China has also invested in Latin America, providing more than $100 billion in loans to the region. It has become a member of the Inter-American Development Bank (IADB) and engages with several regional organisations such as MERCOSUR, the Pacific Alliance and OAS (Santander 2020). Initially its application for the IADB was blocked by the US in 2008 (Jenkins 2018), which is very significant considering how support for Latin America should be seen as a welcome initiative by North America.

To summarise, for several decades the main trade partners of Latin America were the US and EU. However, in recent years China has become its second largest trade partner (after the US). For some countries (Brazil or Chile) it is the first (Santander 2020). Latin America's economic dependence on China has increased as a consequence of the focus of Europe on domestic matters even though the EU is keen to refocus again on the Americas, the US having lost interest in the region since Obama's administration and given the high interest in China of several countries from Argentina to Mexico (Santander 2020).

This degree of dependence does not help the industrialisation of Latin American countries and goes against the integration of the continent (Santander 2020). It is undeniable that the presence of China in Latin America is becoming an issue that both the EU and the US need to take into consideration when developing further trade negotiations and investment opportunities.

Brazil

In relation to the limits of the influence of Brazil on the American continent, the geographical division would be the division between South America and the rest, clearly excluding Mexico and the US (Long 2018). The summit of the presidents of South America left Mexico out of the important gathering, which can be seen as Brazil trying to shape its leadership (Caballero Santos 2011). Brazil's representatives tend to use the term South America instead of Latin America (Caballero Santos 2011). Other countries that have attempted to counterbalance the leadership include Venezuela, thanks to its exports of oil, and Argentina, due to the historical rivalries that have affected Brazil's goal of becoming a permanent member of the UN Security Council (Caballero Santos 2011).

At the same time Brazil has had a visible influence in the region. Brazil's leadership in the 1990s can be seen within MERCOSUR. However, the economic crisis of 1999 had a negative impact (Krapohl et al. 2014). Brazil has projected its power in South America through key moments in various regional integration projects, including the case of the adhesion of Venezuela to MERCOSUR (Gómez Arana 2017). At the same time Brazil has tried to place itself between ALBA and the US which has increased its influence (Long 2018). In fact, by being the pivotal player between the US and other Latin American countries, it has ended up becoming a regional leader (Long 2018). However, if there is a group that has given Brazil an international platform, it is the BRICs. Becoming a member of the BRICs probably helped Brazil to finally be recognised globally (Caballero Santos 2011).

The success of Brazil as a regional power in South America, without offering many material resources in the process, is linked to the fact that the US was not competing and had focused its foreign policy on other countries after 9/11 (Long 2018). However, Brazil has funded several projects that have benefited other Latin American countries over the years. With a budget of $10 billion from 2003 to 2010, Argentina benefited from the enlargement of a gas pipeline, Venezuela from an enlargement of the metro lines and the construction of a hydroelectric power station and Bolivia and Chile from the construction of roads etc. (Pinheiro and Gaio 2014). These projects, at the same time, have helped to diversify trade, and from 2002 to 2011 Brazil's exports to its neighbours increased by over 500 per cent from $7.4 billion to 54.2 billion (Pinheiro and Gaio 2014). The co-operation projects funded by Brazil from 2003 until 2012 cover mainly the transfer of good practices in several sectors including health, agriculture and other issues related to extreme poverty (Pinheiro and Gaio 2014). Overall, Brazil has taken on the role of regional leader but its aims include the development of an international profile (Gómez Arana 2017). Since Bolsonaro became president, a similar pattern to Trump's foreign policy can be perceived in their rhetoric, including on topics such as the pandemic. However, in practice, Bolsonaro seems to be more pragmatic than the former president of the US, perhaps due to the difference in relative power.

Contextualising trade agreements

This last section will discuss how the BRICs both as a group and individually have had a direct impact on both the EU and the US, who decided to combat this redistribution of power by negotiating far-reaching trade agreements that include new regulations and would consequently give some power back to the North. However, this agreement never materialised after Trump became president. With Biden as the new president and his pro-multilateralism agenda, perhaps new trade agreements will be negotiated again with Europe. In relation to the Trans-Pacific Partnership (TPP), Biden might also reconsider joining it again.

The acceleration in the growth of trade agreements since the end of the Second World War does not signify that all of the agreements have the same pattern. The number of countries in the WTO has grown, which affects the possibility of reaching an agreement. With China joining in 2001 and Russia in 2012, it has decreased in success, as the ongoing problems with the Doha Round demonstrate. China's membership of the WTO was linked to the idea of balancing the control that the wealthiest members held at the time, referring to the US, Canada, the EU and Japan (Prashad 2013). The pressure of developing countries and in particular the role of two of the BRIC countries, Brazil and India, and the lack of agreements between the EU and the US, have made this Round more difficult when it comes to success (McGrew 2008). The negotiations stopped after the round in Cancun in 2003.

This failure demonstrates both the economic and the political barriers that the WTO will find difficult to overcome. From an economic point of view, any negotiation that covers complex issues, such as the intellectual property rules that are associated with the fight against HIV, is likely to create long-term disagreements (Prashad 2013). Where an alliance of the EU and the US is not enough to achieve an agreement in a forum with 153 countries, this demonstrates the redistribution of power (Ritzer 2009). The agricultural sector is still a difficult aspect of the negotiation, and India, Brazil and South Africa led on a new group, the G21 created in 2003. This was in order for these countries to have more negotiating power in this area (Ritzer 2009). This also means an accumulation of formal or informal power by some of the countries from the South in organisations created in the North. The struggles between the North and the South provoked the failure of G20 (Prashad 2013).

Despite the lack of success of the last Doha Round, the WTO still affects its members' bilateral agreements. This is because the development of preferential trade agreements by members of the WTO means that they have to respect some of the articles including XXIV and V of the GATT (Stoll 2017). With the base created by the WTO, additional rules are sometimes referred to as WTO-plus, which ends up creating a sort of hybrid legal structure (Stoll 2017).

In the case of regional agreements such as MERCOSUR where there were also members of the WTO, dispute settlements could be complicated. MERCOSUR was created in 1991 with a short treaty that covered only a few ideas. The structure of what it is today was developed and implemented over the years (Gómez Arana 2017). A full detailed discussion on MERCOSUR can be seen in Sanahuja and Rodríguez's Chapter 6 below. Brazil and Argentina, both members of MERCOSUR and the WTO, ended up in a trade dispute with two potential forums to discuss it in. Brazil and Argentina had a dispute in relation to anti-dumping matters regarding products in the poultry sector. The outcome after bringing it to the dispute settlement existent in MERCOSUR was not satisfactory for Brazil and it was taken to the WTO (Stoll 2017). Interestingly, the WTO panel disagreed with the outcome of the dispute provided by MERCOSUR (Stoll 2017). The protocol of Brasilia was applicable at the time of the dispute and it included a provision that clarified the use of the MERCOSUR and WTO dispute settlements for the same cases. It was the protocol of Olivos from 2002 that included a clarification with a clause called "Choice of Forum" to avoid bringing the case to both forums (Stoll 2017). In other cases the EU appealed to the WTO as a consequence of the behaviour of Brazil in MERCOSUR. In the case of Brazil-Tyres the complaint was related to the EU concerns about Brazil imposing restrictions for environmental reasons on the importing of used tyres, while MERCOSUR members were exempt from the ban as a consequence of a decision made by MERCOSUR's tribunal (Stoll 2017). This shows how intricate the legal structures created through multilateralism, regionalism and inter-regionalism can be.

Mega-regional agreements

Despite the level of complexity of the regional groups and the WTO, the push for further trade interdependence continued. Until 2016 the progress in trade agreements went a step further and attempted to develop what are known as "mega-regional agreements". The reasons behind these agreements are linked to the lack of progress within the WTO but it is unclear if this pattern of trade liberalisation will help the WTO to reinitiate the negotiations or if it will help to make it more obsolete (Stoll 2017).

It is difficult to have a precise definition of mega-regional agreements but, broadly speaking, they are associated with very inclusive agreements on the non-traditional aspects of typical trade agreements. These agreements include negotiations on the less traditional trade sectors. For example they include chapters on sustainable development as well as the labour environment. (Stoll 2017). They also include other actors such as non-governmental organisations and representatives of civil society (Stoll 2017). The term arose to highlight the level of ambition that the agreements try to cover (Stoll 2017). Examples of mega-regional agreements include the TPP and the TTIP as well as the Regional Comprehensive Economic Partnership (developed by the ten countries of ASEAN)[1] and six other countries that already trade with them including Australia, China,[2] India, Japan, South Korea and New Zealand (Stoll 2017).

Transatlantic Trade and Investment Partnership

The US and the EU decided to launch very ambitious trade negotiations called the TTIP. Both negotiators were dealing with the consequences of the financial crisis. Within the EU several countries required bailouts that were conceded by the EU Troika composed by the EC, the European Central Bank and the IMF. In 2012 the European Central Bank focused on managing the Euro but the growth in European countries was extremely reduced

(Peterson 2016). Both the EU and the US had to deal with the rise of the BRICs and the failure of the Doha Round negotiations. The economic projection of the US and the EU had clearly declined and an agreement boosting their economic growth could be seen as a way of counterbalancing the economic growth elsewhere, in particular in South-East Asia. The TTIP attempted to stimulate the recovery of their economies as well as creating the chance to create rules for international trade in complex areas that were not being advanced in the WTO as a consequence of the lack of success of the Doha Round (Peterson 2016). It was an opportunity for the US and Europe to influence global governance (Peterson 2016). The EU has operated as an external regulator in the past (Young 2015).

The EU and the US together covered in the mid-2010s around 45 per cent of the world's trade. With an agreement that would cover regulations and access for businesses, the outcome could potentially have helped to act as an impulse for the multilateral agenda while setting the rules for BRIC countries if they wanted to have access to the same sectors (Pavlova 2015). By covering environmental issues as well as social standards, both the US and the EU were attempting to implement their values at the international level (Pavlova 2015). Obama was attempting to avoid the influence of China when establishing international regulations (Pavlova 2015). The TTIP negotiations started in 2013 with Obama, and three years later, with the administration of Trump, they were ended unsuccessfully when the new president decided to develop a more isolationist approach. How these matters will be resolved depends on Biden's approach to a trade agreement in the aftermath of the pandemic.

Trans-Pacific Partnership

The other attempt to develop a mega-regional agreement by Obama to deal with the rise of China was the Trans-Pacific Partnership. It initially included eleven countries (Pavlova 2015). After a trade agreement between Brunei, Singapore, New Zealand and Chile was achieved in 2005, three years later Bush announced that the US would start negotiations with them (McBride and Chatzky 2019). Obama continued with these negotiations and other countries joined them afterwards including Australia, Vietnam, Peru, Canada, Japan, Malaysia and Mexico (McBride and Chatzky 2019). The TPP and the TTIP together could have covered around 60 per cent of the world's GDP (Pavlova 2015). The TPP also helped to put pressure on the EU in relation to the TTIP, especially before the end of Obama's presidency (Pavlova 2015).

MERCOSUR countries were not included in these negotiations, which would add more isolation at international level (Caballero Santos 2014). The pressure exercised by the negotiations of the TTIP puts further pressure on properly relaunching the negotiations with the EU (Gómez Arana 2017). The pressure of the TPP could certainly add even more (Caballero Santos 2014). The negotiations between MERCOSUR and the EU were concluded in 2019. At the same time this isolationism could act as an impulse for the the trade relations between MERCOSUR countries and China (Caballero Santos 2014).

The TPP was agreed in October 2015 and signed in 2016. However, it was too late for the US since both main political parties had criticised it during the electoral campaign and it was not ratified by Congress (McBride and Chatzky 2019). However, it included thirty chapters that covered different areas including intellectual property and environmental standards. By 2015 TPP countries already represented 40 per cent of the trading partners with the US (McBride and Chatzky 2019). When Donald Trump became the President of the US, he left the TPP. The rest of the countries continued with the project and created the Comprehensive and Progressive Agreement for Trans-Pacific Partnership (CPTPP). This is similar to the TPP but without some of the requirements that the US initially demanded (McBride and Chatzky 2019). It is too soon to fully understand Biden's policy in this area but there is room for optimism.

Conclusion

The first two decades of the twenty-first century have included a financial crisis that has affected mainly the US and the EU. There has also been a movement towards populism in some countries in the North that has brought with it economic protectionism and nationalism. At the same time several countries in the South have become major players, counterbalancing to some extent the economic and political power of the North. The degree of interdependence is not going to decline even after protectionist measures have been enacted by some countries. If the BRI becomes successful, it will be in part thanks to the participation of other great powers such as the other BRIC countries and the EU, through the leadership of China (Nordin and Weissmann 2018).

A unipolar world in which the US is a hegemonic partner and where the control of international institutions is done by western countries, is becoming part of history. There are three poles: the EU, the US and the BRIC countries (Wade 2011). Mexico is becoming, together with South Korea and Turkey, one of the countries that could be joining the BRICs (Wade 2011). At the same time these three poles could be reduced to one. Having the largest economy in the BRICs group, China's commitment to multipolarity is significant (Prashad 2013). In fact Chinese officials have explained that

China is not in favour of hegemony. Some scholars indicate that the alternatives offered by this country are not so different in concept (Nordin and Weissmann 2018). Considering the recent events in relation to China since Biden became the president of the US, it is certainly clearer that there has been an increase in confrontation between the EU and the US on one side, and China on the other. The economic sanctions launched from both sides symbolise a high level of tension in a multipolar world.

This chapter has considered this new multipolar world and discussed the role of mega-regional agreements as a potential solution that Obama tried to reach in order to deal with the rise of China. However, since 2016 the US has favoured isolationism. It is in these new circumstances that Latin America and the EU can further develop their trade agreements and political commitments. At a time when multilateralism needs to be re-established to create political stability, growth through external trade is needed and the avoidance of unintended isolationism a required measure to survive the TPP and BRI. And both Latin America and the EU need to find allies that can be trusted. With Biden and the EU on one side and China on the other, it is uncertain where Latin American countries will place themselves in this new Cold War.

References

All websites last visited 30 September 2021.

Bethell, L. (2018). "Brazil and Latin America", in *Brazil: Essays on History and Politics*, pp. 19–52. London: Institute of Latin American Studies. www.jstor.org/stable/j.ctv51309x.

Brand, A., McEwen-Fial, S. and Muno, W. (2015). "An 'Authoritarian Nexus'? China's alleged special relationship with autocratic states in Latin America", *European Review of Latin American and Caribbean Studies / Revista Europea de Estudios Latinoamericanos y del Caribe*, 7–28. www.jstor.org/stable/43673489?seq=1#metadata_info_tab_contents.

Caballero Santos, S. (2011). "Brasil y la región: una potencia emergente y la integración regional sudamericana". *Revista Brasileira de Política Internacional* 54 (2), 158–72. https://dx.doi.org/10.1590/S0034–73292011000200008.

Caballero Santos, S. (2014). "El acuerdo Transpacífico y su efecto en América Latina", *Meridiano* 47 (141), 51–9. https://periodicos.unb.br/index.php/MED/article/view/4835.

Ciccarillo, S. G. (2016). "The Russia–Latin America Nexus: realism in the 21st century", *Student Scholarship & Creative Works by Year*. 47. https://scholar.dickinson.edu/student_work/47/?utm_source=scholar.dickinson.edu%2Fstudent_work%2F47&utm_medium=PDF&utm_campaign=PDFCoverPages.

Climate Home News 4/11/2019 "Trump begins formal US withdrawal from Paris Agreement". www.climatechangenews.com/2019/11/04/trump-begins-formal-us-withdrawal-paris-agreement/.

Ellis, E. (2014). *China on the Ground in Latin America: Challenges for the Chinese and Impacts on the Region*. Berlin: Springer.
Garavini, G. (2012). *After Empires: European Integration, Decolonization, and the Challenge from the Global South 1957–1986*. Oxford: Oxford University Press.
Farah, D. and Babineau, K. (2019). "Extra-regional actors in Latin America". *PRISM* 8 (1), 96–113. https://cco.ndu.edu/News/Article/1767399/extra-regional-actors-in-latin-america-the-united-states-is-not-the-only-game-i/.
Farah, D. and Reyes, L. E. (2016). "Russia in Latin America". *Prism* 5 (4), 100–17. https://cco.ndu.edu/Portals/96/Documents/prism/prism_5-4/Russia%20in%20Latin%20America.pdf.
Gómez Arana, A. (2017). *The European Union's Policy towards Mercosur*. Manchester: Manchester University Press. https://manchesteruniversitypress.co.uk/9780719096945/.
Jeifets, V. (2015). "Russia is coming back to Latin America: perspectives and obstacles", *Anuario de la Integración Regional de América Latina y el Caribe–América Latina y el Caribe y el nuevo sistema internacional*. Miradas desde el Sur coordinado por Andrés Serbin (CRIES, Buenos Aires), Laneydi Martínez (CEHSEU, La Habana) y Haroldo Ramanzi, pp. 90–112. www.cries.org/wp-content/uploads/2016/02/06-Jeifets.pdf.
Jenkins, R. (2018). *How China Is Reshaping the Global Economy: Development Impacts in Africa and Latin America*. Oxford: Oxford University Press.
Krapohl, S., Meissner, K. L. and Muntschick, J. (2014). "Regional powers as leaders or Rambos? The ambivalent behaviour of Brazil and South Africa in regional economic integration", *JCMS: Journal of Common Market Studies* 52 (4), 879–95.
Kurtenbach, S. (2019). *Latin America – Multilateralism without Multilateral Values*. (GIGA Focus Lateinamerika, 7). Hamburg: GIGA German Institute of Global and Area Studies – Leibniz-Institut für Globale und Regionale Studien, Institut für Lateinamerika-Studien. www.giga-hamburg.de/en/publications/12611005-latin-america-multilateralism-without-multilateral-values/.
Long, T. (2018). "The US, Brazil and Latin America: the dynamics of asymmetrical regionalism", *Contemporary Politics* 24 (1) 113–29. doi: 10.1080/13569775.2017.1408167.
McBride, J. and Chatzky, A. (2019). What Is the Trans-Pacific Partnership (TPP)? 4 January. In Council for Foreign Relations, www.cfr.org/backgrounder/what-trans-pacific-partnership-tpp.
McGrew, A. (2008). "Globalization and global politics", in Baylis, J., Smith, S., and Owens, P. (eds), *The Globalization of World Politics: An Introduction to International Relations*. Oxford: Oxford University Press.
Nordin, A. H. and Weissmann, M. (2018). "Will Trump make China great again? The belt and road initiative and international order", *International Affairs* 94 (2), 231–49. https://doi.org/10.1093/ia/iix242.
Pavlova, P. (2015). "Beyond economics: the geopolitical importance of the Transatlantic Trade and Investment Partnership", *European View* 14 (2), 209–16. DOI 10.1007/s12290-015-0376-0.
Peterson. J. (2016). "Introduction: where things stand and what happens next", in Alcaro, R., Peterson, J. and Greco, E. (eds), *The West and the Global Power Shift: Transatlantic Relations and Global Governance*. London: Springer, pp. 1–18.
Pinheiro, L. and Gaio, G. (2014). "Cooperation for development, Brazilian regional leadership and global protagonism", *Brazilian Political Science Review* 8 (2), 8–30. Epub September. https://doi.org/10.1590/1981-38212014000100009.

Prashad, V. (2013). "Neoliberalism with Southern characteristics. *The Rise of the BRICS*", Rosa Luxemburg Stiftung, New York Office. www.rosalux-nyc.org/wp-content/files_mf/prashad_brics.pdf.
Reis da Silva, A. L. and Volpato, V. (2019). "The Brazil–European Union strategic partnership: advances, convergences, and challenges", Working Paper – October. UFRGS Leuven: Leuven Centre for Global Governance Centre. https://ghum.kuleuven.be/ggs/research/eucross/eucross-wp-andre-reis-and-vitoria.pdf.
Ritzer, G. (2009). 'Structuring the Global Economy', in *Globalization A Basic Text*. New York: Wiley-Blackwell. pp. 171–205
Rodrik, D. (2011). *The Globalization Paradox: Democracy and the Future of the World Economy*. New York: W. W. Norton & Company.
Santander, S. (2020). "The Atlantic Triangle in the era of China's rising power in Latin America", in Telò, M. and Feng, Y. (eds), *China and the EU in the Era of Regional and Interregional Cooperation*. Brussels: Peter Lang, pp. 239–56.
Schaefer, M. and Poffenbarger, J. (2014). *The Formation of the BRICS and Its Implication for the United States: Emerging Together*. New York: Palgrave Macmillan.
Segovia, D. (2013). "Latin America and the Caribbean: between the OAS and CELAC", *European Review of Latin American and Caribbean Studies / Revista Europea de Estudios Latinoamericanos y del Caribe* 95, 97–107. www.jstor.org/stable/23595694?seq=1#metadata_info_tab_contents.
Stoll, P. T. (2017). "Mega-regionals: challenges, opportunities and research questions", in Rensmann T. (ed.), *Mega-Regional Trade Agreements*. Cham: Springer, pp. 3–24. https://doi.org/10.1007/978-3-319-56663-4_1.
Vahalík, B. (2015). "Analysis of export diversification development of the European Union and BRICS countries", *Central European Review of Economic Issues* 18, 59–69. http://er-cerei.cz/download/archive/analysis-of-export-diversification-development-of-the-european-union-and-brics-countries.pdf.
Wade, R. H. (2011). "Emerging world order? From multipolarity to multilateralism in the G20, the World Bank, and the IMF", *Politics & Society* 39 (3), 347–78. https://journals.sagepub.com/doi/pdf/10.1177/0032329211415503.
Young, A. (2015). "Liberalizing trade, not exporting rules: the limits to regulatory co-ordination in the EU's 'new generation' preferential trade agreements", *Journal of European Public Policy* 22 (9), 1253–75, doi: 10.1080/13501763.2015.1046900,

Notes

1 Brunei, Cambodia, Indonesia, Laos, Malaysia, Myanmar, the Philippines, Singapore, Thailand and Vietnam.
2 China was a member of ASEAN.

2

EU–LAC: a relationship beyond trade: political dialogues between unequal partners

Susanne Gratius

Introduction

Political dialogue and development co-operation have been the distinctive element in EU trade agreements with Latin America and the Caribbean. Treaties include a democracy clause and are based on shared values and compensations for trade asymmetries by development or technical assistance by the EU. None the less, the three main topics in EU–LAC relations – trade, development co-operation and political dialogue – follow different paths and confront difficult times since the beginning of the pandemic Covid-19 in 2020.

Except for Central America and the Caribbean, the EU's development and political partners in the region do not necessarily coincide with its trade counterparts. For example Brazil, CELAC and MERCOSUR maintained high-level political dialogues with the EU, until the validation of the EU–MERCOSUR agreement, signed in June 2019, without trade liberalisation or development co-operation, whilst Chile, Colombia, Ecuador and Peru or Central America and the Caribbean signed FTAs and do not celebrate summits and/or political dialogues with the EU like its strategic partners Brazil (2007) and Mexico (2009).

Both trade and political dialogues have in common that they are built no longer around regional or sub-regional schemes – according to the EU paradigm of "pure inter-regionalism" between two integrated blocs that speak with a single voice – but around multilevel formats, according to the changing nature of regionalism (Ayuso and Caballero 2018; Gratius 2021). Whilst political dialogue started in the 1980s, in the midst of the Cold War, in a context of global interdependence, from the 1990s on trade has been at the core of European–Latin American relations, and shaped inter-regional progress until the financial crisis in 2008, when the stagnation of bi-regional co-operation coincided with China's rise in Latin America.

Six recent agreements between the EU and its partners Colombia, Peru, Ecuador, the Caribbean, Central America, Cuba, Chile, Mexico and the EU–MERCOSUR agreement signed in 2019 certify the importance of trade in bi-regional relations. In times of new trade wars and US protectionism under the Trump administration, the EU and Latin America shared a strong vocation for trade liberalisation, despite the remaining obstacles in the EU–MERCOSUR trade agreement that might probably never be implemented (Ayuso and Gratius 2017b and 2020).

Differently from US free trade deals with Latin American partners (the same as those of the EU), the EU complemented trade interests with development co-operation to compensate economic asymmetries, and with political dialogue to underline a horizontal partnership beyond the exchange of goods and services that served, among other goals, to build and maintain a regional order now under stress (Nolte and Weiffen 2020).

This chapter argues that there is a constant mismatch between inter-regional political dialogue vis-à-vis trade, and an oversized political network compared to real trade (and other) declining asymmetric interdependences. A second hypothesis sustains that "pure political and economic inter-regionalism" failed and is replaced by bilateral trade agreements and political dialogues with larger powers, particularly Brazil and Mexico as strategic partners of the EU.

The next section explores the goals and evolution of political dialogues. The following section categorises different types of political dialogue forums, taking into account the academic literature on diplomacy, peacebuilding and diplomacy, on the one hand, and the debate on inter-regionalism, on the other. Another section compares EU–LAC political dialogues with other forums and organisations, particularly with the US and China as major challengers for the EU engagement in the region. Concluding remarks will explore recent trends in political dialogue and trade and retake the two hypotheses.

Goals and evolution of EU–LAC political dialogues

Which are the goals of political dialogue? In general they are a soft power instrument of foreign policy that, in the case of inter-regional formats (Börzel and Risse 2009), serve different goals such as to co-ordinate positions based on affinities, to solve conflicts and controversies, to promote ideas and identities, to create an alliance against others (counterbalance), to push for new international norms and principles, or simply to underline the importance of the partnership.

In the case of EU–LAC dialogues, they mainly preserve historic and cultural affinities aimed at promoting global governance by adopting common positions (EC 2009), promote European values, norms and principles incorporated into the Latin American history, and to create an alliance against China and Russia (for example in the Venezuelan crisis), and, sometimes, against the hegemonic aspirations of the US like Washington's coercive policy towards Cuba. None the less, the result of this ambitious and complex agenda has been rather modest. In contrast to the past, when interdependences were strong and political relations weak, the opposite happens today: a high number of multilevel political dialogues contrast with declining trade and development relations due to the financial crisis in 2008 and the economic costs of the pandemic 2020–21.

Function follows form?

Political relations between the EU and Latin America were constructed from above, by an intergovernmental political dialogue that began during the Central American crisis during the Cold War period of the 1980s. This dialogue's principal motivation was to establish peace and democracy in a region that became a battlefield of the Cold War's struggle for power between the United States and the Soviet Union (Roy 1992).

At that time the EU's engagement for peace did not follow the logic of regionalism and inter-regionalism but was driven by the negative consequences of the ideological bipolar confrontation in secondary regions like Central America. From the beginning, "EU" political dialogue was linked to a regional initiative, at that time the Contadora Group integrated by Colombia, Mexico, Panama and Venezuela that, over the time, transformed first into the Rio Group and became in 2011 the Latin American and Caribbean Community of States (CELAC) between thirty-three countries of the region (Ruano 2018). The EU held regular political consultations with all three partners: the San José peace conferences on Central America with the Contadora Group, ministerial meetings with the Rio Group and since 2013 summits with CELAC.

From a Latin American perspective, European political engagement from the 1980s onwards meant two things. Firstly, a diversification of external relations previously centred on the two superpowers, and particularly the US; and, secondly, the chance to build an independent regional order for peace and democracy, supported and guaranteed by Europe as an emerging bloc and example for integration in a bipolar world. From an EU perspective political dialogue as a core instrument to promote own ideas, identities and norms serves to diffuse regional integration and human rights, among other things (Börzel and Risse 2009). As a soft power instrument, political dialogue seeks to convince developmental partners outside European borders to share the preference for regionalism and globalisation including the dismantling of trade barriers, at that time through the Generalised System of Preferences (GSP) and the special trade regime "GSP drugs" for the Andean countries that was later extended to Central America.

Elite political dialogue between the EC, Central America and the Contadora Group, the San José Process that started in 1983, offered Europe the opportunity to contribute to a peace process and counterbalance US and Soviet influence in a region under Washington's domain. The Central American peace process, based on a regional initiative was the starting point for a regular political dialogue between the regions including democracy, development and integration.

Later on, the Contadora Group transformed into the Group of Eight and, in 1986, into the Rio Group, the origin of today's CELAC that held its second (and apparently last) summit with the EU in 2015. Other regional initiatives, particularly UNASUR, created in 2000 in Brazil and under pressure since six Latin American countries[1] decided to temporarily leave the organisation (Ayuso and Caballero 2018), has not established a regular political channel with the EU, but celebrated summits with its African, Arabic and Asian counterparts.

Regular political dialogue generated a closer relationship between Europe and Latin America, and CELAC served to co-ordinate separate policies on Latin America (traditionally not an associated region of the EU) and the Caribbean (as part of the ACP group and the Cotonou agreement). At the end of the 1990s, parallel to the US initiative to create a Free Trade Area of the Americas (FTAA), the EU signed trade-plus (dialogue and co-operation) agreements with Mexico (1997) and Chile (2002), and later on with Central America, Colombia–Peru (and Ecuador), and the Caribbean, parallel to negotiations with MERCOSUR. In that framework CARICOM, the Central American integration system SICA, MERCOSUR and the Andean Community opened regular political dialogues with their European counterparts.

Peace-driven "political interregionalism", supported from its very beginning by the EU, or "pure interregionalism" (Hänggi 2006; Gardini and Malamud 2014), refers to a group-to-group dialogue, since 1999 at its highest level (EU–CELAC summits). Independent from that process, "economic regionalism" also generated inter-regional political dialogues through the free trade-plus and other preferential agreements that the EU signed with sub-regional partners or individual countries (Table 2.1), represent "hybrid inter-regionalism" (Hänggi 2006).

Until the 1980s the lack of regular diplomatic region-to-region contacts contrasted with strong societal interdependences between Europe and Latin America by migration flows in both directions (including the exile community during the Latin American dictatorships), close cultural links, and high levels of trade and investment flows. Migration flows in both directions are

Table 2.1 EU–LAC political dialogues

Bilateral	Sub-regional	Regional
Partner (agreement) • Brazil (SP 2007) • Mexico (SP 2009) • Cuba (PDCA 2014) • Chile (FTA) • Colombia (FTA) • Ecuador (FTA) • Peru (FTA) • Mexico (FTA upgraded 2018)	• SICA (FTA 2012) • Caricom (RPA 2014) • MERCOSUR (AA 2005) • Andean Community (1991)	• LAC and CELAC (Summit 2013 and 2015) • Eurolat (inter-parliamentary meetings) • Sector dialogues (drugs, justice, migration, environment, social cohesion) • dialogues with non-governmental actors (private sector, civil society, academic meetings) • EU–LAC Foundation
Main issues SP (bilateral and global), PDCA (trade, co-operation, human rights), FTAs-plus (trade, development, others)	Trade, co-operation, human rights, democracy, climate change	Regional, inter-regional and global issues
Outcome Brazil: no clear progress, Mexico. Upgrading of FTA, Cuba: human rights dialogue, others: FTA	SICA and Caricom: trade and development, human rights and public security, Andean Community: drugs	No follow-up of Declarations and Action plans, EU–LAC Foundation (EU–LAC Summits)

Source: Author's own elaboration

probably the strongest pillar of societal relations. The first modern wave of migration occurred in the first half of the twentieth century from Europe to Latin America (mainly to Brazil and Mexico) during the dictatorships in Spain and Portugal. The second wave took place in the 1970s: authoritarian regimes in South America pushed many Latin Americans into European exile (Germany, France, Portugal, Spain, Switzerland or Scandinavian countries), where they contributed to creating stronger political links (Ayuso

2009a: 21) that served, for example in the case of Chile during and after the Pinochet dictatorship, to build European support for democracy. It also fostered trade links between the regions. For example, in 1981 (five years before the accession of Spain and Portugal in 1986 to the EU, Latin America had a share of over 6 per cent in the EC's total trade, and Europe represented in 1990 more than 20 per cent of LA exports (González Blanco and Maesso Corral 2000).

At that time relations were built up bottom-up-wise, and societal interdependences (by migration and a common history) between the regions were asymmetrical but strong. Until the 1990s EU–LAC relations followed the motto "form (political dialogue) follows function" (trade interdependences) (paraphrasing David Mitrany) by establishing a political dialogue based on close links between societies that shared the preference for democracy, co-operation and integration.

Today, trade relations are less relevant: in 2016, Asia (China, India, Taiwan, Malaysia, South Korea) had a share of over 20 per cent of Latin American imports and exports. The EU lost its second position to China, which represented in 2016 more than 16 per cent of total LAC trade, compared to the EU's percentage of 14.4 per cent – three times less than the US's 45.6 per cent (EC 2017).

Declining trade relations contrast with a dense network of political dialogue forums (see Table 2.1) that lack a concrete agenda and a regular monitoring system. An extraordinary dense network of multilevel dialogue forums between the two parties contrasts with decreasing interdependences in terms of trade and other interdependences (migration flows, investment and development co-operation).

Today the EU remains top trading partner for only Cuba and Brazil – all other countries have either China or the US as their top trade partner. In an inter-regional context characterised by declining trade relations and a closer partnership between Latin America and China, function (trade interdependences) follows form (political dialogue), i.e. political dialogues that are seeking an agenda have become the hallmark of EU–LAC relations today.

Types and functions of political dialogues

Until the beginning of the 2000s Latin America and the Caribbean engaged in "open regionalism" (a concept developed by the ECLAC) by creating new arrangements such as MERCOSUR, UNASUR, CELAC and the Pacific Alliance, parallel to reforms in former regional entities like the Central American Common Market, CARICOM or the Andean Community (Ayuso and Caballero 2018). The EU supported Latin American states in these initiatives.

Open regionalism of the 1990s favoured FTAs with the EU and the US. To differentiate from the US vision of pure North–South agreements without compensations, the EU included political dialogue and development co-operation at different levels (with governments, parliaments, trade unions or NGOs) in its association or free trade-plus agreements with Latin American partners.

The multiplication of dialogue forums with bilateral, sub-regional and individual partners was a response to fragmented Latin American regionalism (Ayuso and Caballero 2018), but also to the increasing complexity in EULAC co-operation that covers a large number of issues that are difficult to follow up given the broad range of action plans and declarations in each dialogue forum.

Table 2.1 indicates a recent trend towards a bilateralisation of political dialogue forums and trade and/or (as in the Cuban case) co-operation agreements. "Pure regionalism" was worked out with small partners like Central America or the Caribbean, whilst the Andean Community has not signed collective FTAs with the EU, whereas MERCOSUR reached in June 2019 a first step in the long process of negotiating a bioregional association, by signing the "agreement of principles". Brazil's strategic partnership and summits with the EU were launched in 2007 – under Lula's proactive foreign policy – to compensate paralysis in trade negotiations with MERCOSUR. Two years later the EU defined a strategic, "like-minded" partnership with Mexico also based on democratic principles and a shared global responsibility. None the less, since 2014 no bilateral summit with either Brazil nor Mexico has taken place.

Less visible, but more successful, has been the regular inter-parliamentary co-operation between both parties that continues under the umbrella of the long-standing Eurolat forum between the two regional parliaments EP and Parlatino. Different from the incapacity of both partners to reactivate the EUCELAC summits and to overcome their differences on Venezuela, the Eurolat meetings are held regularly and produce common declarations which are, none the less, purely declaratory with a limited influence on the agenda-setting in relations.

These dialogues could be divided into three types: (1) a global-governance-based inter-regional CELAC–EU and Brazil–EU dialogue (EC 2009), (2) a democratic conditionality-driven dialogue as part of the trade, co-operation and association agreements (Chile, Mexico, Colombia–Ecuador–Peru, MER-COSUR and Central America), and (3) a shared problem-focused sector dialogue on concrete issues (drugs, migration, social cohesion, environment etc.). None the less, these ideal types of political dialogue clash with overlapping agendas given that the same issues (migration, drugs, trade) appear in all three types without a systematic follow-up system.

Global governance-based inter-regional dialogues

The EU's idea of inter-regionalism and an increasing global weight of Latin America in terms of presence in international organisations[2] and ranking (Brazil's position as the ninth largest economy in 2019, according to the World Bank) motivated the celebration of the first ever summit with CELAC in 2013. The two EU–CELAC Summit Declarations (2013 and 2015) include a long list of good intentions to co-operate on nearly all regional and international topics. In its 77 points, the final Declaration of the II EU–CELAC Summit, held in June 2015 in Brussels, envisaged "more effective and inclusive global governance". The Action Plan included ten priorities: science and technology, sustainable development, regional integration, migration, education, higher education, drugs, gender, investment and citizens' security. Trade was not part of the list.

The lack of a monitoring mechanism and the division of CELAC (and post-2008-crisis fragmentations within the EU) evidence the limits of political inter-regionalism as a formula to push global governance by co-ordination between two blocs. The limits of inter-regional global governance are evident. Firstly, CELAC is not a regional actor, and positions within the bloc are divided, at the regional level, on the internal conflicts in Venezuela or on Nicaragua, or, at the global stage, on the nuclear conflicts with Iran and North Korea. Secondly, a declining leftist ALBA and the ideologically opposed Lima Group (twelve Latin American countries participate) represented different positions which proved the limits of inter-regional global governance.

Since 2015 high level meetings have not taken place, because of a major political conflict over the political and economic crisis of the authoritarian Maduro government in Venezuela. The dispute on EU sanctions against the Maduro government, imposed since 2017,[3] on the one hand, and a major division on Venezuela within CELAC, on the other, stymied the III EU–CELAC Summit in 2017 and, again, in 2018, and 2021. Internal and inter-regional divisions deepened after 2019, when twenty-five EU member states and a majority of Latin American countries recognised Juan Guaidó as legitimate president, and a minority group of two EU member states (Cyprus, and Italy) and four Latin American countries (Bolivia, Cuba, Mexico and Uruguay) did not recognise him (Gratius and Puente 2019). The Venezuelan tragedy contributed even more to the ideological political division within and between the regions.

The "non-summit" that was replaced by a foreign ministers' meeting held in July 2018 in Brussels reflects differences on the interpretation of sovereignty within and between the regions and reveals the difficulties of an inter-regional dialogue between two unequal partners: the EU and a group of highly diverse Latin American countries. Inter-regionalism clashes with the trend towards bilateral patterns of political dialogue and co-operation with Bolivia, Brazil, Chile, Colombia, Cuba, Ecuador, Mexico and Peru.

Even though the potential for close co-ordination and common positions at the international stage is large (Ayuso and Gratius), the results of global governance-based political dialogues are scarce. Only climate change, a less sensitive issue in relations, offered the opportunity to co-ordinate international positions, for example during the negotiations of the Paris agreement in 2015, when particularly Brazil was a close partner of the EU. None the less, convergence on climate change ended under the government of the right-wing President Jair Bolsonaro, who claimed national sovereignty for the Amazon and defends its exploitation, against the climate-change interests of the EU. This conflictive issue has also negatively affected the ratification of the agreement of principles signed on 19 June 2019 by the EU and MERCOSUR.

Apart from climate change, the EU strategic partnership with Brazil, established in 2007 under the Portuguese presidency, went nowhere. The initial enthusiasm on both sides vanished when Brazil under the leftist Partido dos Trabalhadores (PT) governments came closer to the BRICs and, later on, lost its former economic dynamism and emerged into a deep crisis (Gratius 2017) that, under the conditions of the Covid-19 pandemic, lasted until 2021.

The seven summits held in ten years (2007, 2008, 2009, 2010, 2011, 2013, 2014) produced large final declarations and two ambitious action plans. Most commitments have never been met and relations have stagnated since 2014 (Gratius 2017). Trade as the real strategic element in relations (Brazil is the EU's largest economic partner in Latin America) has not been addressed in bilateral summits, because of parallel EU-MERCOSUR negotiations that lasted for twenty years without having concluded the association (Ayuso and Gratius 2020; Gomes Saraiva 2017; Gratius 2017).

Democratic conditionality driven political dialogues (agreements)

In line with its status as a normative actor, the EU includes democracy clauses in all its trade and co-operation agreements with third partners. Because of the long period of dictatorships until the beginning of the 1980s, Latin America has been a privileged destination of EU democracy and human-rights promotion policies.

Against the traditional hypothesis of the EU's policy of "one size fits it all" (Börzel and Risse 2009), Brussels adapted to the different circumstances and conditions of its trade and co-operation partners. The first two agreements with Chile and Mexico reflect the EU policy to sign comprehensive economic (and trade liberalisation) agreements that assign a large space to the diffusion of democratic principles through conditionality and political dialogue.

Particularly with Mexico, the democracy clause and political dialogue represented an initial obstacle in negotiations, at a time when Mexico began its transition from the PRI hegemony to liberal democracy with competitive elections in 2000. Before negotiations ended, in 2002, Chile was already a like-minded partner of the EU with similar views that facilitated the inclusion of international issues in the bilateral political dialogue of the association agreement. Both agreements with Chile and Mexico were recently updated and adapted to changing global conditions. For historical reasons (the EU's engagement in the region's peace process) also the agreement with Central America has a strong political character specified in several paragraphs of the treaty.

Agreements with Colombia–Peru–Ecuador (see Chapters 3 and 4 below) and Cuba are different cases. The first case is an exclusive FTA. Although it includes a democracy clause, political dialogue develops at a bilateral and sub-regional level. The EU agreement with Cuba includes political dialogue in its title, but, as a result of decades of unfruitful democracy promotion by the EU's Common Position, approved in 1996, it does not have an explicit democracy clause. Similarly to Brussels's agreements with other socialist-governed countries such as Vietnam, the PDCA foresees a regular and specific political dialogue on human rights (Ayuso and Gratius 2017a).

Exceptions are the individual FTAs with Colombia, Ecuador and Peru that followed bilateral paths under the broad umbrella of the Andean Community, but are also part of the PDCA, signed in 2003 and including a democracy clause. Political dialogue and democracy, as a main pillar of relations, are integrated as an essential instrument (mainly with the purpose of diffusing European ideas and their emulation) in all agreements that the EU has signed with Latin American partners.

Shared problem-focused sector dialogues

Sector dialogues (most of them defined at EU–LAC summits, and thirty-three in EU–Brazil relations) are the least developed and least monitored type of political dialogue. To start with, there is almost no public information (agendas, declarations etc.) on sector dialogues with Latin American partners. The so-called political-sector dialogues are held in secret and there is no systematic follow-up of their results or failures by the EU–LAC Foundation or other bio-regional entities.

At different moments the EU and Latin American partners have established issue-specific political dialogues on issues of mutual interest such as drugs, migration, social cohesion and environment. On none of those dialogues has the EU or Latin America offered public information on meetings, partners and outcomes. The closed-door character of those meetings has the advantage of allowing problems in relations to be discussed in a more confident environment, but the disadvantage that visibility and the participation of civil society actors remain low.

The crisis of the triangle model dialogue–development–trade

EU–LAC dialogue forums can be divided into three major categories: (1) pure inter-regionalism by a group-to-group format (EU–CELAC, EU–MERCOSUR, EU–CARIFORUM, EU–SICA); (2) bilateralism, classified as "hybrid inter-regionalism" by Hänggi (2006); and (3) trans-regionalism (Gardini and Malamud 2014) by sector dialogues on thematic issues where countries participated individually but in a broader regional (LAC) format.

The three elements trade, development co-operation and political dialogue (triangle model) between the EU and Latin America followed the EU foreign policy doctrine of inter-regionalism. Three ideal types have been defined (Hänggi 2006; Gardni and Malamud 2014): pure inter-regionalism, the exchange between two actors who speak with one voice; hybrid inter-regionalism, when a region interacts with a country; and trans-regionalism between two regions that represent individual countries. The matrix in Figure 2.1 offers a picture of the combination between the three main issues in EU–LAC relations and the three types of inter-regionalism.

This ideal type model of inter-regionalism changed with the economic crisis in 2008, when China's rise as an external partner of the region dropped the EU from the second to the third position, and the first export market for countries such as Brazil and Chile for Peru. Parallel to declining trade relations (symbolised by the paralysis of the ratification process of the EU–MERCOSUR agreement signed in 2019), the golden decade of primary exports and social politics helped to upgrade eleven[4] Latin American countries to the club of nations with middle or high income, falling out of the EU's list of priorities (Ayuso and Caballero 2018: 74). Political dialogue also lost impulse. For example, Brazil and the EU celebrated their last summit in 2014, and CELAC and the EU in 2015. Stagnation in trade, less development co-operation and the crisis of globalisation and global governance reduced the motivation for a closer association between the two partners.

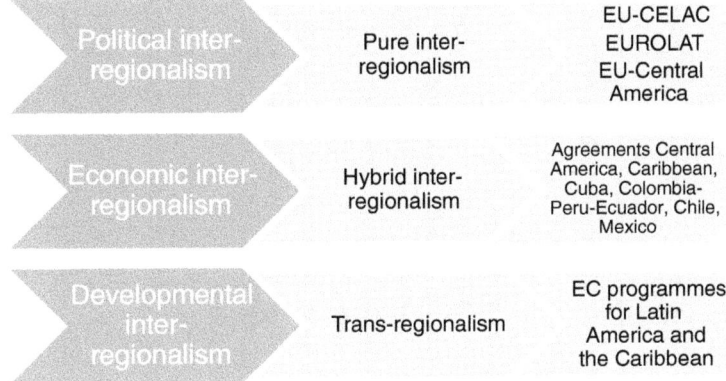

Figure 2.1 Types of inter-regionalism by issue, form and partners
Source: Author, based on the categories of inter-regionalism by Hänggi 2000 and 2006

Traditionally, the EU followed a three-pillar policy towards Latin America: political dialogue, development co-operation and trade or investment relations. These three elements, included in EU's agreements with Latin American partners and nearly all political declarations and development programmes, interacted in a complementary way until the beginning of the twenty-first century. After that period the triangle model came under stress by the setback of globalisation and regionalism, and the emergence of external actors like China and India in detriment of traditional partners like the US and the EU.

The disassociation of the triangle model of EU-LAC relations (trade, development and dialogue) occurs parallel to declining economic exchange and development co-operation that are no longer the main pillars of political dialogues. These do not serve as an umbrella for interdependences but lack a concrete agenda and follow the pattern function follows form (and not, as in the past, form follows function, according to David Mitrany).

None the less, the maintenance of a multilevel political dialogue (Table 2.2) with governmental and non-governmental actors, despite declining trade and development co-operation, confirms the initial hypothesis that institutionalised dialogues (form) are more important than the contents (function). Nearly all fifteen dialogue forums reflect a diffuse multilevel political regionalism, more by accident than as a result of a decision-making process. Most dialogues lack concrete results and a clear agenda. Scarce results are a comparative disadvantage compared to other external actors like China that increased its engagement in trade agreements and political dialogue with Latin America and the Caribbean, and continued its political dialogue with CELAC.

Table 2.2 Political dialogues as part of EU–LAC agreements

	Type of agreement	Conditionality and/or political dialogue	Scope and issues of political dialogue
Mexico	Global agreement (2000), upgraded (trade) in 2018	Conditionality and political dialogue (part II of the agreement)	Regular and institutionalised political dialogue, broad range of issues
Chile	Political and economic association agreement (2002), upgrading under negotiation	Conditionality and political dialogue (part II of the agreement)	Regular political dialogue on international issues, security, human rights, migration, association parliamentary committee
Central America	Association agreement (2012)	Conditionality and political dialogue (part II of the agreement)	Human rights, migration, security, democracy
Colombia–Peru–Ecuador	Trade agreement (2012)	Conditionality, but no political dialogue	Not included in the trade agreement but part of the EU relation with the Andean Community and individual countries
Caribbean			
Cuba	Political dialogue and co-operation agreement (2016)	No conditionality (end of common position), but political dialogue on human rights	Human rights (political, economic and social), mutual approach.

Source: Author's own elaboration

EU-LAC multilevel dialogue forums competing with others

EU–LAC trade relations and political dialogues compete with other external actors, mainly the US and, more recently, China and other emerging global powers. In the 1990s and early 2000s the EU and Spain (through the Iberoamerican summits that have been held regularly since 1991) were perceived as privileged political partners of Latin America and the Caribbean by sustaining a horizontal, multilevel dialogue (bilateral, sub-regional and inter-regional) with different partners and formats. Since its EU membership in 1986, Spain and, to a lesser extent Portugal have been the main driving forces of Brussels's relations with Latin America. The EU's Cuban policy, for example, has been heavily influenced by Spanish interests and domestic relationship between the socialist PSOE (against sanctions) and the PP. The latter imposed in 1996, under the Aznar government, the EU Common Position on Cuba, increasing democratic pressure for twenty years, until its replacement by the PDCA between Brussels and Havana. Other less prominent examples for Spain's special interests and relations with Latin America have been the inclusion of the region in development schemes or the up-grading by regular summits.

Partly as a result of Spain's and Portugal's late accession, EU engagement in Latin America came late. Moreover, non-institutionalised political dialogues between shifting governments and civil society actors cannot compete with the solid institutional structure of the inter-American system under a still hegemonic US leadership, albeit in decline due to internal ideological divisions on Venezuela and the imposition of Trump's candidate Mauricio Claver-Carone as president of the IADB. Firstly, the Organisation of American States is a regional organisation (the first ever created); secondly, it works as a community of states based on cultural and geographical conditions (similar to the Iberoamerican system); and thirdly, the US has been the hegemonic, and more recently, the strongest power in the Inter-American System.

Despite all criticism (for example Legler 2015) of Washington's prominent role and recent weaknesses, the OAS is the oldest and most experienced regional body in the world. The large number of legal documents signed by its thirty-four member states and the dense institutional network, including the IADB, reflect still strong political and economic interdependences in the Americas.

By his absence from the 2018 Summit of the Americas in Lima, President Donald Trump neglected or ignored it, but he was not able to dismantle the inter-American system. Despite all political differences on Venezuela and failed attempts to exclude the country by applying the democracy clause, the OAS approved a critical Resolution on fraudulent Presidential elections held in May 2018 (presidentials) and December 2020 (legislative elections), although it was unable to take the lead in the 2019 crisis, when the leader of the National Assembly, Juan Guaidó, self-proclaimed president, challenged Nicolás Maduro. Not the divided OAS but the informal Lima Group, composed of twelve Latin American states, Canada and the US, took the lead, and supported the opposition leader (Gratius and Puente 2019). Different from the EU–CELAC process that had not managed to organise a high-level meeting for the last five years, the dispute on Venezuela and its final exclusion from the Summit of the Americas in Lima did not hinder its celebration.

The geographical and historical distance between Europe and Latin America facilitated the emergence of a more horizontal but also less institutionalised political dialogue aimed at resolving conflicts in bi-regional relations, promoting peace, integration, development and democracy and, in a post-Cold War context, to identify common positions at the global stage in areas such as drugs and climate change. Drugs and climate change are probably the most prominent issues in global EU–LAC relations. Firstly, the concept of co-responsibility, alternative development and the de-penaliation of certain drugs are part of a shared approach towards the global drugs problem, discussed at the UN General Assembly Special Session (UNGASS) on drugs in 2016. Secondly, the regions converged on sustainable development and in 2015 signed the Paris Climate Change Agreement.

Despite those basic agreements, the outcome of EU–LAC dialogues are limited and they are not institutionalised. The small EU–LAC Foundation created in 2010 and based in Hamburg connects the regions, but its limited scope and budget cannot be compared to the OAS or other inter-American institutions, mainly financed by the US. The lack of institutionalisation and binding commitments (comparable to the OAS or Democratic Charta) constitutes a clear disadvantage, compared to the Inter-American System integrated by the OAS and its related bodies and the IADC.

The low level of institutionalisation, the horizontal approach (despite power and trade asymmetries) and the focus on development co-operation of EU-LAC political dialogue comes closer to the China–LAC dialogue established in 2014 to follow up and deepen economic relations. Thus China and the EU held separately a high-level political dialogue with CELAC. None the less, China's pragmatic approach contrasts with the EU's normative ambitions, mainly the export of integration and political values. The latter seem to have had a negative effect on political relations between the EU and LAC.

Whilst the EU–CELAC summit projected for 2018 failed because of serious differences on how to deal with Venezuela, in line with the principle of non-interference in domestic affairs China ignores the political conditions of its Latin American and Caribbean counterparts. The holding of the second

Ministerial Meeting China–CELAC in January 2018 in Santiago de Chile focused on economic co-operation (technology, innovation, trade, investment and infrastructure) contrasted with the failure to agree on a new edition of the EU–CELAC summit.

The recent political dispute on the crisis in Venezuela (between defenders and opponents of the Maduro government, and for or against sanctions) indicates that the normative approach of EU–LAC dialogues seems to be rather an obstacle than an advantage when it comes to building consensus. Pragmatic political dialogue between CELAC and China, focused on trade, innovation and development in its third edition in 2018, contrasted with a North–South-driven political dialogue driven by EU institutions.

Recent trends in EU–LAC political dialogues

Political (dialogues) and economic (trade) inter-regionalism follow different paths. Whilst "pure economic inter-regionalism" by establishing a region-to-region free trade area, similar to the ambitious FTAA project, has never been envisaged either by the EU or by Latin America, despite the failure to celebrate its third edition, the EU-CELAC Summits are still perceived as the highest form of political inter-regionalism by a group-to-group dialogue. Formally ongoing EU–MERCOSUR negotiations are the last relic of the EU paradigm to sign agreements with trade blocs, but its main partners in Latin America have been individual countries or small sub-regions.

The selection of different partners (Brazil, Mexico and Cuba have been singled out as partners with a special or high-level political dialogue) confirms the initial hypothesis of a mismatch between political dialogue and trade. None the less, trade agreements and political dialogues are part of a liberal world order based on inter-state co-operation and interdependences, principles that are shared between the EU and its Latin American and Caribbean partners. In a context of new unilateral trade barriers imposed by the Trump administration on several countries, trade and political dialogues are key instruments for the defence of open regionalism and global governance that suffered a constant decline as a result of the withdrawal of the US.

In its future Latin America strategy, the EC will stress common challenges and the co-ordination of positions at the global stage. Global inter-regionalism (Ayuso and Caballero 2018) based on trade liberalisation and political dialogues on shared problems, such as climate change, conflict prevention, trade openness and other issues, should be a goal pursued by both, the EU and Latin America, in their own interests to preserve the global liberal order now under pressure from nationalist, populist and xenophobic governments and movements.

In theory the EU and Latin America are ideal partners for a political association based on close trade relations. None the less, neither political nor economic inter-regionalism is in a good shape, and, as a result of a growing Latin American middle class, apart from the poorest countries of the region (Haiti in the Caribbean or Bolivia in Latin America) development is no longer a key issue in relations. This is why the multilevel dialogue forums created before the financial crisis of 2008–9 are losing dynamism and a concise agenda. To reactivate the political and economic partnership between the regions requires innovation and political compromise to recover the level of interdependences of the past based on the form-follows-function principle (contents determine institutions) and not the opposite, function follows form (institutions determine contents).

Benign neglect or other external priorities on both sides might be one explanation for the lack of progress in political dialogue and trade, and geographical distance another, but the current stagnation or even decline in relations also reflects the limits of the EU's paradigm of inter-regionalism that is still present in its Global Strategy (EC, EEAS 2016). Group-to-group dialogues on trade liberalisation work better with small countries (Central America and the Caribbean), whilst bigger states require hybrid inter-regionalism or bilateralism (see Gratius 2017c on Brazil). Political dialogue can be part of those agreements, but is not a necessary condition, as has been proved by the Colombia–Peru–Ecuador trade deal.

The idea of pushing global governance, stressed in the EC Communication on Latin America (2009), introduces a more horizontal approach to the traditional North–South type of relationship characterised by asymmetric inter-regionalism (Ayuso and Caballero 2018). Sector dialogues on drugs, migration, social cohesion and the environment reflect the attempt to use the cultural "community of values" for defining common positions at international organisations and forums. In times of a declining liberal order, the EU and LAC should use the variety of political dialogues to define a limited and realistic number of priorities in relations aimed at advancing global governance against the protectionist position of the US.

Concluding remarks

Compared to rising co-operation with Asian partners, in the twenty-first century EU–LAC relations experienced a decline in trade flows despite the establishment of free trade areas with Central America, the Caribbean, Colombia, Chile, Ecuador, Mexico and Peru. Albeit historic links are still reflected in a dense, flexible, multilevel political dialogue by sector and sub-region or country, results are limited and contrast with the large number of declarations and action plans. Retaking the first hypothesis of an oversized political dialogue compared to real interdependences (migration, trade, investment, societal exchange), the EU and LAC should reduce political co-operation to those issues that are of real mutual interest and inter-regional convergence like drugs or climate policies. At a country-by-country level (hybrid inter-regionalism) the EU and its partners should select strategic topics that reflect the key topics in relations like citizens' security in Central America, diplomacy and humanitarian aid in Venezuela, economic relations and climate change in Brazil, development assistance in Bolivia, etc.

Although these issues are prominent in relations, the "one size fits all" approach of EU policies towards Latin America, and, separately, towards the Caribbean, reflects the relatively low level of interest of Brussels in a deeply divided region in terms of development, size, political ideology and partners (South America's closer relations with Asia, and Central America's and Mexico's asymmetric interdependence with the US). On the other hand, the maintenance of "pure inter-regionalism", as stated in the EU Global Strategy, has negative consequences for relations: the twenty-yearyears negotiation process with MERCOSUR or the failure to organise a new bi-regional summit with CELAC that is deeply divided in right- and left-wing governments and had been unable since 2015 to prepare a new high-level meeting with its European partners.

The lack of a systematic follow-up by an inter-regional institution responsible for the monitoring of declarations and action plans contributed to a constant weakening of political and economic co-operation, Without co-ordination by an "EU–LAC OAS" or similar institutions, the network of dialogue forums got lost in vague declarations of good intention that bring few concrete results. Clear road maps and long-term objectives would also help to structure political dialogues and avoid overlapping agendas and partners. A constant follow-up would also help to increase the low level of visibility and presence of Europe in Latin America and the Caribbean, compared to China, that uses individual and collective formats (CELAC) to upgrade relations with Latin America and the Caribbean beyond economic interests (Ríos 2019).

References

All websites last visited 30 September 2021.

Ayuso, A. (2009a). *Migration in the Context of Relations between the European Union, and Latin America and the Caribbean*. Brussels: Directorate General for External Policies, European Parliament. www.europarl.europa.eu/thinktank/en/document.html?reference=EXPO-AFET_ET(2009)410198.

Ayuso, A. (2009b). "Encuentros y desencuentros de la asociación estratégica eurolatinoamericana: equilibrios y asimetrías", *Revista Cidob Afers Internacionals* 85–6, 185–201. www.cidob.org/es/articulos/revista_cidob_d_afers_internacionals/ encuentros_y_desencuentros_de_la_asociacion_estrategica_eurolatinoamericana_ equilibrios_y_asimetrias.

Ayuso, A. and Caballero, S. (2018). *El interregionalismo de la Unión Europea con América Latina*. Bogotá: Universidad Cooperativa de Colombia. https://ediciones.ucc.edu.co/index.php/ucc/catalog/book/66.

Ayuso, A. and Gratius, S. (2017a). *Nueva Etapa entre Cuba y la UE. Escenarios de Futuro*. Barcelona: CIDOB.

Ayuso, A. and Gratius, S. (2017b). *EU–Brazil Economic Relations*. IAI Working Paper. Rome: IAI. www.iai.it/en/pubblicazioni/economic-agenda-between-brazil-and-eu.

Ayuso, A. and Gratius, S. (2020). "Capítulo 5: Las Relaciones de la Unión Europea con Brasil y el MERCOSUR", in Beneyto Pérez, J. M. (ed.), *Tratado de Derecho y Políticas de la Unión Europea. Tomo X: Las Relaciones de la Unión Europea con Áreas Regionales y Terceros Estados*. Pamplona: CEU, Thomson Reuters Aranzadi, pp. 213–41.

Börzel, T. and Risse, T. (2009). *The Rise of (Inter-) Regionalism. The EU as a Model of Regional Integration*. Working Paper, APSA 2009 Toronto Meeting Paper, https://ssrn.com/abstract=1450391.

European Commission (2009). *The European Union and Latin America: A Partnership between Global Actors*. Brussels. https://eur-lex.europa.eu/legal-content/EN/ALL /?uri=CELEX%3A52009DC0495.

European Commission (2017). *European Union, Trade in Goods with Latin American Countries*. Brussels: EC. http://trade.ec.europa.eu/doclib/docs/2006/september/ tradoc_111527.pdf.

European Commission, EEAS (2016). *Global Strategy: Shared Vision, Common Action: A Stronger Europe*. Brussels: EC. https://eeas.europa.eu/archives/docs/ top_stories/pdf/eugs_review_web.pdf.

Freres, C., Gratius, S., Mallo, T. and Sanahuja, J. A. (eds) (2007). *¿Sirve el diálogo político entre la UE y América Latina?* Madrid: CEALCI, Fundación Carolina. www.fundacioncarolina.es/wp-content/uploads/2014/08/DT15.pdf.

Gardini, G.-L. and Malamud, A. (2014). "Debunking interregionalism: concepts, type and critique – with a transatlantic focus", Working Paper 38. Barcelona: Atlantic Future. www.cidob.org/en/publications/publication_series/project_papers/ atlantic_future_papers/working_paper/debunking_interregionalism_concepts_types_ and_critique_with_a_transatlantic_focus.

Gómez Saraiva, M. (2017). "The Brazil–EU strategic partnership: from Lula to Dilma Rousseff: a shift of focus", *Revista Brasileira de Política Internacional* 60, 1. www.scielo.br/j/rbpi/a/97kDddYzP7rxN6fKbFZbQBL/?lang=en.

González Blanco, R. and Maesso Corral, M. (2000). "Las relaciones comerciales entre la Unión Europea y América Latina De la marginación al entendimiento", *Boletín Económico del ICE* 2649, 23–34.

Gratius, S. (2018). "Brazil and the EU: from liberal interregionalism to realist bilateralism", *Revista Brasileira de Política Internacional* 61, 1. www.scielo.br/j/ rbpi/a/QqJvfpYCwBqBckSL4LZKmZR/?lang=en.

Gratius, S. (2021). "The European Union, Latin America, and the Caribbean", in Vanden, H. E. and Prevost, G. (eds), *The Oxford Encyclopedia of Latin American Politics* . New York: Oxford University Press, Online January 2020, oxfordre.com/politics.

Gratius, S. and Puente, J. M. (2019). "Las claves de la crisis venezolana", *Foreign Affairs Latinoamérica* 19 (2), 5–15. https://revistafal.com/numeros-anteriores/fal-19-2/.
Hänggi, H. (2006). "Interregionalism as a multifaceted phenomenon. In search of a typology", in Rüland, J., Hänggi, H. and Roloff, R. (eds), *Inter-regionalism and International Relations*. London and New York: Routledge.
Legler, T. (2015). "Beyond reach? The Organization of American States and effective multilaterlism", in Domínguez, J. and Covarrubias, A. (eds), *Routledge Handbook of Latin America in the World*. New York: Routledge, pp. 311–68.
Nolte, D. and Weiffen, B. (eds) (2020). *Regionalism under Stress: Europe and Latin America in Comparative Perspective*. London and New York: Routledge.
Ríos, X. (2019). *El estado de las relaciones China–América Latina*. Documentos de Trabajo 1/2019. Madrid: Fundación Carolina. www.fundacioncarolina.es/el-estado-de-las-relaciones-china-america-latina/.
Roy, J. (1992). "The identity of the new Europe and the San José Process", in Roy, J. (ed.), *The Reconstruction of Central America: The role of the European Union*. Miami: North-South Center, University of Miami.
Ruano, L. (2018). "La Unión Europea y América Latina y el Caribe: Breve Historia de la Relación Birregional", *Revista Mexicana de Política Exterior* 112, 69–87. https://biblat.unam.mx/en/revista/revista-mexicana-de-politica-exterior/articulo/la-union-europea-y-america-latina-y-el-caribe-breve-historia-de-la-relacion-birregional.

Notes

1 Argentina, Brazil, Chile, Colombia, Paraguay and Peru.
2 For example, the Mexican Angel Gurría, as long-standing Director of the OECD, or the Brazilian leadership at the WTO (Roberto de Acevedo), the FAO (José Graziano da Silva), and the country's participation in the powerful BRICs group.
3 Smart or selected sanctions include the freezing of assets of members of government, an arms embargo and financial restrictive measures. Sanctions approved by the Council of the EU had been approved on an annual bases until November 2019.
4 Argentina, Brazil, Chile, Colombia, Costa Rica, Ecuador, Mexico, Panama, Peru, Uruguay and Venezuela.

3

Interlinkages in EU–Andean Community trade negotiations

Daniel Schade

Introduction

This chapter focuses on the EU's trade negotiations with the Andean region in Latin America. It considers the EU's negotiations for a so-called association agreement with the Andean Community,[1] and the shift in those negotiations which ultimately led the EU to conclude an FTA with Colombia and Peru, only. This meant that both the goal of negotiations for an association agreement, which would have covered many more policy elements than a mere FTA, and the aim for a comprehensive agreement with all Andean countries in an inter-regional format were abandoned. The chapter then goes on to analyse the unlikely accession of one further Andean country, Ecuador, to the existing FTA between the EU and Colombia and Peru.

As this chapter argues, both the EU's choice of negotiating agreements in the region in the first place and the change of the EU's aims are significant and cannot be understood from within the dynamics of these negotiations only. In line with the book's overarching analytical framework (see the Introduction) this chapter follows an analytical perspective which emphasises that the complexity of contemporary trade policy-making requires researchers to consider more than traditional trade agreements and their negotiations to explain the development of trade ties between trade partners in an increasingly complex international economic setting. The chapter therefore also takes into consideration interlinkages, defined here as (trade) political developments formally outside of the scope of EU–Andean Community negotiations but ultimately influencing their overall scope and the preferences of both sides. In particular the case is made that the evolution of trade relations is influenced by broader patterns in multilateral trade policy-making, the evolution of the trade policy of major players such as the US and the EU itself (Meissner 2018, also García, Chapter 4 below), as well as growing links to other aspects of international relations. To this one needs to add domestic dynamics within both the EU and individual

Latin American countries that can radically alter the underlying conditions for the development of EU–Latin American trade relations.

The chapter also considers the effects of the EU's evolving trade ties with individual Latin American partners on others, as most of these negotiations occur in a setting that can be described as asymmetric trade negotiations. In such negotiations the power of the involved actors differs importantly (for an introduction to the concept see Tussie and Saguier 2011). Ultimately, the chapter argues that it is complex factors such as these which can help explain the unusual development of the trade negotiations under consideration here.

The remainder of the chapter is structured as follows. It first discusses the unlikely context for the launch of EU–Andean Community trade negotiations and how interlinkages with other political processes have contributed to their rapid launch. The second section of this chapter then considers the actual negotiation phase, including the decision to abandon the association agreement and regional framework for bilateral FTA negotiations with some Andean countries only. The last section then deals with the unlikely accession of Ecuador to the existing FTA in a context of asymmetric negotiations.

The context of EU–Andean Community negotiations

From the perspective of the early 2000s the EU's attempts to negotiate association agreements, with the Andean Community and a raft of other partners in Latin America and beyond, appears surprising. Rather than championing FTAs with individual partners (which are a core element of each association agreement), the EU's long-term focus was on progress in the realm of the WTO, and the Doha Development Agenda, in particular. This EU preference for negotiations in the multilateral realm even led the EU under the then Trade Commissioner Pascal Lamy (during the Prodi Commission) to instate a de facto moratorium on the negotiation of new EU FTAs (Woolcock 2007: 5). This is due to the fact that any future EU FTA would necessarily be influenced by the outcome of those broad negotiation under the auspices of the WTO.

It was only after it became clear that the Doha Development Agenda would not be concluded successfully after the WTO's meeting in Hong Kong in December of 2005 that the EU's perspective on FTAs changed once again.[2] The European Commission's Directorate General for Trade (DG Trade) voiced this shift of view in its 2006 *Global Europe* communication, which emphasised that the EU now considered new FTAs as an important stepping stone until further liberalisation could be achieved at the multilateral level (DG Trade 2006: 10).

Whilst the document then sets out to mention the Andean Community as one of multiple partners for a future FTA, the only negotiation priority in the Latin American region specifically referred to were negotiations with Mercosur (DG Trade 2006: 10–11). This was logical for two reasons: on the one hand, the EU's enlargement round in 2004 had meant that its geographic outlook had changed, as its new member states had comparatively few interests in the Latin American region.[3] On the other, the EU's capacity to undertake trade negotiations was and remains limited by the human resources of DG Trade. These resources are therefore usually allocated in such a way as to favour the EU's most important negotiations.[4] The EU's initial lack of enthusiasm for negotiations with the Andean region can then primarily be explained by the small size of the economies of the countries concerned. With the EU's trading arrangements with many more significant partners still not being governed by FTAs at the time, the small EU trade volume with the Andean countries hardly made negotiations with them a priority.

Any consideration of negotiations with the Andean region was also complicated by a long-standing dispute between banana-exporting countries and corporations from the US owning the plantations, on the one hand, and the EU as a key importer of this commodity, on the other (for an overview of the origins of this dispute see Josling and Taylor 2003). Given the EU's overseas territories and its privileged ties to certain former colonies in the Africa Caribbean and Pacific (ACP) grouping, it had shielded its market from Central American and Andean banana exports, leading to litigation under the auspices of the WTO. This conflict which dated back to the early 1990s was ultimately resolved only in 2009 (Fattore and Allison 2013). It had dragged on for such a long period of time as the EU's domestic preference structure on the matter led it to react only strategically and slowly to litigation under the WTO system (Young 2011: 124). When negotiations with the Andean Community were seriously considered for the first time after *Global Europe* in 2006, this conflict had reached a new stage. Ecuador had initiated a renewed complaint at the WTO to which Colombia became a party. This led the EU Trade Commissioner Peter Mandelson to initially rule out such negotiations, arguing that 'it is not possible to litigate and negotiate at the same time' (Agence Europe 2006).

There are also political considerations which complicated the opening of negotiations with the Andean Community. Whilst there may have been some interest in negotiating an FTA with countries in the Andean region, the European Commission's 2005 Latin America strategy clearly stated that this was supposed to occur on an inter-regional basis (European Commission 2005), in line with similar such efforts across the globe at the time (Börzel and Risse 2009). This meant that any consideration of such negotiations

Interlinkages in EU–Andean Community trade negotiations 47

by the EU were initially dependent on the member states of the Andean Community progressing with their own economic integration first (US Embassy Peru Lima 2006; 2005). This was partly due to the Andean Community not yet being sufficiently integrated economically for region-to-region negotiations. More importantly, however, this represented political leverage by the EU to entice further Andean Community integration. This political conditionality was also linked to concerns over the political orientation of the governments led by Hugo Chavez in Venezuela (which even announced its intent to withdraw from the bloc at the time) and that of the newly elected Evo Morales in Bolivia who entered office at the beginning of 2006 (US Embassy Belgium Brussels 2006). These governments' opposition to FTAs along the lines proposed by the EU made the beginning of EU–Andean Community negotiations ever more unlikely.

Despite all this, EU–Andean negotiations were then envisioned, and the process launched relatively quickly on the EU's side for a start of negotiations in 2007. To understand this development, one has to look further than the failure of the Doha Development Agenda. This is related to a change of approach in the external economic policy of the US akin to that observed for the EU. Initially the EU expected little trade competition from the world's largest economy. This is due to the fact that a previous major US initiative on improving its trade relations with all of Latin America, the negotiations for a so-called Free Trade Area of the Americas (FTAA), had dragged on incessantly and ultimately failed in 2005 (Nelson 2015: 183) over major trade political divergences between some Latin American countries and the US. In return the US was quick to shift its attention from this regional approach to one favouring its ties with individual Latin American countries: in 2004 negotiations with numerous Latin American countries, including Colombia, Peru and Ecuador, as well as the Central American nations, were launched.

By 2006 all of these had come to fruition with the exception of Ecuador, promising an immediate improvement of trade ties between the US and two of the Andean Community's major economies – to the detriment of the EU's ties to those countries. Despite the small size of these countries' economies the existing rivalry between the EU and the US over trade influence (Meissner 2018; Sbragia 2010) made it much more likely that the EU would follow suit (Dimon 2006: 214; Meissner 2018: 181). Furthermore, whilst EU officials were initially unconvinced as to the negotiation capacity of the Andean countries, the successful negotiations of Colombia and Peru with the US convinced them that these would be capable of handling a complex negotiation with the EU despite the prior concerns (US Embassy Peru Lima 2006). Whilst the Andean countries remained far from the EU's most important trading partners, the interlinkage with the US's trade policy thus radically altered the prospect for negotiations in a relatively short timeframe. After all this would be able to put the EU's trade access on a par with the US in the region, and the Andean countries' prior negotiations with the US had demonstrated that the Andean countries were capable of partaking in relatively complex negotiations.

Whilst the above captures an altered set of external incentives for the EU's negotiations with the Andean region, it is also important to consider how this change of focus was able to propagate within the EU's institutions. Here consideration of institutional politics within the EC can provide further answers as to how DG Trade's initial concerns were overcome. It is important to note that this is largely related to the activism of another institutional actor, namely the Commission's Directorate-General for External Relations (DG RELEX) and its responsible Commissioner. Given this DG's focus on political aspects of the EU's external relations, this institution had a natural interest in developing closer ties to the Andean Community countries. This was matched by Colombia's and Peru's long-standing advocacy for Andean Community negotiations with the EU.[5] As DG RELEX was also keen to be seen as a promoter of regional integration, language in support of such negotiations gradually made its way into various declarations on EU–Latin American relations, including the conclusions of regular EU–Latin America summits. Considering the 2002 Madrid declaration of the EU–Latin America summit of that year, only vague promises for a future Association Agreement were included (Council of the European Union 2002: 3). By the Guadalajara Declaration following the 2004 EU–Latin America summit this language had become much more supportive of such negotiations already, albeit conditional on the prior conclusion of the Doha Development Agenda (Council of the European Union 2004: 8). The conclusions of the May 2006 EU–Latin American summit held in Vienna then promised that preparatory work for negotiations would be finished by July of that year (Council of the European Union 2006: 12). This can be attributed to the summit being one of the key events of Austria's rotating Council presidency in 2006 (Federal Ministry of Foreign Affairs 2005: 28). The then RELEX Commissioner Benita Ferrero-Waldner had also previously served in the same Austrian government as foreign minister and was a keen advocate of EU-Latin American ties.[6]

All this advocacy could not overcome the remaining hurdle of a lack of unity in the Andean Community and concerns over the views of the Venezuelan government. These concerns were largely removed in 2006, however, when said country formally announced that it would leave the Andean Community and join MERCOSUR instead. The Venezuelan government cited Colombia's and Peru's signature of their FTA with the US as a breach of the fundamentals of the Andean Community as the primary reason for this (Maihold 2008: 23). It is more likely, however, that the underlying concerns were primarily related to the country's quest for influence in the region.[7] The withdrawal of Venezuela from the organisation somewhat reduced the economic incentives for the EU to conclude an agreement with the Andean Community and threw it into disarray at least in the short term. Nonetheless this development had similarly removed the largest political hurdle to such negotiations.

This was reflected in the gradual convergence of member states' views that led to a de facto "permissive consensus"[8] amongst member states to develop the EU's trade ties to Latin America in general, and the Andean Community in particular. On the one hand this was due to the fact that the prospects for reaching an agreement with Latin America's most important economic integration mechanism, MERCOSUR, and its member countries, remained dire after these had essentially been frozen in 2005 (Agence Europe 2004).[9] Spain and some Eastern European countries were initially sceptical of opening negotiations with the Andean Community while Venezuela was one of its members.[10] Spain's socialist government that came into power in 2004 then gradually altered its position (US Embassy Spain Madrid 2005), especially after Venezuela's decision for unilateral withdrawal from the Andean Community.

What was still at stake then was the lack of a joint position of the remaining Andean Community members on beginning association agreement negotiations with the EU (US Embassy Bolivia La Paz 2006). The ambivalent stance of Bolivia under its new president Evo Morales was particularly problematic in that regard. Due to the EU's double desire of fostering its trade ties with the region, all while strengthening Andean integration, it still insisted that a prerequisite for the launch of negotiations would be further Andean integration, all while pressuring Bolivia to be part of the process (US Embassy Colombia Bogotá 2006). Ultimately, this proved fruitful with Bolivia giving in to the views of the other Andean states at a joint meeting in July 2006 at which the organisation formally decided to undertake negotiations with the EU (US Embassy Ecuador Quito 2006). At a meeting between EU and Andean Community officials shortly after, both sides then indeed agreed to the launch a process of negotiations under the condition that the Andean Community undertake further steps in regional integration (EU–CAN High Level Meeting 2006).

A number of complex interlinkages can thus explain the EU's decision to undertake negotiations with the Andean Community. Whilst the EU's changed approach in the aftermath of the failure of the Doha Development Agenda was an enabling factor in the general sense, parallel developments in the trade policy of the US created specific incentives to negotiate with Andean Community countries. To this one has to add the political manoeuvring of DG RELEX in support of regional integration, which had gradually prepared the EU to alter its position on Andean negotiations.

The actual decision for this negotiation was then taken by the EU's Council of Ministers in parallel to a raft of other negotiations. These are notably negotiations for an association agreement with Central America, as well as three negotiations in Asia with the Association of South East Asian Nations (ASEAN), South Korea and India (Agence Europe 2007). Furthermore, the green light for Andean negotiations by the Council once more came with strings attached: the negotiation process was still meant to consider progress in the political and economic integration of the Andean Community and the prior conclusion of the dispute over bananas at the WTO (COREPER 2007: 13). Whilst the Andean countries were not the principal movers of this dispute, the possible scope for any EU trade agreement with banana-exporting countries would ultimately depend on its outcome. Despite this the Commission was enabled by the Council decision to begin the process of negotiations within the red lines set out by the Council. Ultimately the negotiations with the Andean Community would then occur in sync to those with the Central American countries.

The power of interlinkages: moving away from inter-regionalism in EU–Andean negotiations

The actual negotiations between the EU and the Andean Community were marred by the continued divergent views of the latter's remaining member countries, on the one side, and the EU's dual aim of furthering its trade interests, all while wanting to promote regional integration, on the other. The lack of progress in the Andean region's political integration ultimately led to the abandonment of the original negotiations in a region-to-region format and to the conclusion of an EU–Colombia–Peru FTA only. Whilst the aim for reaching at least an agreement on political, rather than trade, matters with all of the Andean Community's members was upheld by the EU in theory, attempts at reaching such an agreement quickly vanished as the negotiations for a pure FTA progressed. This change of the EU's approach towards the negotiations can be attributed to some of the broader economic interlinkages identified above, as well as a gradual disillusionment within the EU as to the prospects of promoting regional integration.

Whilst the positions of first the Venezuelan government and then of Bolivia were the main initial hurdles to the opening of negotiations with the Andean Community in 2006, the inauguration of Rafael Correa as president of Ecuador in January 2007 would complicate the actual negotiations phase further. Much as in Bolivia under Evo Morales, his new government was sceptical of the aims of the negotiation process. This meant that now only Colombia and Peru, two of the Andean Community's four member states, were unreservedly in favour of the negotiations at hand, which increasingly worried EU negotiators (US Embassy Peru Lima 2007). Nonetheless, the initial phase of negotiations after their official launch in June 2007 appeared relatively fruitful as the EU's side managed to emphasise that the association agreement sought with the Andean Community would be much more than a mere FTA governing trade relations (US Embassy Ecuador Quito 2007).

In this initial phase of the negotiations this indeed appears to have been one of the EU's main aims as it continued to insist that further Andean Community integration was necessary for their successful conclusion (EU–Andean Community Ministerial meeting 2007). The EU's new political strategy for the region also emphasised that any development aid should be targeted at strengthening regional integration (European Commission 2007: 15). Thereby the EU attempted to combine various of the policy tools at its disposal in support of regional integration.

This also included attempts by the EU to mitigate divergent demands by various Andean Community countries. Whilst Peru and Colombia came to be increasingly vocal about their desire for a bilateral agreement with the EU (Noriega 2007), Bolivia continued to be highly critical of the FTA aspect of any possible agreement. The EU attempted to mitigate this by promising Bolivia side-payments in return for its continued participation in negotiations, all while explaining to the Colombian side that a region-to-region agreement would receive less scrutiny in the European Parliament over Colombia's human rights track record (US Embassy Colombia Bogotá 2008a). This overall initial EU approach proved so successful that Ecuador initially served as a mediator between the different Andean Community parties and thereby kept the negotiation process afloat (US Embassy Ecuador Quito 2007).

Nonetheless, by the spring of 2008 the views of Bolivia and Ecuador had evolved so far that their demands were increasingly at odds with the initial negotiation aim. This included proposals to limit the scope of the FTA, or wanting to exclude the planned inclusion of a sustainable development chapter within it (US Embassy Ecuador Quito 2008; US Embassy Colombia Bogotá 2008a). Whilst the EU's negotiators initially attempted to accommodate the evolving positions of both countries, this became much more difficult as the change of political tone in both countries politicised the negotiations. This standoff peaked when Bolivia and Ecuador accused the EU of racism over the so-called Returns Directive, a piece of EU migration law (Phillips 2008). Whilst this piece of legislation indeed would affect a number of Bolivian and Ecuadorian nationals resident in the EU, their concerns were ultimately exaggerated, unrelated to the process of ongoing negotiations, and served the Bolivian government's goal to slow down the pace of negotiations while it was struggling to define its own negotiation preferences.[11]

The country's government struggled, in particular, with how its socialist-inspired domestic politics could fit with the notion of an economically beneficial yet ultimately liberalising FTA.

The true difficulty for those negotiations, therefore, remained over diverging trade priorities amongst the Andean countries, based on a Bolivian desire to gain as many exceptions as possible from the proposed FTA, continuously altering preferences of Ecuador, including the negotiation team itself, as well as increasingly wary Colombian and Peruvian negotiators.[12] The Returns Directive, or any other political developments, did not feature prominently in the actual negotiation process, meaning that the political angle provided a mere smokescreen for the trade aspects of the negotiations. In this context a last-ditch attempt was made to save the inter-regional negotiations on the margins of a May 2008 EU–Latin America summit, where it was agreed between the negotiating sides that negotiations would be flexible as to individual countries' preferences and that 'special and differentiated treatment' (CAN–EU troika summit 2008) would be afforded for the particular circumstances of Bolivia and Ecuador.

It was at this point in the negotiations that the economic interlinkages with the trade policy of the US altered the EU's preference structure. On the one hand, it became clear that the political diversity of the Andean Community countries made further regional integration increasingly unlikely. On the other, the deepening of the US's trade relations with Colombia and Peru, as well as the latter countries' aggressive FTA agenda, brought economic concerns to the fore within the EU. Here the conclusion of bilateral FTAs by Colombia and Peru were an increasing hurdle for any further economic Andean integration, as this made regional politics more complex. The most important example here is the FTA between the US and Peru, which was ratified by the US Senate in 2007, and was due to enter into force by 2009. Whilst a US–Colombia FTA had similarly been negotiated, human rights concerns by parliamentarians in the US held up the ratification until 2011, much as would later be the case in the European Parliament for the EU-Colombia–Peru FTA. At the same time, both Colombia and Peru also aimed to reach FTAs with Canada (US Embassy Colombia Bogotá 2007; 2008c), and Colombia furthermore negotiated with the European Free Trade Area countries (US Embassy Colombia Bogotá 2008a). Therefore the EU's negotiators were increasingly worried that the inter-regional set-up for negotiations with the Andean Community threatened the EU's trade position within the region. These concerns and the EU's keen awareness of its competition with the US can be seen in a comment by the EU's chief negotiator to US counterparts wherein the EU lowest aim for negotiations with Colombia and Peru is defined as matching the terms of trade of the respective agreements between those countries and the US (US Embassy Colombia Bogotá 2009).

It is in this context that a cancellation by the EU of an inter-regional negotiation round scheduled for April 2008 needs to be considered. Whilst initially interpreted as an attempt by the EU to force the Andean countries to present a unified position, in reality this unilateral cessation of negotiations would prepare the EU's move away from the inter-regional format of the negotiations. In fact, what followed on the EU's side was a process led by DG Trade which emphasised the necessity to progress on FTA talks with the willing countries of the Andean Community to ensure continued market access.[13] This was further underlined by renewed demands from Colombia and Peru that the EU show itself willing to do so. Both demanded this through increased lobbying which culminated in a joint letter signed by both presidents demanding bilateral negotiations with the EU.[14] Whilst at first DG RELEX was concerned about what this would mean for the EU's commitment to regional integration, increasingly there was a change of view that a prolonged cessation of negotiations would alienate the countries most willing to negotiate with the EU (US Embassy Colombia Bogotá 2008b). In the end it was the thus the preferences of DG Trade (silently supported by most member states) which prevailed, all while DG RELEX gradually adapted its position over a fear of alienating Colombia and Peru.[15]

Ultimately a carefully orchestrated change of position by the EU emerged by October 2008. The EU committed itself to negotiating a collective FTA with all willing members of the Andean Community, whilst simultaneously upholding negotiations for a political agreement with the Andean Community itself. This approach was seen as compatible with the initial negotiation mandate of the EC, thus saving the time needed to gain a new mandate. Simultaneously the parallel efforts for a region-to-region agreement allowed the EU to uphold the claim that it was acting in support of regional integration in the Andean region (US Embassy Colombia Bogotá 2008b). This latter perspective was further strengthened by the EU formally demanding the Andean Community for its approval of such a changed approach, allowing it to claim that it was merely following Andean Community interests.[16] After said approval was given at an Andean Community summit in October 2008, efforts for negotiating a political agreement on a region-to-region basis then rapidly faded. This underscores the importance of trade, rather than political concerns at this stage of the negotiations.

The renewed FTA negotiation process initially continued with Colombia, Peru and even Ecuador in early 2009, whilst Bolivia had left the negotiation table from the outset. This would rapidly change, however, as Ecuador left the process entirely in July 2009, citing the then still ongoing banana dispute at the WTO (Fritz 2010). Once more it is likely that rather than being an actual concern this served more as an expedient reason to hide the country's shifting political views. After all Ecuador's political rhetoric increasingly aligned with that of Bolivia, accusing the EU of wanting to impose its supposed neoliberal economic model on the region (Agence Europe 2009).

The actual negotiations with Colombia and Peru then progressed speedily. This was due to the countries' strongly held beliefs in the necessity for an FTA with the EU, as well as the political will of the EU's member states. Spain, in particular, wanted to make these negotiations the centrepiece of a showcase of the EU's evolving ties with Latin America in time for the May 2010 EU–Latin America summit (Trueb 2012: 277–8). The final agreement between the EU, on the one side, and Colombia and Peru, on the other, could then indeed be initialled at said summit. Whilst the ratification of the agreement in the Council then proceeded largely without incident, the newly emboldened EP after the Lisbon Treaty nonetheless briefly threatened to block it. This had much to do with concerns over the human rights situation in Colombia, as MEPs were lobbied by Colombian NGOs and unions over the matter (Fritz 2010: 7). Ultimately this was resolved by the Commission applying some pressure on MEPs to ratify the agreement,[17] all while Colombia agreed to a (non-binding) 'roadmap' to improve its human rights track record.[18] As the FTA was a so-called mixed agreement, it then still required ratification by the EU's member state parliaments, all while most of its provisions have been applied provisionally since March 2013 for Peru and as of August 2013 for Colombia. Final ratification by the EU has been blocked since 2018, as Belgium's final ratification is still pending (Council of the European Union 2020).

If one is to compare this experience with the parallel negotiations for an EU Association Agreement with Central America, then the different importance of interlinkages in said process becomes clear. Whilst the US had also negotiated FTAs with countries in the region, the relatively small size of their economies compared to those in the Andean region meant that individual bilateral negotiations would have significantly increased the workload of the EU, and thereby reduced their utility from a cost-benefit standpoint. As a consequence, in those negotiations the EU's trade aims remained in sync with those in support of regional integration. The EU thereby insisted on the initial negotiation format which incentivised Central American governments to put pressure on one another and to co-operate so as to enable an agreement with the EU. This strategy ultimately proved to be fruitful, and negotiations for the EU–Central America association agreement also concluded successfully by the time of the 2010 EU–Latin America summit, with the agreement being in provisional application as of 2013 (Council of the European Union 2020).

Contrasting the negotiations with the Andean Community with their preparation, it becomes clear that interlinkages with political developments in some Andean countries, as well as the increasingly relevant issue of trade competition with the US, altered the EU's preferences which explains the move away from an interregional association agreement format.

EU–Ecuador negotiations: political power in asymmetric negotiations

The opening of negotiations between the EU and Ecuador on an FTA in January 2014 and their speedy conclusion in July 2014 is a distinct yet connected piece in the puzzle of exploring the evolution of the EU's trade ties with the Andean region. This sudden development, which saw the country return to the negotiation table with the EU under the same government that had initially rejected those talks in 2009, cannot be understood when considering the negotiation process in and of itself. Instead it is once more necessary to consider the interlinkages that this negotiation process has with wider developments in international trade relations, and the ripple-on effects from other EU trade negotiations, in particular. The ensuing changes to Ecuador's standing in the world economy weakened the country's position vis-à-vis the EU. It is thus illustrative of power dynamics in asymmetric trade negotiations. Ultimately this section of the chapter demonstrates how the policy space of relatively smaller participants in the world trading system, as is the case for most Latin American countries, is constrained by the activities of its major players such as the EU (see also Schade 2016).

Little had changed politically in Ecuador or in the EU's negotiation position that could explain the country's return to negotiations in 2014. To the contrary President Rafael Correa had been re-elected for a third term with a comfortable majority of 57 per cent in February 2013, winning a larger majority than in the previous presidential election in 2009. At the same time the EU's prior successful conclusion of the FTA with Colombia and Peru meant that any negotiation with Ecuador would now amount to a mere negotiation on the accession of the country to the existing agreement, rather than a fully fledged negotiation of all terms.

It is instead two changes outside of the direct framework of EU–Ecuador FTA negotiations which contributed heavily to a change in the country's trade outlook, ultimately motivating its return to the negotiation table. The first was an imminent risk to the country's asymmetrical trading arrangements with the EU under a reform of the latter's Generalised Scheme of Preferences (GSP). Secondly, given the entry into force of the EU's novel FTA with Colombia and Peru, as well as the agreement with Central America, Ecuador's terms of trade for key Ecuadorean exports to the EU were set to worsen considerably compared to its peers.

Ecuador's reluctance to partake in the initial trade negotiations can be attributed to it being a beneficiary of the EU's GSP scheme. It operates under a defined exception to the functioning of the WTO's rules for bilateral trade in absence of an FTA. This exception allows developed participants in the world trading system to grant asymmetrical tariff-free or low-tariff access for less developed countries. Given that Ecuador had signed a number of international human rights and labour conventions, it even benefited from an advanced version of this scheme titled GSP+, which meant that in 2013 more than 60 per cent of its exports to the EU were covered by it (DG Trade 2014). This ensured that the country's exports to the EU were charged $353 million less in tariffs compared to trading under ordinary WTO rules (Enríquez 2014).

Granting Ecuador this advanced status was the result of a reform of the EU's GSP system in 2012, which made the country one of only ten initial beneficiaries of GSP+ when the scheme entered into force in 2014 (European Commission 2013a). Nonetheless, the technical criteria for GSP and GSP+ eligibility, which are based on the classification of a country's economy by the World Bank, would see the growing economy classified in three consecutive years as an upper-middle-income economy. This threatened Ecuador's eligibility for GSP as of 1 January 2015 (European Commission 2013b: 2).

Whilst the underlying GSP reform that led to Ecuador's impending loss of GSP eligibility was unrelated to considerations of EU–Latin American trade ties, a possible increase of the EU's leverage in asymmetric trade negotiations with countries now due to graduate from GSP status after the reform was noted by the EP's rapporteur on the dossier, Christofer Fjellner at the time. He stated that "this proposal could of course lead to increased leverage for the EU in these negotiations" (Fjellner 2011: 3). Similar views have also been voiced in research on the GSP reform (Siles-Brügge 2014). Both these issues are intrinsically intertwined with the negotiations on Ecuador's accession to the EU's existing FTA with Colombia and Peru. Whilst not one of the aims of the GSP reform process, a potential increase of the EU's leverage in trade negotiations was an important, yet largely unintended, consequence arising out of the reform itself.

Another factor influencing the EU's leverage over Ecuador to return to the negotiation table is the ripple-on effects of the previously concluded FTA with Colombia and Peru. The agreement had been provisionally applied with Peru as of March 2013, and with Colombia as of August of the same year. Similarly the trade parts of the EU's association agreement with the Central American region gradually entered into force provisionally for individual countries in the region between August and December of 2013 (Council of the European Union 2020). The provisions of the underlying FTAs would see the terms of trade of these countries' exports to the EU increase substantially over those of Ecuador, especially after it would lose its GSP status. Given that most of these countries can produce similar agricultural goods as Ecuador, and bananas, in particular, there was thus a risk of loss of Ecuador's market share for these kinds of exports to the EU, as the others' terms of trade would improve as a result of their FTAs with the EU.

The combination of these two factors put a significant share of Ecuador's exports at risk, as in 2014 the EU was the country's second most important trade partner (after the US). Of its goods exports 13.5 per cent were to the EU, with 95 per cent of those being agricultural exports (DG Trade 2018b). The exports of bananas alone made up more than 30 per cent of the total at the time (DG Trade 2014). A consideration of trade patterns since the entry into force of the above-mentioned FTAs shows the extent of this risk, as Peruvian and Colombian agricultural exports to the EU have increased substantially (DG Trade 2017b: 4–5), with the exports from some Central American countries also seeing an increase (DG Trade 2017a).

Under these conditions, joining the existing FTA between the EU and Colombia and Peru was now a much more attractive – and indeed necessary – proposition than it had been when the original agreement was negotiated. This was even true for Ecuador now having to join an existing agreement, rather than being able to shape it on its own. Its eventual accession to this agreement was possible given that it was designed with the possible extension to Ecuador and Bolivia in mind. Its article 10 specifically concerns the issue of regional integration in the Andean region and recognises the right of all Andean Community member states to join eventually. Article 329 even sets out specific conditions under which these can join the agreement (Official Journal of the European Union 2012). Notably, this article states that actual negotiations would be limited to details on the modalities of the accession, such as the definition of a specific tariff schedule. Whilst the other Andean signatory countries would be given an ultimate right of regard, the negotiations themselves would take place between the EU and the acceding country only. The specifics of this arrangement mean that in practice no true negotiation on a country's accession is possible given that the flexibility for this is severely hampered by the legal provisions of article 329. These specifics of the accession process can ultimately explain why the actual negotiations phase between Ecuador and the EU was so short.

The truly important factor in the process leading to Ecuador's accession to this agreement was, thus, not the negotiation phase but the process leading to Ecuador's return to the negotiation table. DG Trade, the EU's negotiator, was keenly aware of its increased leverage in negotiations due to Ecuador's worsening terms of trade compared to its neighbours. It even used the threat of Ecuador's GSP loss as a negotiation tactic as early as 2011 when the GSP reform had not even been adopted (Schade 2016: 82–3). As Fernando Yépez Lasso, Ecuador's former ambassador to the EU, has described in his own words in a diplomatic cable, the GSP issue was used as: "an element of pressure by the European Commission [...] for Ecuador to join the FTA [...] with Colombia and Peru as our only alternative to avoid a loss of market access and the eventual economic, commercial and social repercussions" (Yépez Lasso 2011: 4, own translation). While exaggerating as to the direct link between the EU's GSP reform and the EU's negotiation leverage, this still accurately describes the attitude exhibited by DG Trade in the process.

DG Trade's willingness to bring Ecuador back into the negotiation process despite the relatively small economic relevance of the country to the EU and the lack of parallel US-Ecuador FTA negotiations, can be explained primarily by the institutional circumstances surrounding this process (Schade 2016: 80–1). To this one can add that bringing another Andean country into the agreement would also get the EU closer to achieving the EU's original goal of signing a trade agreement with all Andean countries. Whilst negotiating entirely novel FTAs is a time- and resource-consuming activity for this institutional actor, this was not the case here. The means of accession set out in the existing FTA between the EU and Colombia and Peru, as well as the continued validity of DG Trade's prior negotiation mandate for said agreement, meant that the actual workload related to the negotiation would be limited compared to the negotiation of an entirely novel FTA.[19] Furthermore this presented an opportunity for DG Trade to demonstrate its relevance in the post-Lisbon set-up which saw some of the Commission's former external relations responsibilities externalised to a new institutional actor, the European External Action Service (EEAS) (Schade 2020: 75).

Despite an overall "pragmatic turn" in Ecuador's trade policy by 2013 (El Comercio 2014) that would see the country embrace free trade more openly, its return to the negotiation table in early 2014 can be understood only when considering the numerous interlinkages mentioned above. Given those factors, it is ultimately unsurprising that the ensuing negotiations were extremely quick. Nonetheless, some interesting developments accompanied the negotiations which demonstrated the importance of those external factors for the negotiation process. The first relevant element influencing the pace of negotiations was the looming deadline of Ecuador's loss of GSP status by the end of 2014. As even speedy negotiations could not have ensured an entry into force of Ecuador's accession to the existing FTA in time, the EU promised that it would pass provisional and temporary legislation delaying Ecuador's loss of GSP status by two years in the case of a successful negotiation (Schade 2016: 84). After the swift agreement had been found with Ecuador the EU indeed upheld this promise and Ecuador's exports to the EU were not disrupted until the entry into force of its accession to the FTA with Colombia and Peru on 1 January 2016.

Ecuador's accession to the existing FTA meant that out of the four Andean Community countries now only Bolivia has not joined this framework. Given its outlier status it is relevant to briefly explore why this country has not similarly changed its position. On the one hand, this is due to the fact that the Bolivian government's economic agenda had been significantly more sceptical of free trade as espoused by the EU than the Ecuadorean government. After all, Bolivia together with the socialist governments of Venezuela and Cuba experimented with alternative means of economic integration in the so-called ALBA alliance (Erisman 2011: 115ff). More importantly, however, is the state of Bolivia's economic ties to the EU which differs radically from that of Ecuador. Given that the country is rich in natural resources, its export patterns to the EU differ importantly from that of Ecuador, with agricultural exports accounting for only 28.9 per cent of its exports in 2017 compared to Ecuador's 88.2 per cent (DG Trade 2018b: 4; 2018a: 4). Instead, 38.8 per cent of the country's exports to the EU is crude materials, which cannot be easily replaced. As a consequence of this the country was not facing similar pressure from the entry-into-force of the EU's other FTAs with Latin American countries. Furthermore, as one of Latin America's least developed countries (European Commission 2018b: 16) it continues to benefit from the EU's GSP scheme, having gained GSP+ status in 2014 (European Commission 2018a: 3).

Just as the dynamics of the EU's initial negotiations with the Andean Community countries can be attributed to complex interlinkages with other developments outside the scope of EU–Andean Community relations, the process which led Ecuador to join the existing FTA between the EU and Colombia and Peru can be explored by similar links to other complex developments in trade policy-making. This time these are mainly related to activities of the EU, such as its GSP reform or the entry-into-force of the above-mentioned EU trade agreements. It is in this context that Ecuador suddenly faced the risk of a worsening of its terms of trade which ultimately made it return to the negotiation table despite the worse offer now available. The case thus attests once more not only to the importance of interlinkages in EU–Latin American trade relations, but also to how rapidly conditions can change in a context of asymmetric trade negotiations to the detriment of the weaker party.

Conclusion: The importance of interlinkages in EU–Latin America trade negotiations

This chapter has shown that EU–Latin American trade negotiations, and those between the EU and Andean Community countries, in particular, cannot be understood when analysed in isolation. Whilst a focus on the actual negotiation phase between the EU and its individual Latin American partners is able to provide important insights into the preferences of both actors, the larger context of negotiations, including the choice to enter into them, as well as the chosen format for such negotiations can be understood only when considering numerous interlinkages with developments outside the narrow context of the specific negotiations at hand.

These factors are notably other aspects in global trade policy, such as the failure of the Doha Development Agenda, changes to the EU's unilateral tariff-free access to its market under the GSP scheme, or the EU's competition with other major players in global trade policy-making (Meissner 2018; García, Chapter 4 below). Domestic political developments in the Andean Community countries that have led two of its members to pursue an aggressive free-trade agenda, whilst two others have been much more reluctant, have naturally shaped the negotiation dynamics between the sides, including the abandonment of the EU's desire to negotiate a comprehensive inter-regional association agreement with the Andean Community. However, as this chapter has argued, this can be understood only when considering the parallel competition for market access by the US and the EU, as well as the EU's internal hierarchy of preferences which increasingly favours commercial interests over developmental or broader political ones (Siles-Brügge 2014). Lastly, individual EU trade negotiations with Latin America are also affected by ripple-on effects from other such negotiations given the similar structure of many Latin American countries' economies and exports to the EU.

The status quo established by Ecuador's accession to the existing EU–Colombia–Peru FTA has held steady since then. These three countries have signed so-called trade continuity agreements with the UK which will ensure that the benefits of the EU's FTA with those countries roll over to the now bilateral trade relationships with the UK. Through an FTA with the EFTA countries Ecuador has even further narrowed the gap in its terms of trade with the European continent. Bolivia, on the other hand, has not changed its approach to FTAs either. Any willingness of outside partners to negotiate with the country under present circumstances would in any case require an end to the political crisis which has grappled the country since the aftermath of its October 2019 presidential election.

References

All websites last visited 30 September 2021.
Agence Europe (2004). "(EU)EU/MERCOSUR – member states call on commission not to give way on agriculture during Buenos Aires talks", *Agence Europe*, 8 June 8. Factiva Document AGEU000020040608e0680000g.

Agence Europe (2006). "'(EU) EU/ANDEAN COMMUNITY: Equador's complaint to WTO in banana case will make negotiations on FTA more difficult", *Agence Europe*, 8 December. Factiva Document AGEU000020061208e2c80000g.

Agence Europe (2007). "(EU) EU/TRADE: Council green light to launch of negotiations for bilateral free trade agreements with ASEAN, South Korea and India", *Agence Europe*, 24 April. Factiva Document AGEU000020070424e34o0000g.

Agence Europe (2009). "'(EU) EU/LATIN AMERICA: Bolivia and Ecuador question free-trade model on which EU/Andean Community talks are based", *Agence Europe*, 26 September. Factiva Document AGEU000020090926e59q00005.

Börzel, T. and Thomas, R. (2009). "The rise of (inter-) regionalism: the EU as a model of regional integration", APSA 2009 Toronto Meeting Paper. http://papers.ssrn.com/abstract=1450391.

CAN-EU troika summit (2008). "Andean Community – EU Troika Summit Joint Communiqué", Lima. http://www.sice.oas.org/TPD/AND_EU/negotiations/flexible_frame_e.pdf.

COREPER (2007). "2180th Meeting of the PERMANENT REPRESENTATIVES COMMITTEE Held in Brussels on 17, 18 and 20 April 2007", COREPER meeting summary 8565/07. Brussels: Council of the European Union.

Council of the European Union (2002). "Madrid Declaration", Final Declaration. Madrid: Council of the European Union. http://eulacfoundation.org/sites/eulacfoundation.org/files/2002_EN_Madrid_Decl.pdf.

Council of the European Union (2004). "Guadalajara Declaration", Final Declaration. Guadalajara: Council of the European Union. http://alcuenet.eu/dms-files.php?action=doc&id=363.

Council of the European Union (2006). "Declaration of Vienna", IV EU–LAC summit declaration 9335/06 (Presse 137). http://register.consilium.europa.eu/doc/srv?l=EN&f=ST%209335%202006%20INIT.

Council of the European Union (2020). "Agreements Database", Council of the European Union. 2020. www.consilium.europa.eu/en/documents-publications/treaties-agreements/.

DG Trade (2006). "Global Europe: competing in the world", Brussels: European Commission. http://trade.ec.europa.eu/doclib/docs/2006/october/tradoc_130376.pdf.

DG Trade (2014). "EU and Ecuador conclude negotiations for trade and development agreement", http://trade.ec.europa.eu/doclib/press/index.cfm?id=1129.

DG Trade (2017a). "'Third annual report on the implementation of Part IV of the agreement establishing an association between the European Union and its member states, on the one hand, and Central America on the other". Brussels: European Commission. https://eur-lex.europa.eu/legal-content/EN/TXT/PDF/?uri=CELEX:52017DC0160&from=EN.

DG Trade (2017b). "Third annual report on the implementation of the EU–Colombia/Peru trade agreement". Brussels: European Commission. https://eur-lex.europa.eu/legal-content/EN/TXT/PDF/?uri=CELEX:52017DC0585&from=EN.

DG Trade (2018a). "European Union, trade in goods with Bolivia". Brussels: Directorate-General for Trade. http://trade.ec.europa.eu/doclib/docs/2006/september/tradoc_113350.pdf.

DG Trade (2018b). "'European Union, trade in goods with Ecuador". Brussels: Directorate-General for Trade. http://trade.ec.europa.eu/doclib/docs/2006/september/tradoc_113378.pdf.

Dimon, D. (2006). "EU and US regionalism: the case of Latin America", *The International Trade Journal* 20 (2), 185–218. https://doi.org/10.1080/08853900600620167.

El Comercio (2014). "Patiño Lidera La 'otra' Politica exterior del régimen", *El Comercio*, 27 July. Factiva Document COMCIO0020140727ea7r00008.
Enríquez, C. (2014). "El régimen ya planea nueva cita con la Unión Europea", *El Comercio*, 28 March. Factiva Document COMCIO0020140328ea3s00007.
Erisman, H. M. (2011). "Cuba, Venezuela, and ALBA: the neo-Bolívarian challenge", in Prevost, G. and Oliva Campos, C. (eds), *Cuban–Latin American Relations in the Context of a Changing Hemisphere*, pp. 101–47 Amherst: Cambria Press.
EU–Andean Community Ministerial Meeting (2007). "EU–Andean Community Ministerial Meeting Santo Domingo 19 April 2007", Joint Communiqué. Santo Domingo. www.sice.oas.org/TPD/AND_EU/negotiations/Ministerial04_07_e.pdf.
EU–CAN High Level Meeting (2006). "EU–CAN High Level Meeting 12/13 July 2006", Joint Minutes. www.sice.oas.org/TPD/AND_EU/negotiations/highlevel2006_e.pdf.
European Commission (2005). "A stronger partnership between the European Union and Latin America", Communication from the Commission to the European Parliament and the Council COM(2005) 636 final. Brussels: European Commission. http://eeas.europa.eu/la/docs/com05_636_en.pdf.
European Commission (2007). "Andean Community regional strategy paper 2007–2013", E/2007/678. Brussels. http://eeas.europa.eu/andean/rsp/07_13_en.pdf.
European Commission (2013a). "Commission delegated regulation No 1/2014 of 28 August 2013 establishing Annex III to Regulation (EU) No 978/2012 of the European Parliament and of the Council applying a scheme of generalised tariff preferences". Brussels: Official Journal of the European Union. http://trade.ec.europa.eu/doclib/docs/2014/january/tradoc_152057.pdf.
European Commission (2013b). "Commission delegated regulation No 1421/2013 of 30 October 2013 amending Annexes I, II and IV to Regulation (EU) No 978/2012 of the European Parliament and of the Council applying a scheme of generalised tariff preferences". Brussels: Official Journal of the European Union. http://trade.ec.europa.eu/doclib/docs/2014/january/tradoc_152057.pdf.
European Commission (2018a). "EU trade policy encourages sustainable development and respect for human rights in vulnerable economies", Fact Sheet. Brussels: European Commission. http://trade.ec.europa.eu/doclib/docs/2018/january/tradoc_156538.pdf.
European Commission (2018b). "The EU special incentive arrangement for sustainable development and good governance ('GSP+') assessment of Bolivia covering the period 2016 – 2017". Brussels: European Commission. http://trade.ec.europa.eu/doclib/docs/2018/january/tradoc_156539.pdf.
Fattore, C. and Allison, M. E. (2013). "Extended endogenous and exogenous protection in the EU–US banana disputes", *The Latin Americanist* 57 (2), 111–29. https://doi.org/10.1111/j.1557-203X.2013.01195.x.
Federal Ministry of Foreign Affairs (2005). "The Austrian EU presidency 2006". Vienna: Federal Ministry of Foreign Affairs. www.eurosfaire.prd.fr/7pc/doc/1134635746_presidence_autrichienne_2006.pdf.
Fjellner, C. (2011). "Working document on a proposal for a regulation of the European Parliament and the Council applying a scheme of generalised tariff preferences", PE472.115v01–00. Brussels: Committee on International Trade.
Fritz, T. (2010). "The second conquest: the EU free trade agreement with Colombia and Peru". Berlin: Forschungs- und Dokumentationszentrum Chile–Lateinamerika – FDCL e.V.
Josling, T. E. and Taylor, T. G. (eds) (2003). *Banana Wars: The Anatomy of a Trade Dispute*. Cambridge, MA: CABI.

Maihold, G. (2008). "Außenpolitik als Provokation: Rhetorik und Realität in der Außenpolitik Venezuelas unter Präsident Hugo Chávez", SWP-Studie 22/2008. Berlin: Stiftung Wissenschaft und Politik. www.swp-berlin.org/fileadmin/contents/products/studien/2008_S22_ilm_ks.pdf.

Meissner, K. (2018). *Commercial Realism and EU Trade Policy: Competing for Economic Power in Asia and the Americas*. Abingdon: Routledge.

Nelson, M. (2015). *A History of the FTAA: From Hegemony to Fragmentation in the Americas*. New York: Palgrave Macmillan.

Noriega, C. (2007). "Alan García se corta solo con la UE", *Página 12*, 1 November. www.pagina12.com.ar/diario/elmundo/4-93878-2007-11-01.html.

Official Journal of the European Union (2012). "Trade agreement between the European Union and its member states, of the one part, and Colombia and Peru, of the other part". http://eur-lex.europa.eu/legal-content/EN/TXT/PDF/?uri=OJ:L:2012:354:FULL&from=EN.

Phillips, L. (2008). "Latin American leaders condemn 'racist' EU law", *EUobserver*, 2 July. http://euobserver.com/foreign/26432.

Sbragia, A. (2010). "The EU, the US, and trade policy: competitive interdependence in the management of globalization", *Journal of European Public Policy* 17 (3), 368–82. https://doi.org/10.1080/13501761003662016.

Schade, D. (2016). 'Coercion through Graduation: Explaining the EU-Ecuador Free Trade Agreement.' *Journal Für Entwicklungspolitik* 32 (3): 71–90.

Schade, D. (2020). *The EU in Association Agreement Negotiations: Challenges to Complex Policy Coordination*. Abingdon: Routledge.

Siles-Brügge, G. (2014). "EU trade and development policy beyond the ACP: subordinating developmental to commercial imperatives in the reform of GSP", *Contemporary Politics* 20 (1), 49–62. https://doi.org/10.1080/13569775.2014.881604.

Trueb, B. (2012). "'Boost or backlash? EU member states and the EU's Latin America policy in the post-Lisbon era", in Cardwell, P. J. (ed.), *EU External Relations Law and Policy in the Post-Lisbon Era*, pp. 265–86. The Hague: T. M. C. Asser.

Tussie, D. and Saguier, M., (2011). "The sweep of asymmetric trade negotiations: introduction and overview", in Bilal, S., Lombaerde, P. de and Tussie, D. (eds), *Asymmetric Trade Negotiations*, pp. 1–26. Farnham: Ashgate.

US Embassy Belgium Brussels (2006). "'Message on Latin America resonates with EU", Wikileaks Online repository. https://search.wikileaks.org/plusd/cables/06BRUSSELS472_a.html.

US Embassy Bolivia La Paz (2006). "EU awaits Andean Community stance toward trade talks", Wikileaks Online repository. https://search.wikileaks.org/plusd/cables/06LAPAZ1565_a.html.

US Embassy Colombia Bogotá (2006). "'U/S Burns' October 24 meeting with Colombian Foreign Minister Araujo", Wikileaks Online repository. https://wikileaks.org/plusd/cables/06BOGOTA10323_a.html.

US Embassy Colombia Bogotá (2007). "Colombia–Canada Trade Agreement Closing Fast", Wikileaks Online repository. https://wikileaks.org/plusd/cables/07BOGOTA8002_a.html.

US Embassy Colombia Bogotá (2008a). "Colombia's trade agenda – moving ahead without us".' Wikileaks Online repository. https://wikileaks.org/plusd/cables/08BOGOTA1926_a.html.

US Embassy Colombia Bogotá (2008b). "EU to initiate trade talks with Colombia and Peru: will the CAN get canned?", Wikileaks Online repository. https://search.wikileaks.org/plusd/cables/08BOGOTA3705_a.html.

US Embassy Colombia Bogotá (2008c). "Colombia to sign trade/investment agreements with Canada and China at APEC Summit", Wikileaks Online repository. https://wikileaks.org/plusd/cables/08BOGOTA4178_a.html.
US Embassy Colombia Bogotá (2009). "EU–Andean FTA talks reawaken after ten-month coma", Wikileaks Online repository. www.wikileaks.org/plusd/cables/09BOGOTA558_a.html.
US Embassy Ecuador Quito (2006). "CAN leaders meet in Quito", Wikileaks Online repository. https://search.wikileaks.org/plusd/cables/06QUITO1477_a.html.
US Embassy Ecuador Quito (2007). "Ecuador supports an EU–CAN association agreement", Wikileaks Online repository. https://search.wikileaks.org/plusd/cables/07QUITO1478_a.html.
US Embassy Ecuador Quito (2008). "CAN–EU talks – Ecuador will negotiate bilaterally", Wikileaks Online repository. https://search.wikileaks.org/plusd/cables/08QUITO1126_a.html.
US Embassy Peru Lima (2005). "EU Ambassador provides readout on South American visit of EU external relations commissioner", Wikileaks Online repository. https://search.wikileaks.org/plusd/cables/05LIMA3341_a.html.
US Embassy Peru Lima (2006). "EU improves Peru's trade preferences but FTA unlikely", Wikileaks Online repository. https://search.wikileaks.org/plusd/cables/06LIMA469_a.html.
US Embassy Peru Lima (2007). "Peru's fervour for global trade marches forward", Wikileaks Online repository. https://search.wikileaks.org/plusd/cables/07LIMA826_a.html.
US Embassy Spain Madrid (2005). "Zapatero Venezuela policy perplexes Spanish MFA officials", Wikileaks Online repository. https://wikileaks.org/plusd/cables/05MADRID569_a.html.
Woolcock, S. (2007). "European Union policy towards free trade agreements", ECIPE Working Paper 3/2007. Brussels: ECIPE. http://www.felixpena.com.ar/contenido/negociaciones/anexos/2010-09-european-union-policy-towards-free-trade-agreements.pdf.
Yépez Lasso, F. (2011). "Entrevista de viceministro de comercio con director adjunto de comercio de la Comision", Diplomatic Cable 1556-BRU/2011. Brussels: Ecuadorian Embassy to the European Union.
Young, A. (2011). "Effective multilateralism on trial: EU lwith WTO Law", in Blavoukos, S. and Bourantonis, D. (eds), *The EU Presence in International Organizations*, pp. 114–31. New York: Routledge.

Notes

1 The Andean Community is a regional integration mechanism built on similar principles as the EU. However, it faces considerable difficulties in furthering its economic integration over the diversity of political dynamics within its member states. At present the Andean Community consists of Bolivia, Colombia, Ecuador and Peru. Until 2006 Venezuela was also a member.
2 The negotiations for the Doha Development Agenda eventually died down fully after the 2008 negotiation session in Geneva.
3 My interviews with Brazilian diplomat to the EU; Former Council of the EU secretariat staff.

4 Former Barroso cabinet staff/diplomat in the UK Foreign & Commonwealth Office Latin America unit.
5 Former Peruvian diplomat; Former Council of the EU secretariat staff.
6 Former Peruvian diplomat.
7 Polish diplomat.
8 European Parliament MEP staffer.
9 French diplomat.
10 Former Council of the EU secretariat staff.
11 Former Peruvian diplomat; Former Council of the EU secretariat staff.
12 Internal 2008 EU briefing note seen by the author.
13 Senior DG Trade official.
14 Former Peruvian diplomat.
15 Former Peruvian diplomat.
16 Former Council of the EU secretariat staff.
17 NGO staffer.
18 Policy adviser in the European Parliament; Policy adviser in the European Parliament.
19 Polish diplomat.

4

The EU–Peru/Colombia trade agreement: balancing, accommodation or driver of change?

María J. García

Introduction

Following years of pressure from Andean states to commence negotiations for an FTA, in 2004 at the Guadalajara EU–Latin America and Caribbean summit a joint high-level group was established to study the feasibility of an agreement. Three years later, in 2007 negotiations were finally launched. Initial attempts to negotiate a deal between the two regional groupings, the EU and the Andean Community, quickly failed as Bolivia and Ecuador indicated they did not wish to pursue negotiations. Trade agreement negotiations then proceeded between the EU and Peru and Colombia. Ecuador returned to the negotiation table a few years later once an agreement with Peru and Colombia had been concluded in 2012, and when its preferential access to the EU's market was threatened by the reform of the EU's generalised system of preferences (see Schade, Chapter 3 above). The shift from negotiations with the Andean Community to a deal with only Peru and Colombia marked a significant moment in the EU's trade policy, representing a break with some of its normative preferences such as inter-regional negotiations, in favour of a logic of economic competitiveness as expressed in agreements aimed at curtailing potential future losses to EU businesses resulting from these states' newly negotiated bilateral trade agreements with the US (García 2015). It is not coincidental that the US had signed trade agreements with Peru and Colombia in 2006. Commercial competition with the US has been an important motivation behind the EU's trade agreement agenda, particularly since the 2006 Global Europe policy that launched a new era of EU preferential trade agreements (García 2015; 2013). Thus the long shadow of the US, and the 'Atlantic Triangle' (Valladão 1999) metaphor, so often used to describe the nature of the EU's relation with Latin America, emerges again in the rationales and negotiations of modern trade agreements between the EU and Latin American states.

This chapter traces the impact of the US and its commercial policy on the EU–Peru/Colombia negotiations, on the outcomes negotiated, and their implementation and feasibility. Firstly, the chapter explores the role of the EU–US competition underlying the EU–Peru/Colombia trade agreement in shaping the context of negotiations as an exercise in geo-economic balancing. Secondly, the chapter turns its analytical focus to the agreement itself and its initial stages of implementation. Modern trade agreements have far-reaching consequences in the domestic economic and social policies of states that subscribe to them. In the Andean countries, a purposeful agenda of engagement in international bilateral trade negotiations has led to domestic reforms to facilitate liberalisation of the economy. With trade agreements incorporating chapters on facilitation of investment, improved access for foreign firms to the domestic public procurement market or provisions on environmental standards, signatory states must be willing to undertake increasingly far-reaching domestic reforms to successfully enter into, and implement, these agreements. The EU and US share a broad trade and investment liberalisation agenda, with many commonalities (liberalisation of service markets, of procurement markets, protection for intellectual property rights). However, there are some marked differences in their approach to some of these matters. Analysing the trade agreements between the EU and Peru and Colombia, and those between the US and Peru and Colombia, reveals the degree to which those liberalisation agendas overlap, but, crucially, the extent to which accommodation of Latin American interests is possible within each approach, and the degree to which the EU–Peru/Colombia trade agreement has had to accommodate US–Peru and US–Colombia trade deals, enabling us to track more subtle and lasting impacts of the long shadow of the US in this context.

Finally, the chapter charts the initial implementation of the EU–Peru/Colombia trade agreement, which has been implemented since 2013. A number of challenges have arisen in the Andean nations when implementing the agreement. In particular divergent expectations, traditions and material resources have compromised the application of certain provisions in the innovative Trade and Sustainability chapter of the agreement (Orbie and Van den Putte 2016). As more meetings of the numerous committees and bodies created and institutionalised in the agreement take place, a marked improvement can be seen in terms of more effective communication and information exchanges, bureaucratic capacity-building, and improved civil society participation in the monitoring of the implementation of parts of the agreement, as envisaged by the agreement. To the extent that these changes pick up pace and become entrenched practices, the agreement can be seen as a driver of change in Andean states. In this way the trade agreement becomes a critical mechanism for the advancement of other aspects of the

EU–Latin American relations agenda, and a cornerstone defining the evolution of transatlantic relations.

Context of negotiations: geo-economic balancing

President Obama's administration (2008–16) pursued an intense trade agreement policy, with a particular focus on setting the rules of trade through ambitious mega-regional agreement negotiations: the TPP with eleven other states in the Americas, Asia and Australasia, and the TTIP with the European Union. Billed as game-changers in terms of crafting regulatory frameworks and disciplines well-beyond the scope covered by the WTO, TTIP negotiations were suspended in late 2016, and President Donald Trump withdrew the US from TPP in January 2017. Although these initiatives were the most significant in terms of attempts by the US to create alternative regimes to further liberalisation outside of the WTO, they followed a legacy, started under President George W. Bush's administration, of seeking alternative agreements with states willing to accept US models of economic liberalisation (e.g. in terms of intellectual property legislation) in exchange for improved access to the US market. This agenda was energised in the early 2000s as the challenging WTO Doha Round negotiations started to falter. Within the Western hemisphere the US negotiated the FTA with the Dominican Republic and Central American states between 2003 and 2006, and commenced negotiations with Peru, Colombia and Ecuador in 2004. Negotiations with Peru and Colombia were concluded in 2006, whilst Ecuador refused to continue negotiations.

The EU's trade policy has also undergone important shifts since the start of the twenty-first century, moving from a staunch commitment to the WTO in the early years to an active agenda of bilateral trade agreements and negotiations (see García 2013). The EU's initial reluctance to embark upon trade negotiations with the Andean Community states can be accounted for by internal leadership in the Directorate General for Trade committed to the Doha Round, and the challenges EU negotiators were encountering with negotiations in MERCOSUR (García 2015: 631). Following the collapse of Doha Round talks in Cancun in 2003, at the Guadalajara Summit of EU and LAC leaders in 2004, the EU's position began to shift. Whilst still refusing to begin negotiations, it conceded the possibility in the future, but made it contingent on greater regional integration:

> The Parties recognize that the prospect of Association Agreements should give a new impetus for strengthening regional economic integration processes. [...]

This process will start, at this stage, with a joint assessment phase of the respective integration processes of the Central American and Andean Community. The assessment will lead, in due course, to negotiations. (Declaration of Guadalajara 2004: 8)

This remained broadly in line with the EU's agenda of developing inter-regional relations and "normalising" the existence of regional groupings as key international actors (Aggarwal and Fogarty 2004; Söderbaum et al. 2005)[1] by emphasising integration to create larger markets and facilitate region-to-region negotiations. However, it also took account of the fact that the US had commenced negotiations with Andean states. Commercial competition with the US has been a key motivating factor behind EU trade negotiations with Latin American states. Negotiations with Mexico for a Global Agreement in the late 1990s were a reaction to the creation of NAFTA and the loss of EU market share in the Mexican market (Barrau 1999, Valladão 1999), whilst the start of negotiations with MERCOSUR and Chile in 1999 were motivated by a desire to maintain competitiveness in these markets at a time when the negotiation of an FTA for the Americas seemed a real possibility (García 2011).

By 2006 the incoming Trade Commissioner Peter Mandelson had launched "Global Europe". This strategy emphasised improving the EU's global competitiveness and refocused attention on bilateral FTAs alongside WTO liberalisation. It was particularly concerned with competitiveness-driven FTAs:

The key economic criteria for new FTA partners should be market potential (economic size and growth) and the level of protection against EU export interests (tariffs and non-tariff barriers). We should also take account of our potential partners' negotiations with EU competitors, the likely impact of this on EU markets and economies. (DG Trade 2006: 11)

This concern permeated EU–Latin American relations as well:

It is important for the strategic partnership that trade between the two regions continues to grow. Although Europe is the leading foreign investor in Latin America, the United States and Asia (China in particular) are gaining ground. (European Commission 2006: 7)

Within this altered background in EU trade policy, EU leaders agreed to launch trade negotiation with the Andean Community (AC). The EU and the AC began negotiations in June 2007, but it soon transpired that a bloc-to-bloc deal was impossible. Rejecting the EU's position on intellectual property privatisations, Bolivia refused to proceed (Gray Molina 2008: 13). Given opposing views of AC members on trade tariffs and the agreement itself, negotiations were suspended in June 2008. In January 2009 negotiations resumed on a bilateral basis with Peru, Colombia and Ecuador. Although

Ecuador withdrew in 2009 over intellectual property clauses (Brown del Rivero and Torres Castillo 2012), in May 2010 the EU–Colombia–Peru Trade Agreement was concluded.[2] The agreement did provide the opportunity for other AC members to join at a later date, which Ecuador did in November 2016:

> Having regard to the aspiration of the Parties of achieving an Association between the two regions, when all the Andean Community member countries become Parties to this Agreement, the Trade Committee will re-examine the relevant provisions, with a view to adapting them to the new situation and supporting regional integration processes. (EU 2010: 11)

The EU's decision to continue negotiations bilaterally is in sharp contrast to the negotiations with MERCOSUR, where its aim was an inter-regional deal (Doctor 2007). The decision also undermined the cohesion of the AC. The EU's new competition-based trade policy, together with the fact that, unlike the MERCOSUR countries, Peru and Colombia already had FTAs with the US, help to put this pragmatic decision into context as an act of geo-economic balancing (see García 2013, 2015; Meissner 2018). This interpretation gains ground when one considers both the limited economic significance of these countries for the EU and the controversial nature of these trade agreements within the EU. In 2017 Peru ranked 44th amongst EU import sources, and 50th as an export destination, accounting for 0.3 per cent of EU imports and 0.2 per cent of EU exports (DG Trade 2018a). Colombia ranked 45th for imports and 41st for exports, representing 0.3 per cent of EU imports and 0.3 per cent of exports (DG Trade 2018b).

Accommodation of positions: content of the agreements

All trade agreements reflect the outcomes of lengthy negotiations between signatory parties, and, by the very nature of negotiations, they cannot incorporate only the interests and positions of a single party. Nonetheless, there is evidence that larger partners in negotiations can leverage the smaller partners' economic dependence to gain a negotiated outcome closer to their preferences (Allee and Lugg 2016). The content of the EU–Peru/Colombia Trade Agreement and the US's trade agreements with these countries includes the elements that the US and EU typically seek to incorporate into their trade agreements: improved market access for goods through lower tariffs, simpler sanitary and phytosanitary measures, greater ease for service companies to sell their services in partner countries. All of the agreements make some accommodation for the fact that Peru and Colombia exhibit a lower level of development than the EU and US. They do so in the sense that they give Peru and Colombia more phasing-in time for tariff removal. However, for many other provisions the US asks them for reciprocal commitments, whilst the EU grants generous special and differential treatment, displaying a greater degree of willingness to accommodate their level of development (De Micco 2014: 6). In terms of market access the US gained immediate liberalisation for a higher value of consumer and industrial product exports: 80 per cent of its exports compared to an immediate liberalisation of 70 per cent of EU exports. However, the EU achieved better access for its electrical goods and machinery, greater commitments on non-tariff barriers for spirits and automobiles, and greater access for transport services, and to public procurement markets (coverage of Colombian sub-state entities) (De Micco 2014: 6). The more gradual removal of tariffs for EU exports reflects the EU's accommodation of preferences of Peru and Colombia based on their lower stage of development, whilst the improved access for certain products (spirits, machinery) reflects core EU negotiation interests, and is facilitated by the sequencing of the agreements. The US agreements predate EU negotiations; thus EU negotiators, on key areas, were able to argue for at least the same market access that had been granted to the US.

Of particular note is the inclusion of commitments to greater openness in service markets, inclusion of tighter rules on intellectual property, language facilitating competition amongst companies and preventing monopoly enterprises, and increased commitments to enable foreign companies to bid for government procurement contracts, i.e. the so-called Singapore issues that were removed from the WTO Doha Round negotiations in 2005 given developing states' opposition to these matters (Wilkinson 2006). Given the inability to negotiate these interests at the WTO, the US and EU have both sought to incorporate these in their trade agreements (Schott 2006; Horn et al. 2010; García 2018). The services chapters provide improved access to the various parties. US agreements use a negative list approach (where all service sectors except the few listed are liberalised) whereas the EU agreement uses a positive list (where the services liberalised are listed). The EU list notably avoids liberalisation in audiovisual services (national maritime cabotage and air transport services) (European Union 2012, Art. 111) but this is due to internal EU constraints in these areas, and a desire to avoid having to liberalise EU limitations on the import of foreign audiovisual services (such as domestic productions quotas for cinemas and broadcasters). In the agreements both the EU and US achieved better access to government procurement markets, and they also secured stronger intellectual property rights (IPR) measures, including criminal measures which are more detailed than those in the WTO Agreement on Trade-Related Aspects of Intellectual Property

Rights (TRIPS) to fight piracy and counterfeiting (De Micco 2014: 11). The key difference lies in the approach to a particular type of IPR, geographic indications (GI), which the EU protects through a register prohibiting the use of certain names (e.g. champagne) if the good is produced outside of the geographic location (French region of Champagne), whilst the US uses a trademark system based on the principle whereby the first trademark to be registered is the one that gets granted protection. This difference in approach means that, whilst the EU persuaded Peru and Colombia to acquiesce to grant protection to a list of EU products from specific localities (Englehardt 2015), in practice EU GIs cannot override US trademarked products that were already being sold in Peru and Colombia, thereby leading to a mixed system on the ground (European Union 2012, Art. 211). The EU agreement does prevent a US trademark from being used to prohibit the sale of EU GI products that share a name. In this aspect the agreement can be seen as accommodating, of necessity, other legal commitments already undertaken by Peru and Colombia.

Other differences in the agreement reflect different approaches by the EU and US to certain chapters. At the time of the negotiations the EU did not have an EU-wide approach to negotiating investment agreements, so the agreement with Peru and Colombia covers only the terms for the establishment of new investments, whereas the US ones incorporate post-establishment protections and mechanisms for resolution of disputes. There are also important differences in the labour and environmental chapters (called Trade and Sustainable Development chapter in the EU agreement). The US agreements cover fewer commitments, but these are legally enforceable as these chapters are subject to the agreement's dispute settlement mechanism whereby financial penalties in the form of removal of trade preferences can be implemented. The EU's Trade and Sustainable Development chapter, whilst covering more commitments, takes a promotional approach to labour and environmental standards, and is not subject to the dispute mechanism of the agreement. Instead the chapter creates its own dispute-resolution procedure based on a panel of experts delivering recommendations. Across trade agreements the EU includes more areas that go beyond anything that has been discussed at the WTO, but covers more areas in non-legally-binding manners, unlike the US (Horn et al. 2010). Unlike the US agreements, the EU one includes respect for human rights as an essential element of the agreement, with full legal enforceability (De Micco 2014: 12). This has been standard practice in EU external agreements since the early 1990s. As Table 4.1 shows, overall, there is great similarity between the agreements. As mentioned above, where differences occur they are the result of differences in EU and US approaches to trade agreements, rather than accommodation of Peruvian or Colombian specificities.

Table 4.1 Comparison of US and EU trade agreements with Peru and Colombia

	US–Colombia	US–Peru	EU–Peru/Colombia
Goods			
National treatment & market access	✗	✗	✗
Rules of origin	✗	✗	✗
Textiles & apparel	✗	✗	
Technical barriers to trade	✗	✗	✗
Sanitary and phytosanitary measures	✗	✗	✗
Customs and trade facilitation	✗	✗	✗
Trade remedies	✗	✗	✗
Services			
Market access	✗	✗	✗
Commercial presence not required	✗	✗	✗
Exclusions[1]			✗
Mining, processing nuclear weapons	some	some	✗
Processing arms			✗
National maritime cabotage		✗	✗
Audio-visual	some	some	✗
Air transport & related services		some	✗
Processing & disposal of toxic waste			✗
National Treatment	✗	✗	✗
Most-favoured nation treatment	✗	✗	✗
Cross-border supply of services	✗	✗	✗
Key personnel (3 years)			✗
Graduate trainees (1 year)			✗
Business people (90 days)			✗
Contractual services & independent professionals (GATS commitments)			✗
Encourage work towards temporary licensing	✗	✗	
Transparency in regulation	✗	✗	
Professional bodies to develop mutual recognition of qualifications	✗	✗	✗
Telecommunications: preventing major supplier from anti-competitive practices			✗

Table 4.1 Comparison of US and EU trade agreements with Peru and Colombia (Continued)

	US–Colombia	US–Peru	EU–Peru/Colombia
Authorisation to provide telecommunication licences			✗
Telecommunication interconnection obligation			✗
Prevention anti-competitive practices in courier services			✗
Financial services	✗	✗	✗
Prudential carve-out			✗
Effective and transparent regulation	✗	✗	✗
Allow new services			✗
International maritime services	✗	✗	✗
Tourism	✗	✗	
Environment and quality standards	✗	✗	
Computer services	✗	✗	✗
E-commerce	✗	✗	✗
Trade administration electronically			✗
Current payments and capital movements	✗	✗	✗
Competition (apply domestic laws)	✗	✗	✗
Public enterprises with exclusive rights allowed but cannot distort trade	✗	✗	✗
Public procurement			
National treatment and non-discrimination	✗	✗	✗
Follows WTO GPA structure and methods	✗	✗	✗
Electronic means for tenders			✗
Intellectual property			
National treatment	✗	✗	✗
Transparency	✗	✗	✗
Trademarks	✗	✗	✗
Patents	✗	✗	✗
Geographic Indicators	✗	✗	✗
Transparency in system and allowing complaints	✗	✗	
Non-granting of GI that confuses existing trademark	✗	✗	

Table 4.1 Comparison of US and EU trade agreements with Peru and Colombia (Continued)

	US–Colombia	US–Peru	EU–Peru/Colombia
Prevalence of GI over trademarks			✗
Enforcement	✗	✗	
Investment			
Investment	✗	✗	
National treatment	✗	✗	
Most-favoured nation treatment	✗	✗	
No imposition of performance obligations	✗	✗	
Investor-state dispute settlement	✗	✗	
Dispute settlement mechanism			
Consultations and mediation	✗	✗	✗
Arbitration panel	✗	✗	✗
Compliance with arbitration panel ruling	✗	✗	✗
Possibility of compensatory measures	✗	✗	✗
Choice of venue: FTA or WTO dispute settlement	✗	✗	✗
Human rights & social clauses			
Trade and sustainability chapter (subject to non-enforceable dispute settlement)			✗
Labour (subject to enforceable dispute settlement)	✗	✗	
Environment (subject to enforceable dispute settlement)	✗	✗	
Respect for human rights, democracy, rules of taw as essential clause			✗

[1]Although not listed as exceptions in Annex II of the US-Peru FTA, Peru reserves the right to enact any measures it chooses with respect to public waters, cultural services, traditional handicrafts and indigenous matters. Colombia in Annex I of the US–Colombia FTA includes some limitations (registration and local presence requirements) for accounting services, offering tourism services, and limitations on mining, artisanal fishing, electricity services, customs services, broadcasting services, postal and specialised courier services. In Annex II, Colombia reserves the right to adopt measures in relation to audio-visual services, public services, handicrafts, law enforcement and security services, and social services, research and development, education services, environmental services.
Sources: European Union 2012, USTR 2009, USTR 2012

Driver of change? Impact of the agreement

Economic impact

The initial years since the implementation of the trade agreement between the EU and Peru and Colombia have seen an increase in trade in certain sectors, mostly agriculture, but have fallen short of expectations, particularly for the Andean countries. Impact assessments commissioned ahead during negotiations estimated overall welfare effects of between 0.5 and 2.0 per cent of GDP for Andean countries derived from increased exports, and only minimal welfare gains for the EU of less than 0.1 per cent of GDP (Manchester University 2009). In practice, however, trade between the EU and Colombia dropped by 23 per cent between 2012 and 2016, although the EU remains Colombia's second trade partner.[3] EU exports to the Andean states have been rising with the agreement, particularly exports of agricultural goods to Colombia which have increased by 782 per cent between 2012 and 2016 (European Commission 2017). EU exports of pharmaceuticals, vehicles and medical devices have also risen, whilst exports of machinery have decreased. As far as Colombian exports to the EU are concerned, fruit exports doubled, coffee exports increased by 49 per cent, and agricultural exports by 32.9 per cent in the period, although minerals continued to be the major export (European Commission 2017). EU imports from Peru have decreased by 4 per cent, whilst EU exports to Peru have risen by the same percentage between 2012 and 2016. EU exports continue to be dominated by machinery, electrical appliances and motor vehicles, whilst pharmaceutical exports have risen by 76 per cent and agricultural exports by 73 per cent; spirits have risen by 60 per cent and food preparations for infants by 227 per cent (European Commission 2017). Peruvian exports to the EU continue traditional patterns with ores and mineral fuels and oils representing the largest exports. Exports of coffee, fruit, fish and molluscs, vegetables and cocoa have increased as a result of the trade agreement, with the highest percentage increases experienced in fruits (120 per cent) and cocoa (226 per cent).

The EU continues to be the top investor in both Peru and Colombia, with foreign direct investment stocks growing in Colombia by 4 per cent and in Peru by 15 per cent between 2012 and 2016. In terms of trade in services, EU service exports represent 30 per cent of services imports in Peru and 16 per cent in Colombia. In the first years of implementation, the economic asymmetrical relationship between the EU and Peru, and especially Colombia, has remained unaltered. All parties to the agreement have experienced growth in agricultural exports, as a result of the tariffs reductions in the agreement, but key exports are still characterised by traditional patterns, despite high rates of FTA preference utilisation (95 per cent for Peruvian and Colombian exports to the EU, 70.6 per cent for EU exports to Colombia). The underwhelming effects of the agreement are in part due to structural circumstances external to the agreement, including a period of low commodity prices and lower demand in Europe due to the lasting effects of the Eurocrisis. In Colombia this is compounded by a history of low exports. Colombia has trade deficits with both the US and EU, which have not been resolved by the FTAs. Agricultural exports to the EU have increased by 22 per cent, but so have imports by 102 per cent, leading farmers' organisations to stage a national strike in May 2016 where they included amongst their demands that the government revise existing FTAs (Fernanda Forero 2016: 6).

Social impact

Even in sectors that have increased their exports as result of the FTA there are concerns about this not translating into increased employment opportunities. Sugar exports from Colombia to the EU have risen by 154 per cent, but this has relied on mechanisation rather than additional employment. In the flower sector, which has benefited from the elimination of all tariffs, rising exports have been accompanied by greater use of informal and short-term labour contracts, according to a joint report of the Transnational Institute (TNI) and Oficina Internacional de Derechos Humanos Acción Colombia (OIDHACO) (Fernanda Forero 2016: 6). Although the trade agreement places emphasis on labour and environmental matters through the inclusion of a Trade and Sustainability chapter, this does not mandate monitoring of employment impacts of the agreement. It does, however, commit the parties to monitoring the labour rights and environmental law situation, and it was hoped that the trade agreement would have a positive impact in Peru and Colombia, as the ratification of the agreement was made contingent on steps being taken in this direction.

During the negotiations of the EU–Colombia/Peru Trade Agreement the European Parliament voiced concerns about the human rights situations in both of these countries. It was especially concerned about Colombia, where, after a prolonged internal armed conflict, the mistreatment of trade unionists was a special cause for concern. In an attempt to bolster the positive impact of the trade agreement on human rights and labour rights in Colombia and Peru, the European Parliament passed Resolution 2628, also known as Roadmap of the EU–Colombia/Peru FTA (hereafter "Roadmap"), on 13 June 2012. This made Peru and Colombia present plans of action regarding institutional and legislative measures they would undertake to ensure the protection of human and labour rights, in exchange for the European Parliament's ratification of the trade agreement. The approach was not unique to the EU, as the negotiations between the US and Colombia were also contingent on improvement of human and labour rights in the country, with another roadmap being defined under the terms of the Obama–Santos Labour Action Plan (Plan de Acción Laboral Obama-Santos) (El Espectador 2011). The outcomes of these initiatives have been mixed, thus far. A number of significant labour law changes and capacity-building activities have been implemented; however, civil society organisations and trade unions continue to report inadequate implementation of new laws.

The Obama-Santos Plan, which includes more detailed and concrete measures than the Roadmap developed for the EU, included a requirement for the reinstatement of the Ministry of Labour, something that took place in 2011 (Schmieg 2018). It also committed Colombia to increasing the number of labour inspectors to 904, which it has gradually done. Labour inspections were important aspects in all the plans, and FTAs have been shown to be correlated with increases in the number of labour inspectors, but with more modest rises in the number of inspections carried out (Dewan and Ronconi 2014). Advances have also been made in terms of pay for labour inspectors, to prevent corruption and guarantee their independence (Fernanda Forero 2016: 7). Despite clear improvements in formal implementation of the Roadmaps and in creating an infrastructure to promote labour standards implementation, trade unions continue to report insufficient advances. A Report by the Colombian Escuela Nacional Sindical (National Trade Unions School) from March 2015 strongly criticises the Colombian government's inadequate implementation of the Roadmap. Its criticisms concentrate in the following areas: labour co-ordination bodies that are not independent trade unions; lack of transition from informal to formal contracted labour; continued violence against trade unionists; and limited civil society involvement.

Between 2012 and 2013 thirty-six agreements were signed that changed the status of 12,030 workers from informal labour to contracted labour. However, this represents only 0.05 per cent of the country's total workforce. Trade unions criticise the fact that these agreements were signed between the Labour Ministry and companies, with no participation of workers or their representatives. They also criticise the lack of transparency in publishing details of the beneficiaries, and the fact that "contracted" merely means that there is a contract in place, and does not differentiate between "fixed-term" and "indefinite" contracts, or between a contract with the company and with a sub-contractor (ENS 2015).

Most worryingly, the report notes continued violence against trade unionists, including twenty murders in 2014, twenty-two attacks, twelve arrests and 181 threats. Although this represents a decline in overall numbers, it reveals the continuation of an important problem. Trade unions have complained about the reactive rather than preventative character of the trade unionist protection programme, which provides bodyguards for trade unionists who have been subjected to threats, rather than focusing on the creation of a violence-free environment. The Unidad Nacional de Protección (UNP – National Unit for Protection) supports 393 threatened union leaders, although trade union CUT complains that there are more unionists who lack protection, and that the UNP's approach is to gradually reduce protection, arguing that the country is now pacified (El Espectador 2018). For its part the government points out that between 2011 and 2017 3,600 risk assessments have been conducted and 362 sentences have been issued condemning violence against trade unionists (El Espectador 2018).

On the ground significant improvements, especially in terms of institutional capacity, have been undertaken, but there is clearly a long road to travel. These reforms have also been motivated by the key ambition of Juan Manual Santos's government (2010–18) to join the OECD (Schmieg 2018). President Santos placed the peace process and accession to the OECD, as a means to undertake major reforms aimed at modernising the economy, improving governance and well-being and increasing the effectiveness of the public sector, as the key priorities for his tenure (OECD 2018). OECD's joining requirements in terms of labour match the content of the roadmaps subscribed in the FTAs with the US and EU (Schmieg 2018). Accession to the OECD has also been used as an additional route to pressure the Colombian government to make progress on the reforms suggested in the roadmaps. The Economic, Labour and Social Affairs Committee of the OECD, responding to evidence presented by Colombian trade unions, with support of the international trade union movement and EU trade unions, has conditioned entry to the OECD on formal procedures for the improvement of the labour situation. Colombia's government will have to report annually on labour standards to the OECD, and developments will be monitored by the OECD General Secretariat alongside trade unions for eight years (CUT 2018). These additional requirements, in spite of the positive view of all twenty-three OECD Committees which enabled the invitation for Colombia to accede to go ahead on 30 May 2018 (OECD, 2018), show continued concerns over the need to improve labour conditions in the country.

The FTA roadmaps, and the measures adopted in the FTA with the EU under the Trade and Sustainable Development (TSD) chapter placed a strong emphasis on the participation of civil society in labour and environmental affairs, and on the adoption of international standards in these matters. The TSD chapter committed the parties to signing up to and implementing the International Labour Organisation's (ILO) Core Conventions on labour rights.[4] ILO standards mentioned under Article 269 of the FTA add nothing substantively new in terms of regulatory demands since the parties had subscribed to them through their ILO membership (Marx et al. 2017). Yet despite their adoption in domestic labour laws, concerns remain around failure to implement these effectively on the ground. Colombia has established a fairly robust legal and institutional framework to protect labour rights, though compliance with this system is problematic. The lack of enforcement of its well-developed legal-institutional framework is in fact a well-known weakness among stakeholders, who attribute this to the challenging geography of the country impeding proper monitoring, and, more importantly, to the fact that labour rights are but one of many human-rights challenges in Colombia, including the peace-building process, making resources to enforce legislation limited (Marx et al. 2017: 97). Whilst Peru ratified all eight ILO Core Conventions, 33 per cent of children in Peru between the ages of five and fourteen remain in employment, and modern-day slavery affects 0.218 per cent of the population (Orbie et al. 2017). Researchers have also raised concerns about the lack of independence of the labour inspectorate from companies, and the continuation of special labour regimes, especially in the agricultural sector, which permit highly flexible contract practices. They also point to insufficient improvements in health and safety at work legislation, as a stringent law proposed in 2011 was deemed too costly by businesses, and was watered down in 2014, lowering criminal responsibility after an accident. Crucially, those changes to the proposal were introduced without proper tripartite consultations to include labour unions (Orbie et al. 2017).

Another important point of contention in the implementation of the TSD chapter has been the implementation of monitoring procedures and mechanisms for the participation of civil society. The TSD chapter under Title XI creates two main mechanisms for civil society participation in monitoring. The first is a Domestic Advisory Group (DAG) constituted of civil-society representatives who monitor the implementation and provides input to the Subcommittee on Trade and Sustainability. The second mechanism brings together civil-society representatives from both sides of the agreement to discuss issues jointly in an annual Civil Society Dialogue that takes place back-to-back to the meeting of the Subcommittee on Trade and Sustainable Development. The chapter states that, where existing domestic civil society consultation groups exist, these can become the DAG, and where they do not exit they need to be created, but it does not stipulate who should be involved or how they should be constituted. Peru has been criticised for not setting up the required DAG (Orbie and Van der Putte 2016), and for refusing to facilitate information to the EU DAG and EU Delegation to Peru when these have asked for confirmation of the number of meetings of the Peruvian DAG (Orbie et al. 2017). Resource constraints have also hampered full participation of civil-society groups in the subcommittee meetings, although the EU Delegations on the ground have set aside funding to facilitate local civil-society participation (García 2016). Perhaps more worryingly, research on the ground has revealed that, particularly in Peru, DAG members are unaware of their role, and in some cases of being part of the DAG (Orbie et al., 2017).

The participation of civil society in the monitoring of the TSD chapter was meant to facilitate adequate information flows regarding the situation on the ground in terms of labour and environmental standards. Apart from exchanging information regarding ratification of international agreements on these matters, and measures for transposition into domestic legislation, the forum is meant to create an opportunity for breaches to be addressed. If these are continuous, the TSD chapter also creates a legally non-binding dispute-resolution mechanism. The dispute mechanism determines that complaints regarding breaches of the clause can be notified to the FTA's implementation Joint Council by civil society, businesses or government representatives of the signatory parties. The Joint Council will then appoint a three-member expert panel to investigate and produce a report with non-binding recommendations for action. The expectation is that, through benchmarking processes and a dispute mechanism based on naming and shaming, voluntary measures will be adopted to ensure high standards. Although civil society did raise a complaint regarding inappropriate environmental impact assessment procedures for a mining project in Colombia, after bilateral consultation it was determined that this did not fall under the remit of the TSD chapter, and therefore was not subject to dispute-settlement procedures (Interview with EU Official, October 2016). To date no complaints have been brought forward under these mechanisms: thus it is impossible to assess the effectiveness of this aspect of the TSD chapter.[5] Nonetheless, the surveillance of the TSD chapter facilitates holding the EC and Peruvian and Colombian governments to account. The European Parliament has demanded that the European Commission explain how concerns raised by civil society within the TSD chapter are dealt with and how it is decided whether the issue falls under the remit of the agreement or not (European Parliament 2018), especially in light of civil-society concerns over environmental laws in Peru. Within the TSD chapter subcommittee the EU has also demanded explanations from Peru regarding its impact assessments procedures. At the December 2018 meeting Peru updated the EU on new guidance it is issuing for these assessments, and how it has been increasing transparency by making all materials and assessments available online to the general public (Sub-Committee TSD 2018), having come under pressure for insufficiently stringent assessments and insufficient public consultation.

With the TSD subcommittee meetings other issues of concern have been raised by civil-society groups. In Peru's case the main concerns, as pointed out by Human Rights Watch (2015), included the use of force against protestors (including thirty-four civilian deaths in 2014), in protests linked to proposed gas pipeline projects. In Ecuador the situation of banana sector workers and a case of a trade union in the sector that was not allowed to register as such, as it did not meet the legally require threshold of members, have also been discussed (Sub-Committee TSD 2018). The subcommittee also monitors Andean states' implementation of ILO Conventions (e.g. Peru's establishment of a special group of labour inspectors to focus on forced labour and child labour) and multilateral environmental agreements (e.g. presenting circular economy plans, an EU-funded project on green entrepreneurship and legal changes to reduce use of mercury in mining). The European Parliament's 2019 Declaration on the implementation of the agreement recognised Colombia's and Peru's continued efforts to implement ILO recommendations, but nonetheless highlighted concerns about the possible effects of environmental legal changes in Peru, and raised concerns about civil-society claims raised within the TSD subcommittee regarding non-implementation of environmental standards. The subcommittee, through the inclusion of civil society, and creation of an external accountability system, which works in conjunction with other international organisations (ILO) and agreements (CITES, COP agreements), serves mainly to magnify pressure on governments to act to improve social and environmental legislation and, crucially, its implementation on the ground, although its ultimate outcomes may be noticeable only in the long term.

Regulatory impact

A key rationale behind the US's and EU's negotiation of FTAs with partners of little critical significance to their economy is to encourage liberalising reforms abroad that are compatible with their own economic governance preferences. Both the EU and US hoped to extend the disciplines covered at the WTO in terms of trade in services, government procurement (the EU) and rules governing IPR. However, concerted action by emerging and developing countries thwarted their ambitious agenda in the Doha Round at the WTO (see Narlikar and Van Hputen 2010; Hopewell 2016). Turning to bilateral agreements, the US Trade Representative at the time, Robert Zoellick, was forthright in declaring that prospective FTA partners had to be willing to undertake domestic economic reforms in order to be able to subscribe the type of WTO-plus FTA that the US demands, including intellectual property, and extensive services liberalisation (Schott 2004). Peru's and Colombia's keenness to negotiate FTAs with the US and EU, as well as aligning themselves with Chile and Mexico within the Pacific Alliance, responded to the coming to power of governments pursuing an active agenda of domestic economic reforms along liberal lines. Their political economy preferences were not shared across the South American continent, and FTAs with likeminded neighbours, and major economic players and markets like the US and EU, were seen as ways both to maximise the effect of reforms by accessing more markets (Araoz 2005: 8; García-García et al. 2014), and to create external binding mechanisms to crystallise reforms. Given these governmental agendas, FTAs were less about impositions from abroad than about reinforcement of domestic choices. Nevertheless, FTAs can require additional adaptation and reforms, which affect existing arrangements. The examples of the legal environment around labour law described in the previous section, and the case of the treatment of spirits below, are the most notable of such adaptations in the case of this trade agreement.

In Colombia's case the reform agenda supported by FTAs was further motivated by the President's aim to join the OECD. The government had to undertake a series of economic reforms to meet entry requirements, which included reforming its justice system and reducing informality in the labour market, and implementing new national policies, such as on water and chemicals management. Colombia also took important steps to improve its governance of state-owned enterprises, including removal of ministers from the boards. To comply with the OECD Anti-Bribery Convention Colombia significantly modified its corporate liability regime (OECD 2018). As in the case of labour law implementation, the accession process to the OECD offered other OECD members an additional route to pressure the Colombian government to enact economic reforms that they deemed desirable, and had included in their FTAs. The US has continued to insist through the OECD on reforms of Colombia's intellectual property regime, as was required to comply with the FTA between the two states (Portfolio 2018). Modified intellectual property laws were proposed by Santos's government but failed to make their way through ratification in the legislature on procedural grounds. Additional explanations by the Colombian government and OECD regarding the ongoing process and need for sufficient time for parliamentary debates on the matter eventually convinced the US not to block OECD accession.

As with the intellectual property clauses, other commitments entered in FTAs can require domestic legal changes in order to be effectively implemented. In the FTA with the EU, the Colombian government committed to lowering import tariffs on spirits from the EU. In the Trade Agreement, Colombia committed to remove discriminatory tariffs within two years of implementation, but failed to do so.[6] Government attempts to change the legislation that protects domestic spirit producers has been blocked by Congress and regional governors despite the Executive's commitment to fulfilling the Trade Agreement requirements. The problem lies in the fact that the Colombian Constitution grants regional authorities a monopoly over regional rum and spirits production and the collection of taxes on these products, giving them a strong economic incentive to maintain the status quo. On 13 January 2016 the EU filed a request for consultations with Colombia on discriminatory measures on spirits at the WTO. Dissatisfied with the outcome of consultations, on 22 August 2016 the EU requested the establishment of a panel on this dispute at the WTO. The panel was established on 26 September 2016, and other countries, including the US, joined the EU's complaint (WTO 2016).[7] In order to comply with the commitments of the FTAs and WTO, and pre-empt a ruling against it at the WTO, Colombia introduced changes to its spirits legislation in early 2017, removing differentiated alcohol taxes on local and imported spirits, and banning regional authorities from implementing additional barriers to imported spirits (such as compulsory introduction contracts) (ElanBiz 2017).

Spirits taxation has also been a controversial issue in the Technical Barriers to Trade Subcommittee with Peru. In this case the controversy surrounds the fact that local *pisco* is considered a cultural good and, as such, is exempt from taxes on alcoholic beverages. All imported spirits are, however, subject to high taxes, and foreign exporters consider this differentiated treatment for *pisco* to be against the spirit and letter of non-discrimination principles of the WTO. European whisky producers, in particular, have complained about this situation through the Europe Active lobby (García 2016). Although the EC delegation in Peru is in constant contact with the Peruvian government over this matter, given the special status of *pisco* (including issues related to national identity) and vested business interests it is likely that a full resolution of this matter will take time.[8] The minutes of the 2018 Joint Committee meeting reveal the EU's continued frustration with the situation and the EU demands for explanations from Peru not only for not acting on this but for enacting new legislation which the EU considers further discriminates against foreign spirits competing with *pisco* (Committee EU–Peru–Colombia–Ecuador 2018).

Other issues that the parties have discussed within the Joint Committee, and technical subcommittees established in the Trade Agreement, have revolved around clarification by the parties of changes in their regulations (for example an EU regulation changing the maximum level of cadmium allowed in food products and cocoa) and ways to facilitate that information getting to the level of producers and supporting them to adapt to these new circumstances. The parties have also updated each other on their strategic plans for greener economies in the future and implementation of international labour and environmental commitments (Committee EU–Peru–Colombia–Ecuador 2018).

Research on the extent to which the EU has been able to export its regulatory preferences through trade agreements reveals a mixed picture. Alisdair

Young (2015) argues that the EU is able to achieve market access and liberalisation, but not acquiescence with its regulatory preferences. Indeed the slow implementation of some key offensive interests of the EU, such as GIs in Peru, has been the subject of intense discussions within the Joint Committee and technical subcommittees (Committee EU–Peru–Colombia–Ecuador 2018), and reveals that, even amongst likeminded partners, the implementation of agreements is not always smooth, as further evidenced by the examples of taxes on spirits. Researchers focusing on labour and environmental clauses, however, argue that, during the negotiation phase, the EU has been able to persuade partners to accede to ILO conventions and multilateral environmental agreements (Bastiaens and Postnikov 2017; 2019). In reality the full impact of a trade agreement can be truly gauged only after significant time has lapsed. Many of the structures the agreement sets up, particularly under the aegis of the Trade and Sustainability chapter, are likely to yield results in terms of better labour standards on the ground only in the long term (Aissi et al. 2018). What matters is that the Trade Agreement has created a long-term institutional framework within which the parties can hold each other accountable for the implementation of the agreement, and within which they have legal recourse to punitive mechanisms (through the WTO dispute-settlement body) for the market access side of the agreement, as exemplified in the EU's request for the WTO to open a case against Colombia's spirits taxes.

Conclusion

The trade agreement between the EU and Andean states, unlike agreements with Asian partners, was not a key strategic priority for the EU. The 2006 "Global Europe" trade agenda that ended a five-year moratorium on new preferential trade agreement negotiations did not mention these states specifically. However, against the backdrop of US trade agreements with Peru and Colombia in the early 2000s, as part of the US strategy to gradually dismantle opposition to its liberalisation agenda at the WTO, the EU sought to maintain its businesses' competitive position in these countries vis-à-vis US competitors. Balancing against the potential US gains was, therefore, a key motivation for the EU to engage in negotiations with the Andean Community, initially, and explains why the EU sought to continue negotiations with just Peru and Colombia, even at the expense of its purported agenda of supporting regional integration in Latin America (García 2015). The agreement can thus be seen as a tool to maintain equal business opportunities to the US. This is reflected in the content of the agreement with similar market access and concessions.

Although preferential trade agreements can be interpreted as part of the international constitutionalisation of a particular neoliberal economic agenda (Gill 1998), the choice to engage in these normally evolves from a government's own domestic reform processes rather than from an external imposition. Throughout the late 1990s and early 2000s the Peruvian and Colombian governments undertook liberal reforms and encouraged an export-led growth model that had been successful for Chile and Asian countries. Within this context, entering into preferential trade agreements with key partners and economic powers like the US and EU becomes far less controversial and complex, as the domestic economies are already more exposed to external competitors and investors. In fact the Andean states' aims in entering into these negotiations revolved around gaining better access to external markets. Existence of a preferential trade agreement is, however, not a guarantee of more trade or GDP. Economic outcomes of the agreement have not been spectacular for now for Peru and Colombia, but that is due to broader economic trends (commodity prices, demand contraction globally), and also the fact that, despite domestic reforms, some domestic firms have not become internationally competitive and have little history of exporting, and therefore have not been in a position to exploit opportunities created by the trade agreement. Within the framework of the trade agreement the EP (2019) has called for a new section to be introduced focusing specifically on small- and medium-sized firms (SMEs) to enable them to reap more benefits from the agreement. Within its broader co-operation relations with Latin America, the EU has also funded programmes to support green entrepreneurship and SME development and internationalisation such as AL-INVEST (Al-Invest 2021). The agreement facilitates trade and investment, but above all it creates and institutionalises a framework for constant monitoring of the implementation of the agreement and co-operation on upgrading the relationship. It is a long-term project and commitment. The long-term nature of the agreement is exemplified in the initial accommodation of different levels of development through longer phase-in tariffs reductions in the Andean countries to enable domestic producers to adapt gradually to increased competition. However, the text of the agreement reflects other EU agreements, and includes key EU offensive interests such as GIs in the intellectual property chapter (Covarrubia 2011), despite this being an area of contestation in the Andean countries. Indeed, in the minutes of the Joint Committee of the Agreement, there are numerous questions from the EU regarding slow implementation of EU GI registration in Peru and complaints about this (Joint Committee 2019). The scope for accommodation of partners in EU agreements exists but is limited, as the EU wants to secure agreements that go beyond the commitments at the WTO and can extend EU commercial benefits in areas where the EU is competitive. The limited accommodation also reflects the aim of such agreements to drive change and approximation to the EU's economic preferences.

In practice, however, the role of this agreement as a driver for change is relative. Despite the EU's pressure and insistence on improvement of labour rights, there remain problems and challenges in this area in Colombia and Peru. This relates to capacity, as both, and especially Colombia, have enacted legislation to meet external commitments. The motivation, however, is not just the agreement with the EU; prior agreements with the US had already demanded such changes, as had the processes for accession to the OECD. The agreement with the EU adds another layer of external scrutiny and accountability on this front, but cannot be credited with having spurred the reforms and commitment to these.

The TSD chapter of the agreement with its non-binding approach has limited impact (although US sanctions-based approach has not done much either). However, it does create a valuable forum for civil society to raise concerns and hold domestic governments to account. There are also ongoing reforms of how the consultations operate aimed at facilitating independent and honest discussion and magnifying the influence of civil society. At the request of civil-society organisations, under the aegis of the TSD committee, European and Andean civil society now have a private meeting, with no government or EU officials, ahead of their meetings with the officials, to allow them a space to co-ordinate positions and maximise their impact (European Parliament 2018). The potential for longer-term change is there, and the trade agreement could play a role in supporting and facilitating these changes, although, for the time being, capacity challenges on the ground prevent full and effective implementation of labour and environmental commitments, as well as other commitments undertaken in the agreement.

The motivation for the agreement may have been a balancing exercise for the EU against the US, but it has created a framework to support ongoing and future processes of change. The agreement per se has not been a driver of change in the short term, but rather a complement to domestic policies and decisions to liberalise the economy and to enter the OECD and international commitments. However, some initial changes on the ground have already commenced as a result of the agreement (for example changes in spirits laws, and tax dynamics between central and regional governments, changes in labour laws and labour inspections, environmental assessments). More importantly, the structures the agreement creates and the commitment to a long-term partnership by both parties should see increased changes on the ground over the long term, and it is in the long term that the impacts of modern trade agreements need to be judged.

References

All websites last visited 30 September 2021.

Adiwasto, E., De Lombarde, P. and Pietrangeli, G. (2006). "On the joint assessment of Andean integration in EU–CAN relations", Background Paper 451. Barcelona: Observatorio de las Relaciones Union Europea – America Latina. https://cris.unu.edu/joint-assessment-andean-integration-eu-can-relations.

Aggarwal, V. (2013). "US free trade agreements and linkages", *International Negotiation* 18 (2013), 89–110.

Aggarwal, V. and Fogarty, E. (2004) "Explaining trends in EU interregionalism", in Aggarwal, V. and Fogarty, E. (eds), *European Union Trade Strategies: Between Globalism and Regionalism*. London: Palgrave, pp. 207–40. https://citeseerx.ist.psu.edu/viewdoc/download?doi=10.1.1.734.4752&rep=rep1&type=pdf.

Aissi, J., Peels, R. and Samaan, D. (2018). "Evaluación de la eficacia de las disposiciones laborales de los acuerdos comerciales: marco analítico y metodológico", *Revista Internacional del Trabajo* 137 (4), 731–61. https://labordoc.ilo.org/discovery/fulldisplay?docid=alma995036989102676&context=L&vid=41ILO_INST:41ILO_V1&lang=en&search_scope=MyInst_and_CI&adaptor=Local%20Search%20Engine&tab=Everything&query=creator,exact,Peels,%20Rafael&facet=creator,exact,Peels,%20Rafael.

Al-Invest (2021) *Al-invest 5*, www.alinvest5.org. Accessed 15 August 2021.

Allee, T. and Lugg, A. (2016). "Who wrote the rules for the Trans-Pacific Partnership?", *Research & Politics* 3 (3), 1–9. https://journals.sagepub.com/doi/10.1177/2053168016658919.

Araoz, M. (2005). *Perú: política comercial e inserción internacional*. Inter-American Development Bank. https://publications.iadb.org/es/publicacion/13479/peru-politica-comercial-e-insercion-internacional.

Barahona de Brito, A. (2000). "Introduction", *Journal of Interamerican Studies and World Affairs* 42 (2), 1–7. www.jstor.org/stable/166279?refreqid=excelsior%3Ae4ccf4bdbb4ffed2a5e582156ae82e2b&seq=1#metadata_info_tab_contents.

Barrau, A. (1999) "Union Européene et Mercosur: marriage ou union libre? Rio, 28–29 Juin 1999", Les documents d'information Assamblée Nationale Délègation pour L'Union européenne. Rapport d'information no. 1721. Paris.

Bastiaens, I. and Postnikov, E. (2017). "Greening up: the effects of environmental standards in EU and US trade agreements", *Environmental Politics* 26 (5), 847–69. https://doi.org/10.1080/09644016.2017.1338213.

Bastiaens, I. and Postnikov, E. (2019). "Social standards in trade agreements and free trade preferences: an empirical investigation", *The Review of International Organizations* 15 (4), 793–816. https://doi.org/10.1007/s11558-019-09356-y.

Brown del Rivero, A. and Torres Castillo, P. (2012). "La relación comercial Comunidad Andina–Unión Europea y la postura de Ecuador", *Latinoamérica. Revista de Estudios Latinoamericanos* 55, 75–99. www.scielo.org.mx/scielo.php?script=sci_arttext&pid=S1665-85742012000200004.

Campling, L., Harrison, J., Richardson, B. and Smith, A. (2014). 'Working beyond the border? A new research agenda for the evaluation of labour standards in EU trade agreements'. Legal Studies Research Paper No. 2014–3. Warwick Law School. https://papers.ssrn.com/sol3/papers.cfm?abstract_id=2420455.

Committee EU–Peru–Colombia–Ecuador Trade Agreement (2018). Minutes of Meeting, Quito 13–14 December. https://trade.ec.europa.eu/doclib/docs/2019/january/tradoc_157665.pdf.

Comunidad Andina, CAN (2015). *Comercio Exterior de Bienes entre la Comunidad Andina y la Unión Europea 2005–2014*, SG de 690, Secretaría General CAN. http://intranet.comunidadandina.org/Documentos/DEstadisticos/SGDE690.pdf.

Covarrubia, P. (2011). "The EU and Colombia/Peru free trade agreement on GIs: adjusting Colombian and Peruvian national laws?", *Journal of Intellectual Property Law & Practice* 6 (5), 330–8. https://doi.org/10.1093/jiplp/jpr018.

CUT Central Unitaria de Trabajadores (2018). "Lo que el gobierno oculta sobre el ingreso a la OCDE", 29 May. https://cut.org.co/lo-que-el-gobierno-oculta-sobre-el-ingreso-a-la-ocde/.

De Micco, P. (2014). *The US and EU Free Trade Agreements with Peru and Colombia: A Comparison*. Brussels: European Parliament Directorate General for External Affairs, Policy Department PE522.326.

Declaration of Guadalajara (2004). *Joint Declaration by Heads of State and Government at the Third EU–LAC Summit, Guadalajara, Mexico, 28 May 2004*, http://eeas.europa.eu/lac/guadalajara/decl_polit_final_en.pdf. Accessed 5 October 2017.

Dewan, S. and Ronconi, L. (2014). "U.S. free trade agreements and enforcement of labor law in Latin America", IDB. https://publications.iadb.org/en/publication/12154/us-free-trade-agreements-and-enforcement-labor-law-latin-america.

DG Trade (2006). *Global Europe: Competing in the World. A Contribution to the EU's Growth and Jobs Strategy*. Brussels: COM (2006) 567.

DG Trade (2018a) "EU–Peru trade statistics". http://trade.ec.europa.eu/doclib/docs/2006/september/tradoc_113435.pdf.

DG Trade (2018b) "EU–Colombia trade statistics". http://trade.ec.europa.eu/doclib/docs/2006/september/tradoc_113367.pdf.

Doctor, M. (2007). "Why bother with inter-regionalism? Negotiations for a European Union-Mercosur agreement", *Journal of Common Market Studies* 45 (4), 281–314.

Ebert, F. C. (2016). "Labour provisions in EU trade agreements: What potential for channelling labour standards-related capacity building?", *International Labour Review* 155 (3), 407–33.

El Espectador (2011). "Texto del acuerdo entre Obama y Santos", 7 April. www.elespectador.com/content/texto-del-acuerdo-entre-obama-y-santos.

El Espectador (2018). "El tema laboral: unos de los retos de Colombia para entrar en la OECD", 31 January. www.elespectador.com/economia/el-problema-que-le-impediria-colombia-ingresar-la-ocde-articulo-736455.

ElanBiz (2017). "Colombian Congress issued a law that eliminates the discriminatory tax system between imported and domestic alcoholic beverages". www.elanbiz.org/colombian-congress-issued-a-law-that-eliminates-the-discriminatory-tax-system-between-imported-and-domestic-alcoholic-beverages.

Engelhardt, T. (2015). "Geographical indications under recent EU trade agreements", *IIC-International Review of Intellectual Property and Competition Law* 46 (7), 781–818.

ENS Escuela Nacional Sindical (2015). "Informe sobre el estado de (in)cumplimiento de la Hoja de Ruta (Resolución 2628 de junio de 2012)". Bogotá: ENS. http://aitec.reseau-ipam.org/IMG/pdf/informe_hoja_de_ruta._28_de_febrero_2015.pdf.

EU (2010). *Trade Agreement between the EU and Colombia and Peru*. http://trade.ec.europa.eu/doclib/docs/2011/march/tradoc_147704.pdf. Accessed 2 October 2017.

EU–Andean Trade Sustainability Impact Assessment, Final Report 2009, http://trade.ec.europa.eu/doclib/docs/2010/april/tradoc_146014.pdf.

EU–CELAC (2015). *Summit 2015 Brussels. Facts and Figures*, 10 & 11 June. Brussels: Publications Office of the European Union.

European Commission (2006). "A stronger partnership between the European Union and Latin America". Brussels: EC. http://eeas.europa.eu/la/docs/com05_636_en.pdf.
European Commission (2017). *Third Annual Report on the Implementation of the EU–Colombia/Peru Trade Agreement. 10 October 2017*, COM(2017) 585, https://eurlex.europa.eu/legalcontent/EN/TXT/PDF/?uri=CELEX:52017DC0585. Accessed 10 May 2018.
European Commission (2021). "Panel of experts confirms Republic of Korea is in breach of labour commitments under our trade agreement", Press Release. Brussels, 25 January. https://trade.ec.europa.eu/doclib/press/index.cfm?id=2238.
European Parliament (2007). "Recommendation of 15 March 2007 to the Council on the negotiating mandate for an association agreement between the European Union and its Member States, of the one part, and the Andean Community and its member countries, of the other part" (2006/2221 (INI)). www.europarl.europa.eu/sides/getDoc.do?type=TA&reference=P6-TA-2007–0080&language=EN.
European Parliament (2012). "Resolution of 13 June 2012 on the EU trade agreement with Colombia and Peru" (2012/2628 (RSP)). www.europarl.europa.eu/doceo/document/TA-7-2012-0249_EN.html.
European Parliament (2018). "Implementation of the EU–Colombia and Peru Trade Agreement European Parliament resolution of 16 January 2019 on the implementation of the Trade Agreement between the European Union and Colombia and Peru" (2018/2010 (INI)). www.europarl.europa.eu/doceo/document/TA-8-2019-0031_EN.html.
European Union (2012). "Trade agreement between the European Union and its Member States and the Republic of Peru and Republic of Colombia", *Official Journal of the European Union*, 21 December. http://eur-lex.europa.eu/LexUriServ/LexUriServ.do?uri=OJ:L:2012:354:0003:2607:en:PDF.
Fernanda Forero, L. (2016). *Repercusiones en Colombia del Acuerdo Comercial con la Unión Europea tras tres años de su implementación*. TNI Transnational Institute and OIDHACO. www.tni.org/es/publicacion/repercusiones-en-colombia-del-acuerdo-comercial-con-la-union-europea-tras-tres-anos-de.
García, M. (2011). "Incidents along the path: understanding the rationale behind the EU–Chile Association Agreement", *Journal of Common Market Studies* 49 (3), 501–24. https://doi.org/10.1111/j.1468-5965.2010.02149.x.
García, M. (2013). "From idealism to realism? EU preferential trade agreement policy", *Journal of Contemporary European Research* 9 (4). www.jcer.net/index.php/jcer/article/view/462/429.
García, M. (2015). "The European Union and Latin America: 'Transformative power Europe' versus the realities of economic interests", *Cambridge Review of International Affairs* 28 (4), 621–40. https://doi.org/10.1080/09557571.2011.647762.
García, M. (2016). *EU Trade Relations with Latin America: Results and Challenges in Implementing the EU–Colombia/Peru Trade Agreement*, PE354.992. www.europarl.europa.eu/RegData/etudes/STUD/2016/534992/EXPO_STU(2016)534992_EN.pdf.
García, M. (2018). "Building global governance one treaty at a time? A comparison of the US and EU approaches to preferential trade agreements and the challenge of TTIP", in Fahey, E. (ed.), *Institutionalisation beyond the Nation State*. Cham: Springer, pp. 213–42.
García-García, J., López-Valenzuela, D. C., Montes-Uribe, E. and Esguerra-Umaña, M. D. P. (2014). "Una visión general de la política comercial colombiana entre

1950 y 2012", *Borradores de Economía* 817, 1–74. www.banrep.gov.co/sites/default/files/publicaciones/archivos/be_817.pdf.
Gill, S. (1998). "New constitutionalism, democratisation and global political economy", *Global Change, Peace & Security* 10(1), 23–38. https://doi.org/10.1080/14781159808412845.
Gómez, R. (2003). *Negotiating the Euro-Mediterranean Partnership: Strategic Action in EU Foreign Policy?* Aldershot: Ashgate.
Gray Molina, G. (2008). "Bolivia's long and winding road". Interamerican Dialogue ANDEAN Working Paper. https://citeseerx.ist.psu.edu/viewdoc/download?doi=10.1.1.554.3843&rep=rep1&type=pdf.
Gray Molina, G. (2013). "Global governance exit: a Bolivian case study, GEC Working Paper 2013/84. The Global Economic Governance Programme, University of Oxford. www.geg.ox.ac.uk/publication/geg-wp-201384-global-governance-exit-bolivian-case-study.
Hardacre, A. (2009). *The Rise and Fall of Interregionalism in EU External Relations.* Dordrecht: Republic of Letters Publishing.
Hopewell, K. (2016). *Breaking the WTO: How Emerging Powers Disrupted the Neoliberal Project.* Stanford: Stanford University Press.
Horn, H., Mavroidis, P. and Sapir, A. (2010). "Beyond the WTO? An anatomy of EU and US preferential trade agreements", *The World Economy* 33 (11), 1565–88.
Human Rights Watch (2015). *Peru Report.* www.hrw.org/world-report/2015/country-chapters/peru.
ILO (2013). *Social Dimensions of Free Trade Agreements.* Geneva: ILO.
ILO (2018). *Conventions and Recommendations,* www.ilo.org/global/standards/introduction-to-international-labour-standards/conventions-and-recommendations/lang–en/index.htm.
International Organisation of Employers (2006). "The evolving debate on trade & labour standards", IOE Information Paper. Geneva: IOE. https://doi.org/10.1177/0256090915573610.
Jinnah, S. and Morgera, E. (2013). "Environmental provisions in American and EU free trade agreements: a preliminary comparison and research agenda", *RECIEL Review of European Community and International Environmental Law* 22 (3), 324–39.
Joint Committee (2019). *Minutes of the 6th Meeting of the Colombia-Ecuador–Peru/EU Trade Committee, 24–25 October 2019.* https://trade.ec.europa.eu/doclib/docs/2019/november/tradoc_158430.pdf. Accessed 15 August 2021.
Manchester University, Development Solutions, CEPR (2009). *EU–Andean Trade Sustainability Impact Assessment.* http://trade.ec.europa.eu/doclib/docs/2010/april/tradoc_146014.pdf.
Marx, A., Lein, B., and Brando, N. (2016). "The protection of labour rights in trade agreements: the case of the EU–Columbia Agreement", *Journal of World Trade* 50 (4), 587–610.
Meissner, K. L. (2018). *Commercial Realism and EU Trade Policy: Competing for Economic Power in Asia and the Americas.* Abingdon: Routledge.
Miller, V. (2004). "The human rights clause in the EU's external agreements", House of Commons, Research Paper 04/33, International Affairs and Defence. https://commonslibrary.parliament.uk/research-briefings/rp04-33/.
Narlikar, A. and Van Houten, P. (2010). "Know the enemy: uncertainty and deadlock in the WTO", In Narlikar, A. (ed.), *Deadlocks in Multilateral Negotiations:*

Causes and Solutions. Cambridge: Cambridge University Press, pp. 142–63. https://doi.org/10.1017/CBO9780511804809.007.

OECD (2018). Accession of Colombia to the Organisation. C(2018)81, 28 May 2018, www.oecd.org/officialdocuments/publicdisplaydocumentpdf/?cote=C(2018)81/FINAL&docLanguage=En. Accessed 15 August 2021.

Orbie, J. and Tortell, L. (2009). "The new GSP+ beneficiaries: ticking the box or truly consistent with ILO findings?", *European Foreign Affairs Review* 14 (5), 663–81. http://hdl.handle.net/1854/LU-1092835.

Orbie, J., Van den Putte, L., and Martens, D. (2017). "The impact of labour rights commitments in EU trade agreements: the case of Peru", *Politics and Governance* 5 (4), 6–18.

Orbie, J., and Van den Putte, L. (2016). "Labour rights in Peru and the EU trade agreement: compliance with the commitments under the sustainable development chapter (No. 58)", Working Paper, Austrian Foundation for Development Research (ÖFSE). http://hdl.handle.net/10419/145974.

Portfolio (2018). "Colombia acelera proceso para entrar en OECD antes de agosto", 22 January. www.portafolio.co/economia/proceso-de-colombia-para-entrar-a-la-ocde-513505.

Sanahuja, J. A. (2000). "Asimetrías económicas y concertación política en las relaciones Unión Europea-América Latina: un examen de los problemas comerciales", *Revista Electrónica de Estudios Internacionales* 1. http://www.riie.org.

Sánchez Bajo, C. (1999). "The European Union and Mercosur: case of interregionalism", *Third World Quarterly. Journal of Emerging Areas* 20 (5), 927–41. www.jstor.org/stable/3993604?seq=1#metadata_info_tab_contents.

Schmieg, E. (2018). "Labour clauses for sustainability? Colombian trade agreements exemplify potential and limits", SWP Comment, 15/2018, Stiftung Wissenschaft und Politik (SWP), Deutsches Institut für Internationale Politik und Sicherheit, https://nbn-resolving.org/urn:nbn:de:0168-ssoar-57011-3. Accessed 15 August 2021.

Schott, J. J. (2004). *Assessing US FTA Policy. Free Trade Agreements: US Strategies and Priorities, 2.* Washington, DC: Institute for International Economics, 359–82.

Schott, J. J. (2006). "Free trade between the United States and Colombia: analysis of the issues", in *Trade Relations Between Colombia and the United States.* Washington, DC: Peterson Institute for International Economics.

Söderbaum, F., Stalgren, P. and Van Langenhove, L. (2005). "The EU as a global actor and the dynamics of interregionalism: a comparative analysis", *European Integration* 27 (3), 365–80. https://doi.org/10.1080/07036330500190297.

Sub-Committee Trade and Sustainable Development EU–Peru–Colombia–Ecuador (2018). "Minutes of Meeting, 10–12 December 2018, Quito". https://trade.ec.europa.eu/doclib/docs/2019/february/tradoc_157701.pdf.

UNCTAD (2015). *World Investment Report 2015.* http://unctad.org/en/PublicationsLibrary/wir2015_en.pdf.

USTR United States Trade Representative (2009). Peru Trade Promotion Agreement. https://ustr.gov/trade-agreements/free-trade-agreements/peru-tpa.

USTR United States Trade Representative (2012). Colombia Trade Promotion Agreement. https://ustr.gov/trade-agreements/free-trade-agreements/colombia-tpa/final-text.

Valladão, A. (1999). "Le triangle atlantique. L'emergence de l'Amerique latine dans les relations Europe–Etats-Unis. Les notes de l'IFRI – n 16". Paris: Institut français de relations internationales.

Wilkinson, R. (2006). "The WTO in Hong Kong: what it really means for the Doha Development Agenda". *New Political Economy* 11 (2), 291–304.
WTO (2016). *DS502: Colombia-Measures Concerning Imported Spirits*, 26 September. www.wto.org/english/tratop_e/dispu_e/cases_e/ds502_e.htm.
Young, A. (2015). "Liberalizing trade, not exporting rules: the limits to regulatory co-ordination in the EU's 'new generation' preferential trade agreements", *Journal of European Public Policy* 22 (9), 1253–75. https://doi.org/10.1080/13501763.2015.1046900.

Notes

1 EU-fostered interregional relations found a particular expression in relations with Latin America, a region rife with integration initiatives (see Hardacre 2009).
2 Once the agreement was implemented in Peru and Colombia, and facing a disadvantageous position vis-à-vis its neighbours, as well as the prospect of losing preferential access to the EU market through the Generalised System of Preferences (GSP), Ecuador negotiated to accede to the agreement, which it did in November 2016. In Chapter 2 above Daniel Schade charts this process and the negotiations with Andean states in detail.
3 Colombia's trade with the rest of the world dropped by 86 per cent in the same period, largely due to the fact that statistics are based on value of traded goods, and in that period mineral commodities, a major component of Colombia's trade, were low.
4 The Eight Fundamental Conventions of the ILO relate to: Freedom of Association and Protection of the Right to Organise Convention, Right to Organise and Collective Bargaining Convention, Forced Labour Convention, Abolition of Forced Labour Convention, Minimum Age Convention, Worst Forms of Child Labour Convention, Equal Remuneration Convention, Discrimination (Employment and Occupation) Convention (ILO 2018).
5 The EU did request a panel of experts under the TSD chapter in its agreement with the Republic of Korea. On 25 January 2021 the experts agreed with the EU's position that South Korea had committed to implementing ILO core conventions and reforming laws around trade union freedoms in the FTA, irrespective of the impact on trade (European Commission 2021).
6 The same situation arose in Colombia's FTAs with the US and Canada.
7 Brazil, Canada, Chile, China, Ecuador, El Salvador, Guatemala, India, Kazakhstan, Korea, Mexico, Panama, the Russian Federation, Chinese Taipei and the United States reserved their third-party rights.
8 From interviews with Sub-Committee members.

5

EU–Mexican relations: adaptation to global trade relations

Roberto Domínguez

Introduction

Extensive asymmetries, geographical distance and limited interdependence define the context of the bilateral relationship between the EU and Mexico. None the less, both parties have sought to develop practices and institutions to increase their political and economic interconnections. Since the early 1990s the EU and Mexico have dealt with the changing global contexts and adapted their relationship to the new circumstances. Two salient moments have defined the relationship in the past three decades. The first moment starts with the end of the Cold War and continues with the ascent of neoliberalism, ushering in a new era of international co-operation defined mainly by FTAs. Whilst the EU embraced the 1993 Maastricht Treaty and Mexico walked on a new path to economic and political development, both parties negotiated and concluded the 1997 Global Agreement (GA), the first of its kind between the EU and a Latin American country. The GA stamped the next two decades of an EU–Mexico relationship characterised by a convergence in public policy visions. Later, in 2008, Mexico became the second EU strategic partner in Latin America. Several shifts have marked the second moment in the international order since the late 2000s: the 2008 financial crisis, the rise of China in global trade, the technological revolution and questions about the durability of US global leadership. To face such a context the EU has reinforced its role as the pre-eminent actor for international free trade and liberal values. Mexico has worked to consolidate its economic and political stability, and both parties have concluded the negotiation for a Modernised Global Agreement (MGA) in 2020.

One of the main goals of this chapter, along the lines of this book's premises, is to explain and discuss the complexity of EU–Mexican trade relations considering the challenges the global trade system is facing today. Under the gridlock analytical framework developed by Hale and Held (2017), this chapter argues that an adverse context and negative incentives motivated the decision to launch the 2016–20 MGA negotiations. In this regard the MGA is a mechanism of adaptation and resilience to advance the free-market liberal agenda between the EU and Mexico. After reviewing the literature about the study of the EU-Mexico relationship and discussing the concept of gridlock, this chapter examines three significant points in the EU–Mexico relationship. Firstly, it provides a contextual overview of the world trade system's leading trends and the potential effects on Latin America. Secondly, it explains the conditions that facilitated the GA's negotiation, its evolution and the subsequent Strategic Partnership (SP). The final section will discuss the rationale for GA's modernisation and some of its unique details.

Through the trade gridlock in the EU—Mexico relationship

The literature about theoretical debates and interpretations of EU external relations in geographical areas where there is a significant interdependence level, such as Russia or the US, is prolific. In contrast the literature regarding EU–Mexican relations has been more empirical and policy-driven than theoretically grounded. Potential explanations for such a practical orientation derive from the modest level of interdependence, asymmetries in political and social development, geographic distance between the EU and Mexico and the US's outsized influence in Mexico. Within this existing literature four interrelated trends emerge to summarise the rationale for the continued and expanding relationship between the EU and Mexico (Dominguez and Crandall 2019; Dominguez 2019; 2020).

The first trend embraces the argument of a growing preference to diversify Mexican external relations to offset the US's dominant role. Several authors (Peña Guerrero 2008; Chanona 2008) argued that the diversification of external economic ties opened new opportunities for Mexico. However, the tangible impact EU–Mexico GA was limited because domestic economic actors were not ready to compete in the new environment generated by the implementation of new FTAs, particularly NAFTA. The second trend in the literature highlights the role of the institutionalisation of the EU–Mexican relationship as a pivot for enduring change in three areas: reinforcing the modernisation process of the Mexican political system; liberalising the economy; and strengthening social inclusion and democratic governance (Peña Guerrero 2008; Dominguez 2008; Oberda Monkiewicz 2017). A third complementary trend focuses on neoliberal institutionalist perspectives and the absolute gains approach. In this regard the EU–Mexico relationship can be considered an exemplar of the absolute gains approach. Both parties pursue differentiated interests that do not necessarily collide or compete, ultimately incentivising co-operation: when a conflict of perspectives emerges, the remedy is bilateral negotiation (Dominguez 2003; Espana Arrieta 2007).[1] The fourth trend of the literature stresses Mexico's relevance as an integral piece in the EU strategy towards Latin America (Chanona 2008). Under this view Mexico and the EU share a long-term vision in favor of free trade and the multilateral rules-based system of the WTO when rising economic nationalism obstructs larger flows of global trade (Ruano 2018b).

This chapter adopts a different approach to explain the EU–Mexico trade relationship. Rather than focusing exclusively on the rationale of action within the bilateral relationship, it observes the MGA as a mechanism to go through the global trade gridlock. Based on the analytical framework developed by Thomas Hale and David Held (2017), the central argument is that, after a long period of construction of global governance mechanisms, the international community has experienced a period of gridlock. The definition of gridlock is "the inability of countries to cooperate via international institutions to address policy problems that span borders" (Hale and Held 2017: 3). Hale and Held identify four specific trends that have made global governance more difficult in the twenty-first century: increasing multipolarity, more complex problems, institutional inertia and growing fragmentation (Klasen 2017). Their argument indicates that global governance is not static and takes place simultaneously in different sectors and societal organisation levels. Actors in global governance move "through" and "beyond" gridlock. These terms refer to positions along the continuum of change in the outcomes of interests. "Through connotes incremental yet significant improvements [...] and beyond, in turn, refers to more fundamental transformation" (Klasen 2017: 12). In other words, "The existence of pathways through gridlock means that a positive difference can be made by bolstering resilient areas of governance and by creatively seeking incremental progress [...] Moving truly beyond gridlock will require far-reaching and radical changes" (Klasen 2017: 252)

Under the gridlock analytical framework, this chapter argues that the 2000 GA took place in a context where the international trade system was moving beyond the gridlock of the 1980s. The positive context and incentives included a global trade system that experienced a deep transformation with the creation of the WTO and the proliferation of FTAs. The global trade system moved beyond the gridlock of the trading system derived from the Cold War. Simultaneously, the GA was also moving through the gridlock due to its limited scope in the global system. In contrast an adverse context and negative incentives motivated the decision to launch the 2016–20 MGA negotiations. Among other things, they included a decade of slow economic growth, no expectations of continuing the Doha Round, the exacerbation of economic nationalism and the contestation to the international liberal order (Trump's trade policies and Brexit, for instance). The MGA results from bilateral efforts to reinvigorate trade eroded flows first and foremost by a decade of slow global economic growth. Following Hale and Held, the MGA is a pathway through the current gridlock in the global trade system of the 2010s. In other words, "the global trade landscape suffers from extensive gridlock [...] at the same time, elements of the trade regime have proven remarkably resilient and adaptive" (Klasen 2017: 80). In this regard the MGA is a mechanism of adaptation and resilience to advance the free-market liberal agenda between the EU and Mexico. On top of all the negative context, the MGA negotiations concluded in the context of the Covid-19 economic slowdown in 2020.

Dealing with the Global trade gridlock

A combination of structural factors, trade policy approaches and the 2020–21 pandemic will prolong the decade-long global trade gridlock into the 2020s. Even before Covid-19, the World Bank projected that potential global growth between 2020 and 2029 would slow to a yearly average of 2.1 per cent, from 2.5 per cent in the previous decade, as a result of ageing populations and lower productivity growth. After considering the likely effects of Covid-19, the World Bank lowered its projection to 1.9 per cent (Hayashi 2021).

Recovery has been far from satisfactory, and the global trade growth has remained erratic for more than a decade. Whilst the 4.6 per cent growth in 2017 merchandise trade volume suggested a departure from the damage inflicted by the 2008 crisis, such expectations fell short with only 3 per cent growth in 2018 and 2.6 per cent growth in 2019 (Azevedo 2019). On the other hand trade freedom dropped to its lowest level since 2006 in the 2021 Index of Economic Freedom (Smith 2020). Even before the pandemic, the average tariff rate in the US nearly doubled between 2018 and 2020 because of new tariffs on nearly all imports from China and alleged national security tariffs on steel and aluminium. In sum, nativist or neo-mercantilist trade perspectives have fanned the flames of uncertainty (Brexit and US unilateral tariffs) in the global trade system and perpetuated the lack of interest in concluding the Doha Round, which predated the 2008 crisis.

Against this background, explaining the global trade system on the basis only of sluggish global trade growth, neo-protectionist perspectives and the Doha Round stalemate would forecast a catastrophic present and immediate future. Altogether the combination of these three elements renders negative inputs and outputs for the global trade system. However, to assume trade actors would remain passive in the face of these challenges is inaccurate and would obscure the analysis. In fact, in prior times of uncertainty, governments worldwide have recalibrated their trade strategies and delivered various policy responses that have stimulated actions at the global, regional and bilateral levels. It is very likely that this time is not different (Gómez Arana, Chapter 1 above).

Despite the Doha stalemate globally, the WTO is still the only organisation overseeing global trade rules. WTO regulations cover around 98 per cent of global trade and provide the mechanisms for countries to monitor and review each other's trade policies and the means to settle any disputes that may arise. Even during the Doha impasse, the WTO has struck significant agreements over the last few years, including the Trade Facilitation Agreement, the expanded Information Technology Agreement and the deal to abolish export subsidies in agriculture (Azevedo 2019).

Whilst the progress led by the WTO is far from its members' expectations, states have found alternative arrangements to advance their trade interests, sometimes complementary, but also often in opposition to the global trade system. As Griller, Obwexer and Vranes (2017) indicated, the rationale of states' action to launch mega-regional, inter-regional and bilateral agreements results from negative incentives. Some include the Doha Round trade negotiations' stalemate, the existing WTO rules that are perceived as unsatisfactory, as they often reflect the lowest common denominator, and trade obstacles due to regulatory issues (behind the border measures). Often, on the other hand, the main affirmative reasons propelling governments to enter into more reduced membership arrangements include improving preferential access to new markets; implementing economic stimulus in an era of tight budgets; upgrading "old" agreements; achieving higher ambition agreements; addressing new issues and creating potential precedents for future multilateral agreements; and improving competitiveness (Schwab and Bhatia 2014).

The proliferation of bilateral and trilateral agreements mushroomed after the early 1990s, and mega-regional agreements also became part of the trade strategies toolbox in the late 2000s. Rather than the number of members, the category of mega-regional agreements includes the group's leverage on the global trade system. Meléndez-Ortiz (2014) defines mega-regional agreement as follows: "deep integration partnerships between countries or regions with a major share of world trade and foreign direct investment (FDI), and in which two or more of the parties are in a paramount driver position, or serve as hubs, in global value chains" (Meléndez-Ortiz 2014: 13). Beyond market access, emphasis in this integration is on the quest for regulatory compatibility and a rules basket to iron out differences in investment and business climates (Meléndez-Ortiz 2014). In other words, beyond trade barriers, which are already low, mega-regional agreements are seen as necessary to advance the agenda on trade in services, investment, and regulatory co-operation, which is considered unmanageable on the multilateral WTO level. In particular the EU and the US seek to establish, through mega-regional agreements, the core of future global regulatory standards by producing a global cascade effect and setting a precedent for potential WTO reforms and negotiations (Griller, Obwexer and Vranes 2017).

The TTIP and the TPP were emblematic of mega-regional agreements' ascending wave. Others (Griller, Obwexer and Vranes 2017) also observed the Trade in Services Agreement (TiSA) as a sectoral megaregional agreement. The TiSA reforms international trade governance and brings about preferential commitments on trade in services between the three largest services markets in the world (EU, US and Japan) that potentially could be incorporated into the WTO/GATT agreement. The success of mega-regional trade agreements was affected by the withdrawal of the US. However, other significant regional agreements were also revisited and modernised in the second half of the 2010s. Three agreements are significant for the EU–Mexican relationship due to one of the parties' memberships or the potential effects on the GA's modernisation: NAFTA-USMCA, TTP-CPTPP and TTIP.

In the context of the mega-regional trade agreements, the US and Mexico have been involved in two. The Trump administration (2017–20) positioned the renegotiation of NAFTA on top place of the trade agenda. Negotiations started in August 2017 and included some of the following areas: improving rules of origin for automobiles, trucks, other products and disciplines on currency manipulation; modernising and strengthening food and agriculture trade in North America; supporting new protections for intellectual property; and new chapters covering digital trade, anti-corruption and good regulatory practices (Office of the United States Trade Representative 2019). The final document of the US–Mexico–Canada Agreement (USMCA) was signed in November 2018 and entered into force in July 2020. On the other hand, Donald Trump withdrew the US's participation in TPP in January 2017 and put a hold on the mega-regionals proposed by the Obama administration (Crespo 2018). In response to the US withdrawal, the other eleven[2] TPP parties embarked upon negotiations to negotiate a CPTPP based on the TPP text. The CPTPP was signed in March 2018 and came into force on 30 December 2018. It incorporates TPP's text generally and suspends only twenty-two provisions from the original TPP agreement (New Zealand Foreign Affairs and Trade 2019). Finally the TTIP negotiations were launched in 2013 and ended without a conclusion at the end of 2016. In April 2019 the Council of the EU decided that negotiating directives for the TTIP was obsolete and no longer relevant. Hence it was appropriate to pursue a more limited agreement with the US to eliminate tariffs on industrial products only and exclude agricultural products (Council of the European Union 2019).

Latin American countries have implemented different strategies to address the slow global trade growth and the reorganisation of trade groups. The inter-regional relationship between the EU and Latin America has mainly been conducted on a bilateral (EU–Mexico or EU–Chile) or sub-regional (EU–Central America or EU–MERCOSUR) basis. In contrast the region-to-region dialogue has experienced a "summitry fatigue", particularly after the 2017 EU–CELAC summit's postponement, which has been unfortunate, as Ruano (2018a) argues. Regarding the impact of mega-regional agreements (CPTPP and TTIP) on Latin American countries, the responses have varied depending on whether each country has trade agreements with CPTPP or TTIP parties and how vital those markets are for their exports (Leycegui 2014). In the case of the CPTPP three groups can be identified: firstly, countries that are part of CPTTP (Chile, Mexico and Peru); countries that have FTA agreements with the US and have increased the presence of Asian trade (Central America and Colombia) and hence may seek negotiations with the CPTPP to offset adverse effects and trade deviation; and other Latin American countries that are less dependent on the US and have a relatively small trade relationship with TPP Asian countries finding CPTPP less attractive (Leycegui 2014). Regarding the TTIP, negotiations were suspended in 2016 and later diluted to include simple tariffs negotiations in 2019. Whilst the TTIP's potential effect on Latin America could have been on the area of regulations, the diluted EU–US negotiations will very likely produce some trade deviation in the area of agriculture.

All in all, mega-regional agreements and gridlock in the global trade system are a moving target for Latin American countries. The global trade variable geometry can change by adding the membership of FTAs and finding co-ordination strategies between the regulatory norms of various trade arrangements. For instance, in this chapter, Mexico is part of the CPTPP and NAFTA/USMCA, whilst the EU is negotiating lowering tariffs with the US. The ripple effect on the EU–Mexico relationship is mostly related to the inclusion of new topics that were not included in the 1997 GA, the adaptation to potential trade deviation and the innovation to reinvigorate regional chains of production. Baldwin (2014) argues that excluded trade actors (EU or Mexico in this case) could also include autonomous trade reforms, seek for membership of mega-regional agreements or initiate negotiations with other important trading partners. The dynamic will enable them to raise the competitiveness of their productive apparatus.

The GA and the consolidation of the Mexican open trade model: moving beyond gridlock

The 1990s global trade context and EU and Mexican public policies' alignment led to the GA's negotiation and implementation. From this chapter's perspective, actors in global governance move "beyond" gridlock when they experience a fundamental transformation in norms and implement far-reaching changes. Five main incentives advanced the negotiations of the EU–Mexico GA. Firstly, the end of the Cold War was a historic, transformational event that produced a debate regarding the most conducive models for economic growth in general and global and regional trade, which led to the proliferation of FTAs around the world. Secondly, the creation of the WTO was emblematic of the direction of the global trade system. Thirdly, NAFTA's prospects and eventual implementation produced uncertainty in the EU and hence motivated European economic and political actors to reduce potential losses due to NAFTA. Internal transformations in Europe and Mexico also strengthened the impetus to negotiate a GA, the fourth and fifth incentives. As Torrent and Polanco (2016) indicate, the EC, either on its own or jointly with its member states, developed a strategy to negotiate bilateral agreements with several countries and regions globally, including Latin America. There was growing consensus within the EC to provide more structured and coherent EU external relations in light of the geopolitical transformations of the early 1990s, and to move forward the EC's initiative to negotiate a new round of agreements with Latin America, first with MERCOSUR as a whole, and then with Chile and Mexico (Dominguez and Crandall 2019).

Mexico's radical internal transformation allowed the EU to look for an enduring partnership with Mexico in the mid-1990s. The administration of Miguel de la Madrid Hurtado (1982–88) shifted the Mexican economic model from a protectionist model to a liberalised model by acceding to the GATT. The administration of Carlos Salinas de Gortari (1988–94) cemented Mexico's economic liberalisation by embracing the open regionalism model. The central principles were opening new markets for Mexican products, attracting foreign investment (Villarreal 2017) and deepening economic modernisation and trade liberalisation (Zabludovsky and Lora 2005). The transformations in Mexico incentivised the EU to deepen the relationship with Mexico. In 1995 both parties signed the Solemn Joint Declaration (also known as the Paris Declaration), which paved the way for formal negotiations, ultimately leading to the GA of 2000. The EU and Mexico signed the Economic, Political, and Co-operation Agreement (Global Agreement) in Brussels in December 1997 and it officially entered into force in October 2000. However, it was implemented in two phases: the trade in goods portion entered into force on 1 October 2000, with the liberalisation of services and investment as well as co-operation in the intellectual property domain to follow on 1 March 2001, after Decision 2/2001 of EU–Mexico Joint Council.

The implementation of the GA opened new and numerous avenues of co-operation between the EU and Mexico. On the other hand, the bilateral

Strategic Partnership (SP) negotiation reinforced Mexico and the EU's relationship. In contrast to the GA, the SP is an EU instrument designed to deepen co-operation with key partners to promote the values and interests of the EU at the global level (Cîrlig 2012). In 2008 Mexico became the second country in Latin America to become a Strategic Partner of the EU (after Brazil). Whilst the main framework of the economic, political and co-operation relationship is based on the GA, the SP has enhanced bilateral dialogue. To guide the EU–Mexico relationship, the SP Joint Executive Plan indicates that both parties agree to work together on common interest issues at the bilateral, regional and multilateral level on global points of common interest. Illustrative of the need to avoid duplication, the SP Joint Executive Plan also indicates that the SP will use the GA's institutional structure to promote bilateral dialogue rather than producing new structures (Council of the European Union 2010). The GA and the SP have institutionalised permanent communication practices and mutual commitment to good governance between the EU and Mexico. Informal and formal mechanisms allow for monitoring policies, exchanging experiences and adapting diplomatic and co-operation instruments to the bilateral relationship's evolving challenges.

From the economic perspective the GA has increased trade volume and offered the EU and Mexico an instrument to deal with regional and global transformations. Yet the pace of bilateral trade growth has slowed down in the past decade due to a combination of numerous factors: the slow economic growth in Mexico and the EU after the 2008 "Great Recession"; the stalemate of the WTO global negotiations; the increasing trend of economic populism in some countries resulting in the contestation of market liberalisation: and the dominant presence of China in the worldwide economy.

Despite these external forces, trade relations have grown more than 300 per cent since the EU–Mexico FTA was established in 2000, with bilateral trade reaching a record of €61.8 billion in 2017 and trade volume growing each year since 2014. The EU represented 8.8 per cent of Mexico's total business in 2017 and was its third trade partner (after the US (62.3 per cent) and China (10 per cent)). From the European perspective Mexico was the twelfth largest trade partner of the EU and represented only 1.7 per cent of its total trade. The trade balance has been consistently in favour of the EU – between €7.1 billion in 2003 and €14.1 billion in 2017. In the case of services EU exports amounted to €9.8 billion and imports to €5 billion in 2016 (DG Trade 2018).

Mexico's largest exports to the EU (value) are machinery and transport equipment (automotive products and office and telecommunications equipment, combined €8.1 billion) and petroleum products (€3.4 billion). The EU's largest exports to Mexico are machinery and transport equipment (€19.9 billion) and chemicals (€6.2 billion). Agriculture and fisheries products received considerable attention during the GA negotiation despite trade in this sector totalling €2.8 billion (DG Trade 2018). The balance of trade in the agricultural sector between the two parties has oscillated, with Mexico achieving a slight advantage since 2014. Agriculture also achieves the most parity of any sector. The GA provided a ten-year window after which all tariffs on agri-food products were to be eliminated. In 1999 only 8 per cent of EU agri-food products could enter Mexico free of tariffs; by 2009 the percentage had climbed to 64 per cent (Copenhagen Economics 2016).

Whilst FDI benefits the investor and the recipient, the FDI flow is significantly higher from the EU to Mexico than in the reverse direction. From this perspective, as often occurs with FTAs, one of the expectations is that the flow of FDI from the more to the less developed economy will produce jobs and contribute to increasing living standards. This premise also applies to the case of EU FDI flows to Mexico. In 2016 total accumulated FDI between Mexico and the EU was nearly €180 billion, with the balance heavily favouring Mexico. €137 billion flowed to Mexico, primarily directed to manufacturing, transportation and construction, followed by the retail and wholesale trade and financial services (European Commission 2018d). The EU is the second-largest investor in Mexico in various sectors and represents around 37 per cent of total FDI in Mexico. For example German companies employ more than 120,000 people in Mexico. German car makers such as Audi, BMW, Daimler and Volkswagen continue to invest billions in opening factories in Mexico, which generates thousands of jobs for skilled workers (Konrad 2015). In 2015 the largest European investors in Mexico were Spain, Germany, Belgium, Italy and France (Mexican Representation to the EU 2017).

From the political perspective Mexico and the EU have created a high-level political dialogue and eight sectoral dialogues on climate change, the environment, macroeconomic issues, human rights, security and justice, higher education, the digital agenda and energy. The high-level political dialogue is the most important type of exchange featured in the SP, and, as of 2018, it had convened five times. These meetings, attended by high-ranking officials from both parties, review the bilateral agenda's most significant aspects (SRE 2018a). International and regional issues have also been examined in the political dialogue, including exchanges of views about Iran, Syria, the Middle East's situation, relations with strategic partners, and the EU's and Mexico's regional contexts.

Each sectoral dialogue is significant in its capacity and domain. Still some are more visible due to immediate social needs and difficulty – particularly on behalf of the Mexican government – in raising the performance and effectiveness of existing oversight frameworks. The High-Level Dialogues (HLD) in Human Rights and Security and Law Enforcement are two examples of sectoral dialogues where Mexico has struggled to make significant progress. Human rights have been an essential and sensitive item on the bilateral agenda for several years. EU annual reports on human rights consistently indicate that Mexico faces considerable challenges in the areas of security and human rights, despite substantial efforts made to strengthen further the country's legislative framework (EEAS 2017a). These challenges include torture, forced disappearances, extrajudicial killings and organised crime infiltration in state institutions (EEAS 2017b). Structural deficiencies in the justice system are unable to lessen impunity, and Mexico ranks among the countries with the highest levels of impunity according to the 2017 Global Impunity Index (Le Clercq Ortega and Rodríguez Sánchez Lara 2017). The observation of human rights in the EU–Mexico agenda was a priority area even before implementing the GA. As of 2018 the HLD on Human Rights has held eight annual meetings (EEAS 2018).

Another vital dialogue is the HLD on Security and Law Enforcement, which has been held since 2011 due to Mexico's increasing violence levels. During her visit to Mexico in May 2016 Federica Mogherini, High Representative of the Union for Foreign Affairs and Security Policy and Vice-President of the European Commission, attended the second HLD on Security and Justice. Her visit was emblematic because it revealed that security and law enforcement are among the most critical bilateral relationship areas. Whilst acknowledging the progress made in Mexico, her remarks during the meeting were firm regarding the shared security concerns and the urgency to work together in the areas with potential for further co-operation (Delegation of the EU to Mexico 2016).

Development co-operation is the third pillar of the GA and has been a very active area of the EU–Mexico agenda. Two significant transformations have reshaped bilateral development co-operation. Firstly, EU development policy changes produced a differentiated approach where countries achieving middle-income-country status would no longer be eligible for EU bilateral aid, only regional and thematic assistance. Thus, given Mexico's position as a graduated country, the EU development partnership with Mexico for 2014–20 no longer included EU bilateral funds. Secondly, over the past two decades Mexico has strengthened its dual nature as recipient and provider of development co-operation through the institutionalisation of this approach by creating the Mexican Agency for International Co-operation for Development (AMEXCID).

Mexico has not been eligible for bilateral assistance since 2014. However, the main bilateral programme under the 2007–13 EU Country Strategy for Mexico (Social Cohesion Lab, phase II) maintained activities with twenty-six critical institutions in Mexico until 2018. Moreover, Mexico remains eligible to receive funding from several EU programs/instruments, such as the

Development Co-operation Instrument, thematic programmes, such as the Partnership Instrument and the European Instrument for Democracy and Human Rights. These programmes are all continental programmes for Latin America and external components of internal instruments (European Commission 2018c). The current EU development co-operation portfolio to Mexico represents some €100 million in grants leveraging an additional €40 million from Mexican institutions and close to €1 billion in development bank loans. Ongoing bilateral programmes include actions co-financed by Mexican institutions and co-ordinated by AMEXCID in the field of social cohesion (€42 million), economic innovation and competitiveness (€18 million) and culture (€5.6 million) (European Commission 2018c).

As a result of the bilateral convergence of approaches to co-operation in development, the EU and Mexico started sharing best practices, knowledge and expertise to strengthen developing countries' capabilities – particularly in Central America and the Caribbean. In December 2018 the Mexican President Andres Manuel Lopez Obrador (2018–24) presented "The Plan for Comprehensive Development to Central America" and the EU Ambassador to Mexico stated that the EU would seek to align its programmes in the region to contribute to the Mexican President's initiative (SRE 2018b).

The modernisation of the GA: innovating and moving through gridlock

The First CELAC-EU Summit in Santiago, Chile, in 2013, was the formal starting point for exploring the potential modernisation of the GA with Mexico, particularly its trade pillar (Secretaria de Relaciones Exteriores 2019). The changing circumstances of the global economy and the increasing limitations of the GA led the former President of the European Commission, Manuel Barroso, the former President of the European Council, Herman van Rompuy and the former Mexican President, Enrique Peña Nieto, to agree to the review and update the Mexico–EU bilateral legal framework: the negotiations started in 2016 and concluded in 2020 (Drazen and Blenkinsop 2020).

In a context of a global trade system facing a gridlock, to follow the argument of this chapter, the modernisation of the GA is significant because it reflects the political will of the EU and Mexico to provide an updated legal framework for areas of common interest that (1) were not included in the GA, (2) were contemplated in a limited way, and (3) needed to be adapted to internal transformations in Mexico, the EU and the international arena (Del Río and Saavedra Cinta 2018). The global factors that have inspired EU–Mexico plans for modernising the GA range from the urgent (the revolution in digital technology) to the subtle (shifts in the international balance of power). The norm-based liberal international order established by the US, which is currently being challenged by populist politics, and the rising influence of China's economic expansion, represent two of the most important incentives for the EU and Mexico to forge a common front (Ruano 2018c). Additionally, transformations in international value chains, where both trade and foreign direct investment are increasingly important, were a significant factor in revisiting the EU–Mexico mechanisms for investment protection, regulatory co-operation and sustainable development, among other things (Del Río and Saavedra Cinta 2018). More positive incentives for the GA's modernisation are the legal and technical innovations of other comprehensive agreements concluded since 2000 by the EU or Mexico, and the increasing competition from third countries, such as China and other Asian countries (European Commission 2015).

After concluding the preparatory work, formal negotiations to modernise the GA were launched in May 2016, ending in April 2018. Negotiations were expected to be completed within a year; however, nine rounds were required to address the main discussion areas (Rodríguez-Piñero Fernández 2018). Table 5.1 presents the sequence of the main achievements in each round of negotiation. Similarly to the original GA negotiation process, the rounds were complicated but not highly contentious. Forty negotiation proposals were submitted by the EU (Harte 2020), with disputes arising in various areas. Remarkably, the Members of the EP and civil-society organisations repeatedly expressed their concern for Mexico's ability to respect human rights and deter the rising impunity related to drugs and migration.

Whilst some EU–Mexico relationship areas have gradually adapted to the international arena's changing circumstances, a few areas of the GA framework needed formal updates. The MGA will be more capable of adjusting to these new circumstances not only because of its focus on political, economic and co-operation areas but also due to the inclusion of new policies and mechanisms of co-operation, such as the Strategic Partnership, the establishment of the Joint Parliamentary Committee (EU–Mexico JPC), the continually expanding scope of HLD (Dominguez 2014) and the adoption of the Investment Tribunal System (European Commission 2018e).

The general spirit of the modernisation effort in trade achieved the highest level of liberalisation possible and securing better rules for all (Harte 2020). To that end the modernised Agreement updated the eleven existing disciplines in the GA and added the following eight additional items: (1) anti-corruption; (2) transparency; (3) trade and sustainable development; (4) technical barriers to trade; (5) trade remedies; (6) small and medium enterprises (SMEs); (7) animal welfare and antimicrobial resistance; and (8) energy and raw materials

Table 5.1 Negotiation of the modernisation of the GA EU–Mexico

Round of negotiations	Achievements and discussions
Round 1, Brussels 13–14 June 2016	Mexico and the EU agreed to design a multidimensional framework that consists of bilateral, regional, bi-regional, and triangular co-operation projects. Definition of methodologies of negotiation.
Round 2, Mexico City Political & Co-operation, 15 May 2017	Agreed on issues relating to political dialogue bilateral and multilateral, as well as international development co-operation.
Round 2, Mexico City Trade, 22–5 November 2016	Mexico and the EU work to modernise the commercial pillar of the global agreement (TLCUEM)
Round 3, Brussels Political & Co-operation, 10 July 2017	A new agreement is to replace the current Economic Partnership Co-ordination and Global Agreement, will help with future investment, trade, and reinforce their partnership.
Round 3, Brussels Trade, 3–7 April 2017	The Ministry of Economics works on commercial agenda to deepen integration of Mexico with its partners. Work was continued on issues such as access to goods, rules of origin, trade facilitation, investment, competition, etc.
Round 4, Mexico City Political & Co-operation, 6 October 2017	Agreements were reached on the majority of the issues from organised crime to climate change along with migration, gender equality and corruption. Negotiations of political and cooperative issues were to be concluded by the end of 2017.
Round 4, Mexico City Trade, 26–9 June 2017	Ministry of the Economy is to organise a Forum on the modernisation of the FTAEU. This will consist of opinions and recommendations from civil society organisations, academic institutions, both industry and economic agents, and chambers of commerce.
Round 5, Brussels Political & Co-operation, 13 November 2017	Delegates reached an agreement towards issues consisting of remaining articles on political dialogue and co-operation. Much of their talk consisted of institutional and final provisions.
Round 5, Brussels Trade, 25–9, September 2017	N/A

Table 5.1 Negotiation of the modernisation of the GA EU–Mexico (Continued)

Round of negotiations	Achievements and discussions
Round 6, Mexico City Political & Co-operation, 29–30 November 2017	Delegates concluded on political and co-operation issues, with no relation to ongoing trade and investment. There is reaffirmation on the commitment of both parties.
Round 6, Mexico City Trade, 27 November – 1 December 2017	Issues that pertained to the competition policy were completed.
Round 7, Brussels Trade, 11–21 December 2017	Efforts towards market access, appellations of origin, intellectual property, GIs, and investment were achieved.
Round 8, Mexico City Trade, 8–17 January 2018	Mexico and the EU agreed to progress with various topics such as access to markets, trade barriers, rules of origin.
Round 9, Mexico City Trade, 20 February 2018	Negotiations on the modernisation of TLCUEM concludes. Topics such as technical barriers, trade, enterprises, subsides, and trade in services were concluded.
April 2018	Both parties reached agreement in principle.
28 April 2020	Conversation between European Commissioner Paul Hogan and Secretary of Economy Graciela Márquez. The EU accepted the Mexican proposal regarding public procurement at the state level. Negotiations concluded.

Source: Author, based on the information in Secretaria de Relaciones Exteriores (2019) and Secretaria de Economia (2020)

(Ecorys 2015). Disciplines 1–3 have crossed over from the EU–Mexico co-operation agenda to become formal institutionalised disciplines under the modernised agreement. Items 4–6 are examples of where the GA was insufficient to enhance trade, and items 7 and 8 represent shifts in global realities requiring international accord.

The trade pillar's modernisation reflected transformations in three areas: trade policy, contemporary EU and Mexican priorities, and limitations of the 2000 Agreement. The new trade agenda's realities required the modernised agreement to address non-tariff barriers (NTBs), sustainability issues, growth in financial services, and e-commerce, among other items (Ruano 2018c). In addition to adding NTBs and sustainability topics to disciplines covered, the modernised agreement dedicated six chapters to address trade in services, including a chapter on digital trade (Rodríguez-Piñero Fernández 2018).

Among other trade innovations, the new agreement will remove customs duties on trade in goods, liberalising 99 per cent of tariff lines (including full liberalisation of trade in industrial goods). In the area of agricultural goods more than 85 per cent of tariff lines would be fully liberalised. Simultaneously, specific sensitive sectors (such as dairy and meat) would remain subject to specific restrictions (including quotas and tariff-rate quotas). The modernised agreement would also protect an additional 340 European GIs in Mexico. Also it includes chapters on rules of origin (including for cars), trade facilitation, trade remedies, technical barriers to trade, and sanitary and phytosanitary rules. On services the modernised agreement would make it easier for EU firms to do business in Mexico (including in the maritime transport, telecommunications and financial sectors) while protecting both parties' rights.

Investment has been one of the driving forces of the EU–Mexican relationship. Whilst both parties agreed on measures to make it easier for EU companies to invest in Mexico, one of the main innovations is adopting the Investment Court System (ICS). The EU has included in its investment negotiations instead of the traditional Investor-State Dispute Settlement. The new ICS will include professional, independent judges bound by a strict code of conduct, will hold hearings in public and will publish documents related to cases online, and specified grounds on which an investor can challenge a state (European Commission 2018a). The inclusion of the ICS in investment negotiations was quite controversial. It opened a legal debate in the EU, particularly regarding the Comprehensive Economic and Trade Agreement (CETA) with Canada. Proposed by the President of the European Commission, Jean-Claude Juncker, in 2014, the ICS became the template for all EU investment negotiations. The European Court of Justice confirmed the ICS's compatibility with EU treaties on 30 April 2019, meaning that no changes would be made to the EU–Canada agreement text, which entered into force provisionally on 21 September 2017. Member states' ratifications can proceed for full-fledged implementation. Equally, no change will be required in the ICS provisions included in the agreements with Singapore (signed in 2018), Mexico and Vietnam (negotiations concluded in 2018) (European Commission 2019).

Public procurement is a very significant area of the Mexican economy. In 2015 Mexico's federal government issued procurement contracts for €30 billion, representing 5.2 per cent of the GDP (European Commission 2018b). The MGA is the first trade agreement that commits Mexico to open its public procurement at the state level to non-Mexican firms. After the MGA conclusion in principle in April 2018, the Mexican government started negotiations with the states and municipalities to enable EU firms to tender for contracts before formally submitting the MGA for ratification (Morales 2019). Whilst the agreement will offer reciprocal access for Mexican suppliers to the European procurement market, including the utility market, the agreement's emphasis is regarding the access of EU firms to the Mexican market. Particularly important is the acceptance of Mexico "to ensure a high level of predictability and transparency of its public procurement process covered by the Agreement by introducing new generation disciplines equivalent to those internationally agreed in the WTO Government Procurement Agreement" (European Commission 2018f: 12).

The modernised agreement would also include chapters on corruption, TSD, transparency, energy and raw materials, small- and medium-sized enterprises, subsidies, competition, good regulatory practices, animal welfare and antimicrobial resistance, as well as annexes on motor vehicles and wine and spirits. Lastly, the modernised agreement would include a review clause on the need to include provisions on the data's free flow. A Commission Impact Assessment determined that a comprehensive and ambitious modernised agreement could increase EU GDP by 0.01 per cent per annum by 2028, as well as rendering improvements in social and environmental standards (Rodríguez-Piñero Fernández 2018).

Following the structure of the 2000 GA, the MGA retained the pillars of Political Co-ordination and Co-operation. About modernising the Political Co-ordination pillar, three existing elements have now been fully incorporated into the revised agreement: (1) the biannual summits of heads of state and government – designed to be the top political structure responsible for managing the most critical aspects of the common agenda and for projecting both sides as Strategic Partners in the global arena; (2) the annual inter-parliamentary meetings (the Mixed Parliamentary Commission EU-=-Mexican Congress) which have met uninterruptedly since 2005 and (3) the dialogue with Civil Society Organisations (Ruano 2018c). Concerning the Co-operation pillar, Mexico and the EU have experienced converging positions on multiple issues on the international agenda. They include sustainable development (in other areas not specifically related to trade); combating corruption; agreements on fisheries, forestry, and biodiversity; labour rights; preventing a race to the bottom; and an expanded human-rights agenda addressing justice and security. Their talks also focused on the possibilities of expanding bilateral co-operation in research and development, especially in renewable energy, and on tools to facilitate mobility and academic co-operation between Mexico and the EU (Rodríguez-Piñero Fernández 2018).

The conclusion of the negotiations of MGA in April 2020 will continue with the legal and technical reviews. The expectation is that the MGA will be officially signed at the VIII Mexico–EU Summit. Later it will be submitted to the European and the Mexican Parliament for ratification. If approved, the ratification would allow the immediate implementation of the agreement's trade section and supranational matters. The process will continue with the ratification of the MGA by the national European parliaments regarding matters of the agreement of national concern.

Final considerations

The evolution of the relationship between the EU and Mexico has been influenced not only by the international context but also by the EU's and Mexico's policy choices. As indicated in the first section of this chapter, actors in global governance move "through" (incremental improvement) or "beyond" (more fundamental transformation) global trade gridlocks. The two turning points in the EU–Mexico relationship (GA and MGA) have taken place in two entirely different international contexts that reveal both parties' capacity to adapt to the changing circumstances.

The 1990s provided an environment conducive to significant transformations in the global trade system. The entry into force of the GA in 2000 marked a turning point in the relationship. Despite substantial differences in economic and political development, the EU and Mexico inked one of the most comprehensive bilateral agreements of its time. More than just a trade agreement, the GA set the EU and Mexico on a path towards institutional convergence of good governance practices. Although negotiations for the GA were long and at times complex, shifting international paradigms compelled both the EU and Mexico towards compromise and agreement. Internal transformations also strengthened their partnership. Whilst Mexico experienced democratic consolidation and adopted the liberalised trade model, the EU expanded its membership and updated its external relations policies, leading to the Strategic Partnership in 2008. The initial GA institutionalised frameworks across trade, political dialogue and co-operation, whilst the SP reaffirmed the principles of the EU–Mexico relationship and expanded co-operation areas to include Latin America.

The 2010s offered a context of recalibration to adapt to a global trade system under stress. Based on the lessons of the implementation of the GA, the negotiations to modernise the GA are the capstone of three decades of EU–Mexico relations, which have experienced an intense acceleration in the last two decades. Although asymmetries in economic and political development still exist, the MGA is reinvigorating EU–Mexico relations at a time when the liberal global order is being challenged, and the leadership role of the US is being questioned. With the MGA consolidating and extending the institutional frameworks that have allowed for the decades-long durability of their relationship, the EU and Mexico are well poised to endure the challenges of contemporary international relations.

References

Azevedo, R. (2019). "Remarks by the WTO Director-General." *Special session in the Senate — "Importance of the multilateral trading system for Mexico in the current economic climate"*, 4 April. www.wto.org/english/news_e/news19_e/dgra_05apr19_e.htm.

Baldwin, R. (2014). "The economic impact", In World Economic Forum (ed.), *Mega-regional Trade Agreements Game-Changers or Costly Distractions for the World Trading System?* Geneva: World Economic Forum.

Chanona, A. (2008). "Inclusion social: eje de la relacion estategica Mexico–Union-Europea," in Guerrero, R. P. (ed.), *Mexico–Union Europea. Asociacion Estrategica para la Gobernalibilidad y la Inclusion Social*, pp. 37–58. Mexico: UNAM.

Cîrlig, C. C. (2012). "EU Strategic Partnerships with third countries", *Library of the European Parliament*, 26 September. www.europarl.europa.eu/thinktank/en/document.html?reference=LDM_BRI%282012%29120354.

Copenhagen Economics (2016). *Impacts of EU Trade Agreements on the Agricultural Sector*. Luxembourg: European Commission, Directorate-General for Agriculture and Rural Development. https://ec.europa.eu/info/sites/default/files/food-farming-fisheries/trade/documents/bilateral-trade-agreements-2016-exec-sum_en.pdf.

Council of the European Union (2010). *Mexico–European Union Strategic Partnership Joint Executive Plan*. Comillas. www.europarl.europa.eu/cmsdata/122322/114467.pdf.

Council of the European Union (2019). "Council decision authorising the opening of negotiations with the United States of America for an agreement on the elimination of tariffs for industrial goods", 9 April. https://eur-lex.europa.eu/legal-content/EN/TXT/?uri=COM:2019:0016:FIN.

Crespo, C. S. (2018). "A Mexican outlook on Nafta, TPP and their renegotiation: investment arbitration's transparency and international supervision at peril?", *Houston Journal of International Law* 40 (3), 937–1002. https://international.vlex.com/vid/mexican-outlook-on-nafta-782309061.

Del Río, F. and Saavedra Cinta, R. (2018). "Modernización de los capítulos de diálogo político y cooperación del Acuerdo Global México–Unión Europea", *Revista Mexicana de Política Exterior* 112 (January–April), 33–48. www.europarl.europa.eu/RegData/etudes/BRIE/2017/608680/EPRS_BRI(2017)608680_ES.pdf/.

Delegation of the EU to Mexico (2016). Visit of Federica Mogherini, Vice-President of the EC, to Mexico, 25.May. https://eeas.europa.eu/delegations/australia/14589/visit-of-federica-mogherini-vice-president-of-the-ec-to-mexico-joint-press-conference-with-claudia-ruiz-massieu-mexican-secretary-for-foreign-affairs_zh-hans.

DG Trade (2018). "Mexico. EU bilateral trade and trade with the world." accessed 5 October.

Domínguez, R. (2003). "The European Union and Mexico: discovering the new south of North America", Working Paper 1 (2). Centro de Estudios Europeos-UNAM. https://ec.europa.eu/trade/policy/countries-and-regions/countries/mexico/index_en.htm.

Domínguez, R. (2008). "El papel de la Uniion Europea en la politica exterior de Mexico", in Gragea, A. C. and Ochman, M. (eds), *Integracion, Desarrollo e Interregionalismo en las relaciones entre la Union Europea y America Latina*, pp. 231–46. Mexico: Miguel Angel Porrua-Tec de Monterrey.

Domínguez, R. (2014). *The Modernisation of the European Union–Mexico "Global Agreement", Directorate-General for External Policies of the Union*. Brussels: European Parliament. www.europarl.europa.eu/RegData/etudes/STUD/2014/534985/EXPO_STU(2014)534985_EN.pdf.

Domínguez, R. (2019). "Strategic partner and model of governance: EU perceptions of Mexico", in Chaban, N. and Holland, M. (eds), *Shaping the EU Global Strategy Partners and Perceptions*, pp. 147–64. New York: Palgrave Macmillan.

Domínguez, R. (2020). "Resilience in the modernization of the EU–Mexico Global Agreement", *Análisis Carolina* 45/2020EN (27 July). https://doi.org/10.33960/AC_45en.2020.

Domínguez, R. and Crandall, C. (2019). "EU–Mexico", in Laursen, F. (ed.), *Oxford Research Encyclopedia of EU Politics*. Oxford: Oxford University Press.

Drazen, J. and Blenkinsop, P. (2020). "EU, Mexico conclude talks to update free trade deal", *Reuters*, 28 April. https://uk.reuters.com/article/uk-mexico-eu/eu-mexico-conclude-talks-to-update-free-trade-deal-idUKKCN22A2L2.

Ecorys (2015). *Ex-post Evaluation of the Implementation of the EU–Mexico Free Trade Agreement. Interim Technical Report*. Rotterdam: ECORYS Nederland BV.

EEAS (2017a). *EU Annual Report on Human Rights and Democracy in the World in 2017*. Brussels: EEAS. https://eeas.europa.eu/sites/default/files/eu_annual_report_on_hr_2017.pdf.

EEAS (2017b). *EU Annual Report on Human Rights and Democracy in the World in 2017*. Country Reports Compilation. Brussels: EEAS. https://eeas.europa.eu/sites/default/files/compiled_country_updates_annual_report_on_human_rights_and_democracy_2017_clean_0.pdf.

EEAS (2018). "Mexico and the European Union reaffirm their commitment to human rights", Joint Press Release, 26 October. https://eeas.europa.eu/delegations/congo-brazzaville/52888/mexico-and-european-union-reaffirm-their-commitment-human-rights_sq.

España Arrieta, O. (2007). "El Acuerdo de Asociacion entre Mexico y la Union Europea: Nuevas oportunidades o nuevos retos", in Arroyo Alejandre, J., Romero Morett, M., Diaz Barrado, C. and Espana Arrieta, O. (eds), *A siete anos de la firma del Acuerdo entre Mexico y la Union Europea*, pp. 111–37. Guadalajara: Universidad de Guadalajara.

EU–Mexico JPC (2013). *Draft Minutes of the 16th Meeting of the EU–Mexico JPC*. Strasbourg: European Parliament. www.europarl.europa.eu/cmsdata/145057/20140515ATT83905EN.pdf.

European Commission (2015). *Executive Summary of the Impact Assessment Accompanying the Document Recommendation for a Council Decision Authorising the European Commission and the High Representative of the Union for Foreign Affairs and Security Policy to Open Negotiations and Negotiate with Mexico a Modernised Global Agreement*: DG Trade SWD (2015) 290 final. https://eur-lex.europa.eu/legal-content/en/TXT/?uri=CELEX%3A52017SC0172.

European Commission (2018a). *EU–Mexico Trade Agreement. Overview*. Brussels: EC. https://ec.europa.eu/trade/policy/in-focus/eu-mexico-trade-agreement/index_en.htm.

European Commission (2018b). *Guide to the New EU–Mexico Trade Agreement*. Brussels: EC. https://trade.ec.europa.eu/doclib/press/index.cfm?id=1833.

European Commission (2018c). "Mexico", *International Cooperation and Development*, 21 December.
European Commission. (2018d). *Mexico. Trade.* https://ec.europa.eu/trade/policy/countries-and-regions/countries/mexico/index_en.htm.
European Commission. (2018e). *New EU–Mexico Agreement: The Agreement in Principle and Its Texts.* Brussels: EC. https://trade.ec.europa.eu/doclib/press/index.cfm?id=1833.
European Commission (2018f). "New EU–Mexico Agreement. The Agreement in Principle," 23 April. https://trade.ec.europa.eu/doclib/press/index.cfm?id=1833.
European Commission (2019). "European Court of Justice confirms compatibility of investment court system with EU treaties", Press Release, 30 April. http://trade.ec.europa.eu/doclib/press/index.cfm?id=2014.
Griller, S., Obwexer, W. and Vranes. E. (2017). "Mega-regional trade agreements. new orientations for EU external relations", in Griller, S. Obwexer, W. and Vranes, E. (eds), *Mega-Regional Trade Agreements: CETA, TTIP, and TiSA*, Oxford: Oxford University Press.
Hale, T. and Held, D. (2017). *Beyond Gridlock.* Medford, MA: Polity.
Harte, R. (2020). "Modernisation of the trade pillar of the EU–Mexico Global Agreement". Briefing International Agreements in Progress. Brussels: European Parliamentary Research Service.
Hayashi, Y. (2021). "Covid-19 aftermath could spell a 'lost decade' for global economy, World Bank says", *Wall Street Journal*, 5 January. www.wsj.com/articles/covid-19-aftermath-could-spell-a-lost-decade-for-global-economy-world-bank-says-11609862404.
Klasen, A. (2017). "Trade. gridlock and resilience", in Hale, T. and Held, D. (eds), *Beyond Gridlock*, pp. 65–82. Medford, MA: Polity.
Konrad, A. (2015). "EU trade and investment in Mexico: facts and figures", *Wilson Center Home*, 15 July. www.wilsoncenter.org/article/eu-trade-and-investment-mexico-facts-and-figures.
Le Clercq Ortega, J. A. and Rodríguez Sánchez Lara, G. (2017). *Global Impunity Dimensions. Global Impunity Index 2017 (GII-2017).* Puebla: Fundacion Universidad de Las Americas. https://papers.ssrn.com/sol3/papers.cfm?abstract_id=3065593#.
Leycegui, B. (2014). "Mega-regionals – how 'mega' will their impact be for Latin America?", in Global Agenda Council on Trade & Foreign Direct Investment (ed.), *Mega-regional Trade Agreements Game-Changers or Costly Distractions for the World Trading System?*, pp. 38–41. Geneva: World Economic Forum.
Meléndez-Ortiz, R. (2014). "Mega-regionals: what is going on?", in Global Agenda Council on Trade & Foreign Direct Investment (ed.), *Mega-regional Trade Agreements Game-Changers or Costly Distractions for the World Trading System?*, pp. 13–17. Geneva: World Economic Forum.
Mexican Representation to the EU. (2017). FDI.
Morales, R. (2019). "Unión Europea fija objetivo de compras públicas con México", *El Economista*, 13 February. hwww.eleconomista.com.mx/empresas/Union-Europea-fija-objetivo-de-compras-publicas-con-Mexico-20190213-0075.html.
New Zealand Foreign Affairs and Trade. (2019). *Comprehensive and progressive agreement for Trans-Pacific Partnership*, New Zealand Foreign Affairs and Trade. www.instituteforgovernment.org.uk/explainers/trade-cptpp.

Oberda Monkiewicz, A. (2017). "Evolution of EU–Mexico relations: time for real partnership?", *Anuario Latinoamericano Ciencias Políticas y Relaciones Internacionales* 4, 187–202.
Office of the United States Trade Representative (2019). *United States, Mexico and Canada Agreement*. Washington, DC: OUSTR.
Peña Guerrero, R. (2008). "A manera de introduccion: hipotesis, objetivos y temas", in Peña Guerrero, R. (ed.),*Mexico–Union Europea. Asociacion Estrategica para la Gobernalibilidad y la Inclusion Social*, pp. 11–36. Mexico: UNAM.
Rodríguez-Piñero Fernández, I. (2018). "Legislative train schedule of the European Parliament". Last modified 14 December 2018. www.europarl.europa.eu/legislative-train/theme-a-balanced-and-progressive-trade-policy-to-harness-globalisation/file-modernisation-eu-mexico-global-agreement.
Ruano, L. (2018a). "Dealing with diversity. The EU and Latin America today", in European Union Institute for Security Studies (ed.), Chaillot Papers No. 148. Paris: EUISS. www.iss.europa.eu/content/dealing-diversity-%E2%80%93-eu-and-latin-america-today.
Ruano, L. (2018b). "Introducción. Europa y su relación con México", *Revista Mexicana de Política Exterior*, 112 (January–April), 9–16.
Ruano, L. (2018c). "The "modernisation" of the global agreement between Mexico and the EU", in Mori, A. (ed.), *EU and Latin America: A Stronger Partnership?*, pp. 47–66. https://revistadigital.sre.gob.mx/images/stories/numeros/n112/introduccion112.pdf.
Schwab, S. and Bhatia, K. (2014). "Why mega-regionals?", in Global Agenda Council on Trade & Foreign Direct Investment (ed.), *Mega-regional Trade Agreements Game-Changers or Costly Distractions for the World Trading System*, pp. 18–20. Geneva: World Economic Forum.
Secretaria de Relaciones Exteriores (2018a). *5th Mexico–EU High-Level Political Dialogue*. www.gob.mx/sre/en/prensa/5th-mexico-european-union-high-level-political-dialogue.
Secretaria de Relaciones Exteriores (2018b). *Unión Europea expresa su interés en participar en el Plan de Desarrollo Integral para Centroamérica. Mexico*. www.gob.mx/sre/es/articulos/union-europea-expresa-su-interes-en-participar-en-el-plan-de-desarrollo-integral-para-centroamerica-185775?idiom=es.
Secretaria de Relaciones Exteriores (2019). *Mexico–EU Global Agreement*. https://globalmx.sre.gob.mx/index.php/en/political-dialogue/mexico-eu-global-agreement.
Smith, T. K. (2020). "2021 index of economic freedom: after three years of worsening trade freedom, countries should recommit to lowering barriers", *Issue Brief No. 6026*, 12 November. www.heritage.org/trade/report/2021-index-economic-freedom-after-three-years-worsening-trade-freedom-countries-should.
Torrent, R. and Polanco, R. (2016). *Analysis of the Upcoming Modernisation of the Trade Pillar of the European Union–Mexico Global Agreement*. Brussels: European Parliament, Directorate-General for External Policies. www.europarl.europa.eu/RegData/etudes/STUD/2016/534012/EXPO_STU(2016)534012_EN.pdf.
Villarreal, M. A. (2017). "Mexico's free trade agreements", in *Congressional Research Service*. Washington, DC. https://sgp.fas.org/crs/row/R42965.pdf.
Zabludovsky, J. and Lora, S. (2005). "The European window: challenges in the negotiation of Mexico's free trade agreement with the European Union", in Working Paper SITI-09, INTAL: Institute for the Integration of Latin America and the Caribbean. https://publications.iadb.org/en/publication/european-window-challenges-negotiation-mexicos-free-trade-agreement-european-union.

Notes

1 In contrast the relative-gains approach employs the zero-sum game logic where one party wins, and the other loses; hence conflict inhibits co-operation.
2 Australia, Brunei, Canada, Chile, Japan, Malaysia, Mexico, New Zealand, Peru, Singapore and Vietnam.

6

Twenty years of EU–MERCOSUR negotiations: inter-regionalism and the crisis of globalisation

José Antonio Sanahuja and Jorge Damián Rodríguez

Introduction

On 28 June 2019 the EU and MERCOSUR, to the surprise of many, concluded the negotiations of the chapter on trade and investment of the association agreement that both parties had negotiated, discontinuously, for twenty years. That date had a double significance. On the one hand, both parties were able to announce that important agreement at the G20 Summit in Osaka (Japan), as a powerful political message in support of multilateralism and free trade, against the bleak scenario for international economy marked by the trade and technology war between the US and China, President Trump's threats of protectionist measures towards the EU and other countries and, more generally, by a globalisation in crisis and a contested international liberal order. On the other hand, exactly twenty years before, on 28 June 1999, the "Rio Summit" – the first summit of heads of state and government between the EU and Latin America and the Caribbean – began a new stage of political dialogue at the highest level and established an ambitious bi-regional "strategic partnership".

It is very likely that the G20 as a political opportunity has been more important than the twentieth anniversary of the Rio Summit for establishing a deadline to close the negotiation between MERCOSUR and the EU, but that coincidence cannot be disregarded, since the EU–MERCOSUR Agreement also means the closing of a cycle of relations between the EU and Latin America and the Caribbean. That cycle began in the mid-1990s, and it was based on an inter-regional matrix, which sought to establish a deep link between the two regions built on a network of "partnership agreements" with three components: political dialogue, development co-operation and, most importantly, reciprocal free trade. The EU–MERCOSUR Agreement, the most significant one within that network, was the first to be proposed, on 29 June 1999. It has also been the most difficult to achieve, after twenty years of formal negotiations, several times interrupted due to impossible differences, and the culmination of the negotiations does not mean that it becomes effective, since in August 2021 the text is still in the technical and legal revision phase, and the ratification process on both sides faces major political obstacles.

In a marked contrast the EU managed to sign association agreements in this same period with, in chronological order, Mexico (1999), Chile (2002), Peru and Colombia (2010), Central America (2012, the first one between the two regional groups), and Ecuador (2014), as well as the 'post-Cotonou' Economic Partnership Agreement with the countries of the Caribbean (2000), and a dialogue and co-operation agreement with Cuba (2016), more limited than the afore-mentioned, lacking a pillar of reciprocal free trade. Moreover, in cases such as Mexico and Chile, the "modernisation" of the original agreements has also been negotiated. Within the narrative dominant in the EU institutions and its member states, the EU–MERCOSUR Agreement remains the principal pending task in order to complete the "bi-regional partnership" designed decades earlier (Sanahuja 2015).

The year 2019 was an important milestone in the relations between Latin America and the Caribbean and the EU both for the signing of this agreement and for the fact that with that signature a new stage in bi-regional relations was opened. In fact, in April of that year, the EC and the High Representative for EU Foreign and Security Policy (European Commission / High Representative 2019) launched a joint communication with the purpose of updating the EU strategy for bi-regional relations, as ten years had passed since the previous communication (European Commission 2009).

The extensive bibliography on EU–MERCOSUR relations (Estevaordal and Krivonos 2000; Bizzozero 2001; Santander 2002; Bouzas 2004; Peña 2010; Sanahuja 2007b, 2011; Gómez Arana 2014, 2017; Cienfuegos 2016) has studied in detail and from various perspectives the difficulties inherent in the negotiating agenda itself, in particular the internal deficiencies of MERCOSUR as an "imperfect customs union" in terms of free circulation and the application of common standards; the agenda of offensive or defensive interests by both parties, and the limitations of respective offers of market access in areas such as agricultural and industrial goods and public procurement; and the scope of non-tariff barriers and trade protection measures. These difficulties explained the suspension in 2004 of negotiations initiated in 1998, as well as a second, temporary suspension in 2012 following their resumption at the 2010 EU–LAC Summit held in Madrid. The literature also analyses how these negotiations have been affected by other factors, such as the evolution and subsequent suspension of multilateral trade negotiations by the WTO, for similar reasons, as well as the different strategies adopted under Latin American and European regionalism.

This chapter revisits these issues and situates them into a broader analytical framework, which the literature on relations between these two regional groups has not addressed enough, particularly the structural changes observed in the international political economy, attending to both structure and agency factors. It is based on the premise that globalisation defines international political economy as a hegemonic "historical structure", in the sense that Robert W. Cox (1981) and Stephen Gill (1987) give to these concepts. In these years this historical structure has evolved from the "regionalised globalisation" of the 1990s, including inter-regional trade agreements between regional groups such as the one between the EU and MERCOSUR, to the arrival of the crisis of the globalisation twenty years later. Within this evolution, the following three phases may be identified.

"Open regionalism" and inter-regionalism: obstacles in the negotiating agendas. When negotiations were launched in the 1990s, the strategies of both parties seemed to be synchronised under an inter-regional logic, around the liberal visions of "open regionalism" and the process of globalisation and within a negotiation matrix based on the "WTO-plus" model of trade agreements. Such agreements, developed in the realm of international law, must be seen as a form of external "constitutionalisation" of national development policies, framed on a markedly liberal cast. Thus, regionalism defined a normative framework favourable to the interests of the business sector in terms of guaranteed access to markets, capital mobility and protection of foreign investments which could not be altered by changes in government. In this framework the limits to negotiation are found in the evident asymmetries in terms of the low institutionalisation, low regulatory quality and narrower scope of MERCOSUR's economic integration as compared to the most advanced of the EU. In particular, deficiencies included MERCOSUR's internal obstacles to free circulation; the absence or weakness of common rules; and insufficient offers for market access, derived from the relative costs implicit in MERCOSUR's economic structure and in the actors and policies particular to each party. Added to these frustrations was the slowdown in MERCOSUR's integration process following the "double crises" of 1998 (in Brazil) and 2001 (in Argentina).

Normative divergences and the attractiveness of third markets. Over the following decade (2003–13) a new cycle of progressive governments in South America gave way to neo-developmentalist policies that were visibly out of line with the EU agenda, critical of its "WTO-plus" model of trade agreements, by then considered "neoliberal". This gave rise to a more social and political MERCOSUR as an expression of a "post-liberal regionalism", whilst the EU did not hide its preference for the liberal model of open regionalism adopted by the countries (Chile, Colombia, Mexico and Peru) that in 2011 formed the Pacific Alliance – with which both the US and the EU were signing FTAs (Sanahuja 2017a) . At the same time the accession to the EU by Central and Eastern European countries featuring a productive pattern similar to that of the MERCOSUR countries also proved unfavourable to agreement. Nor was the export boom of primary products from South America (in response to growing demand from Asia, particularly China) deemed favourable, and the strong economic growth generated by that boom diminished the attractiveness of both sub-regional and European markets. This further discouraged MERCOSUR's own integration process and its negotiations with the EU, feeding the institutional and normative asymmetry that had hampered negotiations since their inception.

Liberal-conservative turn in Mercosur and crisis of globalisation scenario. With the end of the commodities' cycle and the coming to power of liberal-conservative governments in Argentina and Brazil in 2015–16, a liberal strategy of external opening was again adopted. The end of the commodity boom highlighted the external commercial and financial vulnerabilities of the region, again making regional markets and a strategy of commercial diversification attractive. However, this recent shift towards more open positions by MERCOSUR has not eliminated the obstacles present in prior stages, because trade and investment patterns between the two regional groups had not undergone significant change. Hence the position of the EU continues to be anchored in a marked protectionism around agricultural matters; resistance by the MERCOSUR countries to make concessions in the liberalisation of trade in services, public procurement and intellectual property rules; and the MERCOSUR demand, in view of existing asymmetries in development, for recognition of the special and differential treatment provided by WTO regulations.

However, by the time Argentina and Brazil announced their intention to "return to the world" and re-embrace globalisation, globalisation itself had become elusive and entered in a deep crisis. When MERCOSUR sought to attract foreign investment and relaunch trade negotiations, no positive response was forthcoming from the rich world. International trade started to show growing signs of fragmentation, and, since 2016, the rise of new nationalist and far-right political actors has brought protectionism and contestation of multilateral institutions and rules. In this unfavourable scenario two moments stand out: initially, Latin America faced the twin challenges of "mega-regional" negotiations related to the TPP and the TTIP. Had these agreements been signed, they would have had far-reaching consequences for developing and emerging countries' positions. In brief they meant a reaffirmation of the North Atlantic axis against the process of "shifting wealth" towards the Asia-Pacific region, and they lead to a direct questioning of the WTO regulatory and negotiation framework. Concerning the EU–MERCOSUR negotiations, mega-regionalism also represented a significant change in the interests at stake and the potential incentives and costs for both parties.

After 2016, however, the electoral triumph of Donald Trump meant the abandonment of these mega-regional negotiations, and strong protectionist tendencies emerged in advanced countries. It brought the risk of wide "trade wars" and the breaking of multilateral trade rules, and, in sum, a broad contestation of globalisation and multilateralism, which pointed to a broad crisis of globalisation. In MERCOSUR the arrival at the presidency of Jair Bolsonaro, in Brazil, strongly raised the possibility of "flexibilisation" of MERCOSUR to turn it into an FTA, leaving behind the customs union, and making possible bilateral negotiations of its member countries. The renewed impetus given to the negotiations since 2016 had a marked political tone: it is framed in the defence of open trade, regionalism and the multilateral system, and can be seen as a political response to that globalisation crisis. This "re-politicisation" of the negotiation, as will be indicated, has been a decisive factor in explaining that in this phase the agreement was eventually achieved.

Taking these developments into account, the chapter succinctly examines the common framework of EU–LAC relations, from which the bi-regional agreement with MERCOSUR emerged. Next a historical tour of the negotiations is presented, establishing four stages based on the ups and downs of these negotiations and the afore-mentioned conditions of the international political economy. The first stage covers the first negotiation cycle that started in 2000 until its suspension in 2004; the second stage, from 2004 to 2010, is marked by mutual neglect; the third stage begins with the negotiations relaunch of 2010 and ends with the exchange of offers of 2016; the fourth and final stage focuses on the 2016–19 period, emphasising the new scenario of globalisation in crisis and the way in which that factor, along with others, made the agreement possible.

Open regionalism and inter-regionalism: EU–MERCOSUR relations and the EU–LAC "strategic partnership"

The EU–LAC "bi-regional strategic partnership" emerged in the 1990s as a result of the strong renewal in regionalism and regional integration. In both areas the so-called "open regionalism" was affirmed in the economic realm. It asked for regional preferences in terms of access to markets for the partner countries of each group, but with low external protection, in order to attract investment and to promote international competitiveness. At the time a "new regionalism" was proposed as a broader strategy of co-operation and regional political integration to overcome the limits of the nation-state in the face of growing interdependencies that (in areas such as security, the environment and population movements) were producing a novel post-Cold War and globalisation scenario (Coleman and Underhill 1998; Grugel and Hout 1999; Sanahuja 2007a).

This bi-regional strategic partnership was also an expression of "inter-regionalism", a concept referring to relations between regional groups and one of the prime modalities of the EU's nascent foreign policy, established after the Maastricht Treaty of 1992 (Hänggi et al. 2006). According to Hettne and Söderbaum (2005: 540) this policy was based on criteria related to the distance and relevance of partners, according to the next policy matrix: (1) accession, for candidate countries seeking to become part of the EU; (2) the neighbourhood policy, with objectives around stabilization, democracy, peace and security and economic association; (3) "strategic" bilateral relations reserved for major powers such as the US, Japan or Russia, and for those countries not falling into any other of the above categories; and (4) inter-regionalism, by way of regional organisations and groups. The latter has remained the most common modality in the EU's international relations. As a projection of its own integration model, this approach has also adequately reflected the identity of the Union as an international actor (Sanahuja 2007b).

From this framework the EU in 1994 launched a new strategy for relations with Latin America. Discussed at the Councils of Corfu (June 1994), Essen (December 1994), and Madrid (December 1995), the strategy was complemented by communications from the EC regarding this bi-regional relationship and, in particular, relations between the EU and MERCOSUR (Comisión Europea 1994, 1995, 1999). These documents expressly recognised the economic interests at stake, fostered by notable increases in European exports and investment to Latin America, by privatisations carried out within the Washington Consensus policy framework, and by the attractiveness of expanded markets arising from new integration schemes that emerged in Latin America in the 1990s, especially MERCOSUR and NAFTA. In particular the EU expressed fears that NAFTA, like the FTAA project, might put European investors at a disadvantage and induce a trade-diversion effect that would reduce European market share, to the benefit of the US. These fears were not unfounded. According to Eurostat data, between 1995 and 2000 the EU share in Latin American imports and exports decreased from 12.5 per cent to 10 per cent, and the EU share in Latin American imports and exports decreased from 12.95 per cent to 8.5 per cent (Sanahuja 2003: 33).

The new inter-regionalist strategy incorporated broad political dialogue by way of the Summits of heads of state and government, initiated at Rio de Janeiro in 1999. In the sphere of trade, market access for the less developed countries (Central America and the Andean Community) remained under an expanded modality of the GSP, known as the "GSP-drugs" and later as "GSP+", whilst the most advanced countries, including those of MERCOSUR, would be subject to reciprocal "WTO-plus" free trade agreements (Hänngi 2000; Grugel 2002). The new strategy owed much to diplomacy by Spain and to the proposals of the vice-president of the Commission responsible for relations with Latin America, Manuel Marín, who first raised the possibility of a bi-regional zone of free trade, co-operation and integration know-how during a meeting of EU–MERCOSUR foreign ministers in São Paulo in 1994 (Bizzozero 2001: 378–9. This would also be part of a dynamic of "Europeanisation" of Spanish politics towards and within the EU framework (Sanahuja 2012; Gómez Arana 2014, 2017).

This strategy was intended to respond to the regional integration map of that period, as well as to the differing levels of development within each regional group, and of certain countries (such as Chile or Mexico) not included in either group. Although without commitments as to method or timeline, the creation of free trade zones proved to be the main objective of "third-generation" agreements signed by the EU with MERCOSUR, Mexico and Chile between 1995 and 1997 (Arenal 1997; Durand et al. 2000; Sanahuja 2000a; Lebrija and Sberro 2002). This objective generated strong expectations in Latin America, since the possibility of access to European markets was opened for the first time, without the EU's traditional protectionism (Sanahuja 2000b; Díaz Barrado and Fernández Liesa 2000). However, this was also the basis for a selective approach and for a "two-speed" relationship model: the "emerging" markets of MERCOSUR, Mexico, and Chile qualified for a new "association" model of more advanced agreements. As expected, from the first moment this approach was rejected by the Central America and Andean countries.

The moment chosen to launch this strategy could not have been more propitious: EU enlargement towards the East was still a distant prospect, whilst the WTO had already been established and the Uruguay Round of its GATT negotiations had been concluded. This gave way to a favourable scenario for regionalism and inter-regionalism, in particular between the EU and Latin America, through reciprocal FTAs with regional groups or with specific countries of the region, incorporated into what was later termed the "Singapore agenda": facilitation of trade, public procurement, competition policy and protection of investment, among other issues.

This inter-regionalist matrix, based on support for integration processes, was present on two levels: in terms of political dialogue with the region as a whole, and at the commercial level with regional groups and specific countries. The first agreements were signed with Mexico (1997) and Chile (2002). Shortly thereafter the EU had to abandon its initial "two-speed" model and propose two association agreements to the Andean and Central American countries that would include reciprocal free trade, but only after a "joint evaluation" (indeed, a prior conditionality) of their respective integration processes. In 2010 the EU–Central America Agreement was signed. However, it was not feasible in the face of crisis in the Andean Community, caused by the Venezuela withdrawal from this bloc in 2006, and the rejection of new-left governments in Bolivia and Ecuador. Because of this, relations with this group became fragmented: the EU chose to sign bilateral agreements with Peru and Colombia (2010), and later with Ecuador (2016). At the political level the EU also established "strategic partnerships" with Brazil (2007) and Mexico (2009). Thus a hybrid inter-regionalist matrix was defined that co-existed with the bilateral matrix (Domínguez 2015a: 17; Sanahuja 2011: 25, 31), featuring a network of bilateral and inter-regional Association Agreements from which, paradoxically, the EU–MERCOSUR Agreement remained noticeably absent.

First push for negotiations following signing of the EU–MERCOSUR Inter-regional Framework Agreement (2000–04)

Shortly after MERCOSUR gained international legal status, following the entry into force of the Ouro Preto Protocol in 1995, the EC formally undertook negotiations (Bouzas 2004) within the Inter-regional Framework Co-operation Agreement (EMIFCA) signed on 15 December 1995. But it was not until the Rio de Janeiro Summit in June of 1999 that this agreement came into force (Bizzozero 2001, 2006). The first meeting of the Co-operation Council, held in Brussels in November 1999, sought to design the structure, methodology and timetable for future rounds of negotiations.

The EMIFCA formalised the Bi-regional Negotiations Committee (CBN), which since its first meeting in April of 2000 has been the forum for talks held to advance the three components of the EU–MERCOSUR Association Agreement: political dialogue, co-operation, and trade and investments. From that time, and until the formal suspension of negotiations in August 2004, a total of fifteen CBN meetings were held. As of April 2000 agreements had been reached regarding the method and objectives of the negotiation: bilateral and reciprocal liberalisation of goods and services, in accordance with WTO rules; government purchases; opening to and non-discrimination of investments; intellectual property and competition policy; and dispute resolution mechanisms. The creation of three technical working groups was also agreed: one on trade in goods; another on trade in services, intellectual property and measures for the promotion of an open and non-discriminatory environment for investment; and a third on public procurement, competition and dispute resolution.

This negotiating process soon faced its own intrinsic constraints, visible in the limitations of the offers from both parties, as well as in an external scenario deemed to be adverse. Ever since the end of the 1990s, forces in some EU member states have been opposed to trade liberalisation; by the time of the Rio de Janeiro Summit the EU had already distanced itself from strategies established in 1994, and the EU–MERCOSUR negotiations were among the most affected. Agreement with this regional group met tenacious opposition from some member states, especially France (Konold 2010; Gómez Arana 2017: 157), on grounds that it would affect "sensitive" agricultural products on the European side and could entail high costs for the Common Agricultural Policy (CAP) (Comisión Europea 1998; European Parliament 1999). The negotiation mandate with MERCOSUR was approved *in extremis* one week before the Rio Summit in 1999, following three years of blockade in the Commission, the Committee of Permanent Representatives and the Council (to avoid the discredit of going to a meeting with empty hands). This mandate likewise postponed tariff negotiations until 2001 and conditioned them to what would be agreed within the multilateral framework of the WTO, which from 2000 announced the start of what would become its Doha Round (Cienfuegos 2002: 735). This express link with WTO negotiations proved key to this stage and helps to explain its failure (Gómez Arana 2017: 157).

Tariff negotiations effectively begun in mid-2001 with a presentation of the negotiating proposals of both parties, but they stalled by disagreements over their scope. MERCOSUR (and especially Brazil) resisted rapid liberalisation of the manufacturing sector, and the EU's tariff proposal, although very broad regarding sectors, limited itself to the offering of preferential tariff quotas on the CAP's most "sensitive" products (cereals, beef, sugar and dairy), also demanding specific agreements for the wine sector. In order to assess these difficulties, we must bear in mind that the tariff profiles of the two blocs remain very asymmetric, and that (in contrast to MERCOSUR) Chile and especially Mexico export fewer "sensitive" agricultural products to the EU – a fact which facilitated bilateral negotiations in those two cases (Estevaordal and Krivonos 2000). In addition, in the case of Mexico, it had been decided to exclude certain of these products by placing them on a so-called "waiting list"; in the agreement with Chile, tariff quotas and longer transitional periods were established.

Finally, the Brazilian crisis of 1998 and the Argentine crisis of 2001 meant a unilateral rupture or "perforation" of MERCOSUR's common external tariff across various sectors, and these gave rise to a phase of stagnation in MERCOSUR which, unable to establish a common customs territory, cooled the enthusiasm of external actors (Santander 2002). Since that time the EU institutions have reiterated that a strengthening of MERCOSUR will be an essential prerequisite to establishing any association agreement, since the group (despite evident advances) remains an imperfect customs union with serious shortcomings in terms of macroeconomic convergence, proximity of laws, development of common policies, implementation of decisions and resolution of differences.

The result is that the South American bloc, despite its being the regional group with more political and economic links with Europe, did not achieve an association agreement, and so the EU has given priority to Mexico and Chile. These were the two Latin American countries furthest from the integrationist ideal and the first willing to accept FTAs with the US, thus joining the hemispheric FTA known as the FTAA. It is worth to remark that FTAA's failure after 2005 was due to the opposition of progressive MERCOSUR governments. In a way the EU's strategy can be defined as "reactive" to the FTAA project and the FTAs that (like NAFTA, or the accord reached with Chile in December 2002) formed part of that hemispheric project (Gómez Arana 2017: 25). The key factor for the EU seems to have been a fear of being shouldered out of the Latin American market. This had contradictory effects: the EU institutions held that the agreement with MERCOSUR should be a stimulus for the strengthening of that regional bloc. However, the difficulties in negotiation and the cases of Chile and Mexico, followed by Peru and Colombia, seemed to suggest that signing a separate agreement with the US and discarding the inter-regional option was the best incentive to bring the EU to the negotiating table. This was stated at different times by some business and opposition political actors in Brazil, advocating the abandonment of the common external tariff of MERCOSUR and the signing of bilateral agreements with the US or the EU. It was argued that an EU–Brazil trade agreement could serve as a substitute for the EU–MERCOSUR Agreement due to Brazil's weight in trade between the two blocs. It is also the case of Uruguay, a country with scarce industry to protect – although in this case the argument further responded to a need to stand out among the main MERCOSUR partners.

It must be recalled that in 1999 the EU had already opted to start off a new round of WTO trade negotiations, which (after some delays) was launched in November 2001 in Doha; in its ambitious initial agenda were raised certain liberalisation targets similar to those sought by the EU–MERCOSUR inter-regional negotiations. Within this multilateral project, together with the EU member states and Council, the new Prodi Commission (1999–2005) exerted significant influence, and it was less inclined towards strengthening ties with Latin America than the prior Delors and Santer Commissions had been. As indicated, this meant subordinating EU relations with Latin America to what would be agreed in the WTO, where both the EU and Latin America have often found themselves in opposition. This subordination was explicitly stated in the negotiation mandate with MERCOSUR approved by the European Council. In the initial calculations the advantages that MERCOSUR could conceivably obtain in multilateral negotiations against the EU's agrarian protectionism seemed to be greater than those that might come through inter-regional negotiations, which further discouraged the latter.

As is well known, the failure of the Doha Round at the Cancún Fifth WTO ministerial summit in September of 2003 was prelude to the suspension of EU–MERCOSUR negotiations in 2004, and for similar reasons: the limits defined in advance in the "Fischler reform" of the CAP in June of 2003 – very like the US Farm Bill in 2002 – made it impossible to comply with the Doha commitments regarding broad agricultural liberalisation. Thus the EU, like the US, had no margin for making significant concessions in this area, and there was no renunciation of the onerous demands placed on developing countries in terms of access to markets for industrial goods and public procurement, protection of investments and intellectual property rights, or trade facilitation. Developing countries organised around the newly established WTO G22 group against the agrarian protectionism of the EU and the US, endorsing the slogan that "no deal is better than a flawed and bad deal". That argument also hovered over the subsequent suspension of EU–MERCOSUR negotiations, as well as the refusal by Brazil and Argentina to accept the FTAA proposal in the Fourth Summit of the Americas that met in 2005 at Mar del Plata (Argentina), only a few months after the failure at Cancún.

The political and ideological misalignment with the EU and with the dominant liberal vision of globalisation must be seen as an expression of the new cycle of progressive governments affirmed across South America in the middle of the first decade of the 2000s. It was caused by their adoption of neo-developmentalist discourses and economic policies, and "post-liberal" integration proposals, which supplanted the prior model of open regionalism. These new regionalist strategies opted for a more socially oriented and political MERCOSUR, and for the constitution of the Union of South American Nations (UNASUR), an instrument that left out classical economic integration and was configured as a tool to expand autonomy in foreign policy and development for the member countries (Sanahuja 2017b: 105). Meanwhile the EU did not hide its preference for the liberal open regionalism model adopted by the countries that later formed the Pacific Alliance, with which both the US and EU signed FTAs. At the same time the strong economic growth generated by the export boom of primary products (in response to increased demand from Asia, and especially China) reduced the reciprocal interest for both LAC and European markets and thereby discouraged both the Mercosur integration process and negotiations with the EU.

Suspension of negotiations and mutual neglect (2004–10)

The strong disagreement between the two blocs, for ideological reasons as well as for the refusal to make significant concessions to the initial negotiating offers, produced a six-year period without negotiations, although Ministerial-level meetings ratified a mutual interest in their resumption (Domínguez 2016a: 126; Cienfuegos 2016: 241). During this period the EU-MERCOSUR relationship was limited to political dialogue and co-operation for development. In 2007, with the impulse of the then president of the Commission, Durão Barroso, the EU and Brazil established a bilateral "strategic partnership" as a result of the growing international activism contained in the foreign policy of the then President Lula da Silva. This was hastily and wrongly interpreted as a European return to bilateralism (Sanahuja 2011: 31), although this strategic partnership never questioned the inter-regional framework of the EU–MERCOSUR trade negotiations.

The failure of the WTO Doha Round, the global financial crisis of 2008, the economic rise of Asia (especially China) and EU enlargement with new members in Central and Eastern Europe (including countries with large and not very competitive agricultural sectors) all helped to set a scenario in which the mutual interests of the EU and Latin America appeared to diminish. Paralysis at the multilateral level had consequences in bi-regional talks, overriding historical claims of EU protectionism by the MERCOSUR countries. In addition both regions experienced political trends that promoted left-wing governments in Latin America and right-wing parties in the EU, and this redefined (or diluted) their respective integration projects as well as their positions within an international system characterised by profound changes in the distribution of power.

In Latin America the popular vote that inaugurated a new political cycle of progressive governments expressed in part the rejection of neoliberal reforms and the costs of the adjustment policies that accompanied economic recession between 1998 and 2002 (called the "lost half-decade" by the Economic Commission for Latin America and the Caribbean, in reference to the prior "lost decade" of the 1980s, because declines in average per capita income in both phases were similar). These new governments adopted neo-developmental policies aimed at confronting poverty and inequality, and the maps and agendas of regional integration were reconfigured to respond to the exhaustion of open regionalism. New "post-liberal" integration agendas were constructed, emphasising political, security and defence dimensions as well as asymmetries, the co-ordination of energy and infrastructure policies, and non-commercial issues in general. In this framework South–South co-operation was promoted in fields such as infrastructure, energy, communications, education, health, and science and technology. This post-liberal regionalism crystallised in projects like the Bolivarian Alternative to the Americas/Trade Treaty of the Peoples (ALBA-TCP) and UNASUR, which the EU never addressed in its inter-regionalist strategy, still attached to the schemes of the prior stage (Sanahuja 2017b). Brazil maintained its more assertive foreign policy, with aspirations to global leadership by way of the BRICs bloc (Brazil, Russia, India, China and South Africa); along with other developing countries, Brazil held a position against any WTO agreement considered to be unbalanced or contrary to its interests.

Traditional obstacles and new risks of mega-regionalism (2010–16)

In May 2010, under strong political impulse from the Argentine and Spanish presidencies of the Sixth EU–LAC Summit, held in Madrid, it was formally decided that trade negotiations be resumed, again through the CBN, in a cycle that would extend to 2012. Several factors drove this decision. Firstly, despite the fact that similar obstacles persisted in terms of the negotiating agenda, the blockade of WTO negotiations invited a new exploration of inter-regional routes. Secondly, the global economic crisis that began in 2008, and the associated decline in trade and investment, encouraged the search for new strategies and new markets, particularly by the EU. This lessened the asymmetry between the parties – between an EU plunged into recession and a MERCOSUR that had shown greater resilience to the initial shock, followed by an enviable recovery and good macroeconomic indicators, with positive balances in trade and foreign exchange reserves driven by Asian demand for primary goods. Thirdly, mention must be given to the economic progress of China, which had begun to be viewed as a threat to Europe's position in the region in areas including exports and investments in industrial sectors, especially the automotive sector, along with the appearance of Chinese contractors in tenders for large infrastructures, public procurement and mining concessions. Between 2001 and 2017 the EU's share of MERCOSUR foreign trade went from 25 per cent to 17 per cent and that of the US fell from 20 per cent to 12.5 per cent. Meanwhile, China's share rose from 5 per cent to over 17 per cent, dethroning the EU from its first position among MERCOSUR's external partners (Stratfor 2019: 3–4).

On the other hand MERCOSUR by 2016 represented only 2.5 per cent of the EU's foreign trade, falling as a group to ninth place among the EU's trading partners. Trade between MERCOSUR and the EU had increased from €68.9 billion in 2006 to €111.6 billion in 2012, but this declined in subsequent years, to €84.9 billion in 2016. These exchanges continue to respond to the traditional North–South pattern: the EU imports agricultural products and raw materials from MERCOSUR, with these products representing around 70 per cent of imports from that group; meanwhile, 85 per cent of European exports to MERCOSUR consists of manufactures, chemical products and pharmaceuticals. The persistence of these trade asymmetries helps clarify the relatively unchanged obstacles to negotiation (European Commission 2017).

However, the EU represents the largest foreign investor in MERCOSUR: more than 5 per cent of total FDI stock from the EU has been directed to this group. In 2000 this already amounted to some €130 billion; by 2014, it had increased to €387 billion. Conversely, MERCOSUR companies (especially those originating in Brazil) have also substantially invested in Europe, totalling around €115 billion in 2014.

Despite this new political impulse, the internal fracture within the EU regarding agricultural protectionism had not changed. The "agriculture and livestock" coalition led by France (and including Austria, Finland, Greece, Hungary, Ireland, Luxembourg and Poland), together with organisations from those productive sectors, questioned the resumption of negotiations in opposition to a more "liberal" bloc that included Germany, the UK and a more nuanced Spain (Gómez Arana 2017: 185). Within MERCOSUR, Argentina voiced formal support for new negotiations but also assumed the most protectionist positions in the group, against both European exporters and its own MERCOSUR partners.

The resumption of negotiations in July of 2010 began with agreements reached during the prior phase, although the need for new negotiation proposals was also raised. Working groups were also established for markets for goods, rules of origin, IPR, dispute settlements, trade defence, competition policy, customs, trade facilitation, services, and investments and government procurement (Makuc, Duhalde and Rozemberg 2015: 40). In successive rounds progress was made with respect to goals achieved in 2004, but substantial disagreements persisted regarding the concessions to be made, and the scope of the rules to be established, which could not be dispelled by the political energy of Spain's EU presidency and other afore-mentioned factors (Gómez Arana 2014).

As in the prior phase, the EU called for recognition of geographical indications for a large number of agri-food products; very demanding standards for the protection of intellectual property and foreign investment; the abolition of import licences; and the opening of MERCOSUR's public procurement markets. It should be noted that, in the first phase of negotiations, the

EU had been composed of only fifteen member states; by 2010 there were already twenty-eight, which fortified Europe's protectionist coalition and made concessions in the agricultural sector more difficult (Gómez Arana 2014: 157). In a defensive strategy tariff quotas were offered for agricultural products (beef, cereals) from MERCOSUR, which this group considered very limited (Instituto para la Integración de América Latina y el Caribe 2011: 178). MERCOSUR also demanded recognition of the existence of asymmetries of relative development between the parties, and it requested Special and Differential Treatment, under the WTO rules.

MERCOSUR's internal dynamics also posed difficulties. At the MERCOSUR Summit in San Juan, held in August of 2010, the group's long-awaited Customs Code was approved; after several years of blockade, agreement was reached on the abolition of double tariff collection, and on a gradual schedule to be applied between 2012 and 2019, as well as on a revenue system from common external tariffs, with a compensation mechanism for landlocked Paraguay. MERCOSUR would thus finally constitute a common customs territory – a necessary condition for signing an inter-regional agreement with the EU. As negotiators have pointed out, the reopening of negotiations with the EU proved a decisive factor in overcoming differences that had long affected these issues (Peña 2010). However, these ambitious objectives did not materialise until years later, and only partially. During this period marked differences were also observed between the position of Argentina (much more protectionist and reluctant to negotiate) and that of the other MERCOSUR members (Messerlin 2013). The 2012 MERCOSUR summit in Mendoza decided the suspension of Paraguay as a state member, as a sanction for the removal of President Lugo. This fact allowed the full incorporation of Venezuela, since 2006 vetoed by Paraguay, but it became a factor of instability for MERCOSUR, although Venezuela did not participate in negotiations with the EU.

After the 2013 rounds of negotiations the exchange of offers planned for that year was postponed by the EU until 2014. In parallel MERCOSUR made progress in the definition of its national offers, which were presented as a single offer at the Mercosur Summit in Caracas in July of that year. In November the EU reported that it had not yet defined its own offer. In June 2015 the parties agreed that the exchange of offers would take place before the end of that year, although this exchange did not take place until May 2016.

Widespread pessimism around WTO negotiations, which had remained blocked since 2003, and the "graduation" of MERCOSUR member countries under the new EU's GSP, in force from 2014, which worsened access to the European market, proved to be insufficient incentive for advancing the negotiations (Inama 2018). Meanwhile, the new direction adopted by the EU in its global trade policy also worked against resumption of talks (Peña 2014). In 2013 the EU formally initiated negotiations with the US towards the TTIP, complementing the Trans-Pacific Economic Co-operation Agreement, in negotiations since 2008. The first was not signed because of the withdrawal of the US, being abandoned. The TPP was signed, but the US withdrawal led to a different trade agreement, now known as the Integral and Progressive Treaty of Trans-Pacific Partnership (TPP-11). TTIP and TPP posed significant risks for Latin American countries in terms of diversion of trade and investment. Effects would vary depending on the economic structure and commercial strategies of each country (Instituto para la Integración de América Latina y el Caribe 2013), but in the long term the entire region would be negatively affected (Ferbelmayr et al. 2013, 2014; Francois 2014; Freytag et al. 2014; Manrique and Lerch 2015; Schmieg 2015). Still more relevant is the fact that these negotiations weakened the multilateral trading system and the WTO, questioning its dispute settlement system, which has responded relatively well to the demands of developing countries. Both placed trade rules, the definition of environmental and labour standards, digital rights and data standards, and the redress of differences between corporations and states outside the WTO's multilateral framework, meaning more demanding standards on Latin America (Rosales et al. 2013). For all these reasons the TPP and the TTIP significance goes much further afield trade, with clear geopolitical implications, and both could be viewed as a strategic response by the US and EU to the major emerging countries, excluded from these negotiations (Falk and Unmüßig 2014; Dieter 2014; The Economist 2015). In short the TTIP updated the traditional alignment of the US and EU as rule-makers, but from outside the WTO, given that emerging economies had acquired veto power within that organisation. Indeed, if the TTIP were signed, emerging countries would face a real risk of marginalisation within these new mega-regional groupings.

The final stage of negotiations (2016–19): liberal-conservative turn and the crisis of globalisation

The new phase of the trade talks began with the exchange of market access offers of May 2016, the first since 2004, and involved twenty-eight negotiating rounds, in addition to other technical meetings, until its successful closing in a final round on 28 June 2019. Initially, December 2017 was set as the deadline, coinciding with the WTO Summit to be held in Buenos Aires, to take advantage of the "window of opportunity" that was supposed to be open until the presidential elections in Brazil. However, that first deadline, charged with symbolism, was not a sufficient incentive for the parties to overcome the traditional obstacles in the negotiation. After the failure of the WTO Summit in Buenos Aires (December 2017), and the impossibility of reaching the EU–MERCOSUR Agreement on that date, the Argentine President Mauricio Macri made an official visit to his French counterpart Emmanuel Macron in January 2018 in order to settle their differences and take advantage of the remaining months until the October 2018 elections in Brazil, with a view to reaching an agreement before the G20 meeting in Buenos Aires in December of that year. In the meeting, however, the rejection of France to move forward in the negotiations was clear if its "red lines" were crossed (El País 2018).

In June 2018, in Montevideo, the parties concluded the negotiation on the pillars of political dialogue and co-operation, but the trade agreement was still far away. The traditional EU agricultural-livestock coalition, led by France, and seconded by countries such as Ireland and Poland, repeatedly asserted their rejection to agricultural markets liberalisation. Germany, for its part, demanded from Brussels better market access for vehicles and other industrial goods. For its part, the European Confederation of Trade Unions and trade unions in the Southern Cone also expressed their rejection of free trade talks between EU–MERCOSUR invoking development asymmetries and foreseeable adjustment costs in terms of production and employment (Confederación Sindical de Trabajadores/as de las Américas 2018). The Argentinian Industrial Union, the National Confederation of Industries of Brazil, the Paraguayan Industrial Union and the Chamber of Industries of Uruguay, meeting at the MERCOSUR Industrial Council, made an unusual statement against the agreement, asking for a "Industrial development clause", the granting of "special and differential treatment", the rejection of the extension of patents and the protection of test data and the setting of a limit to protection under geographical indications requested by the EU (Consejo Industrial del MERCOSUR 2018).

All this showed that, despite the discourse of support for openness and globalisation, in the two decades of negotiation the classic trade pattern "North–South" that characterises the EU–MERCOSUR exchanges had not changed much, and neither party had managed to penetrate sectors in which they have less presence (Cienfuegos 2016: 231). Thus in 2016 the negotiation had started with an exchange of offers that reflected the traditional agenda of offensive and defensive interests of both parties: in terms of goods, MERCOSUR pointed out that the EU had not significantly improved its offer of access for agricultural products. The EU offered an annual tariff quota for imports of 99,000 tons of beef, which MERCOSUR considered insufficient, claiming duty-free access. For sugar from MERCOSUR, a quota or tariff quota of 150,000 tons per year was foreseen, which MERCOSUR also did not consider adequate. The EU, for its part, demanded that MERCOSUR increase the coverage of the agreement to 90 per cent of the tariff items, including processed dairy products and wines, in which the EU has a very competitive offer of high-value-added products. On geographical indications MERCOSUR was also reluctant to accept the high demands of the EU (Bianco 2018: 123–4). The EU also called on MERCOSUR that the tariff reduction schedules be a maximum of ten years. MERCOSUR raised its defensive agenda in industrial goods, highly protected, and public procurement. There were also differences in the automotive sector (cars and components), which is outside the common external tariff of MERCOSUR, regulated by a complex conglomerate of bilateral agreements, in particular between Argentina and Brazil. Both countries concentrate MERCOSUR's car production and have important regional supply chains (Obaya et al. 2017). MERCOSUR requested an increase in the transition period for the import of European vehicles and auto parts, up to fifteen years, compared to the initial proposal of ten years. Regarding services, MERCOSUR requested the incorporation of a "national treatment" clause, to provide the same conditions to European service companies and its own. Finally, in terms of IPR, MERCOSUR was reluctant to accept the demands of the EU, which claimed a stricter regime and longer periods of protection for medicines and agrochemicals.

If only these economic conditions are taken into account, and above all the limited compatibility of the offensive and defensive interests of the parties, it is difficult to explain that the trade agreement has finally been possible. There are several main reasons that would explain the acceleration of the negotiations since 2018, and that they could be successfully closed in June 2019. Firstly, as indicated, the causes must be sought in major changes in the international political economy – in particular, in the more adverse external context of the globalisation crisis, marked by the contestation of the multilateral institutions and norms and the international liberal order by the US and other rising nationalist and ultra-right forces, also within the EU (Sanahuja and Comini 2018), which encouraged a "defensive convergence" between the EU and MERCOSUR to ensure reciprocal access to their markets.

The second factor is the re-politicisation of trade negotiations, which in this context acquire important normative, political and even geopolitical implications: the EU–MERCOSUR negotiation is seen now as a line of defence of the international liberal order, beyond its commercial significance, and its culmination, as an opportunity for the actors involved to take on a normative role, appealing to values, and to launch a powerful political signal against rising economic nationalism. In this context, as will be indicated, a highly relevant factor has been the greater political closeness of MERCOSUR and EU governments, and the leadership of some of them within each bloc, as well as by the EC.

Thirdly, regarding the two factors already mentioned, timing has been also relevant: the completion of the mandate of the European institutions Commission and Parliament, and in particular the Juncker Commission in October 2019 and elections in Argentina that same month, which could give way to more nationalist political actors and reluctant to free trade.

Finally, fourthly, and more as a consequence than as a causal factor, the negotiating process itself can be mentioned. At least, both parties made significant concessions on a number of key issues, thus making the agreement feasible. Next this chapter will briefly detail how these factors have worked.

The first of these factors, the crisis and the decline in globalisation, is the most important, since it radically alters the calculations and expectations of the parties. The challenge of mega-regionalism, which defined the negotiation scenario until 2016, had a very short course. But since that year, the triumph of Donald Trump in the US, the UK's withdrawal from the EU after the Brexit referendum, and the rise of the far right in many places have led to the abandonment of these mega-regional negotiations, and, beyond that, they express a broad social process of contestation to the norms, institutions, ideologies and elites on which the globalisation process has been based as a contemporary expression of the liberal international order, both multilaterally and regionally. In the short term it entails evident protectionist tendencies and their associated economic risks. In the long term, as noted, these processes should be understood as manifestations of a broad crisis of globalisation, understood as a hegemonic historical structure (Sanahuja 2017b).

In addition to the refusal of the TTIP and the rejection of the TPP, replaced by a less significant agreement, Trump's election led to the revision, from positions of force, of the existing bilateral trade agreements. This has been the case with NAFTA, replaced by a new Treaty, the so-called Agreement of the US, Mexico and Canada. It is more inward-looking, by increasing the requirements regarding rules of origin. Since 2018 the "trade wars" unleashed by the US against China and the EU themselves carry a certain risk of markets closing and a global economic slowdown. China, beyond its free trade discourse, also turns towards a growth model that is more focused on its internal market.

In the EU social and political contestation to free trade is also on the rise, as is shown by the difficulties for the ratification of the CETA agreement with Canada and the rejection of the TTIP by the governments of France and Germany. France looked again with reservations to the EU–MERCOSUR agreement, among others, in response to demands of an electorate increasingly critical regarding free trade and its social effects. Facing this scenario, there has been a radical change with respect to what happened in the previous twenty years, in which MERCOSUR endorsed the slogan "no deal is better than a bad deal" adopted by developing countries against rich countries' demands at the WTO ministerial conference in Cancun in 2003. Now both sides seem to accept that keeping on their positions without reaching an agreement is worse than signing it, even if it meant painful concessions (Zelicovich 2019). In brief what has been assumed is that the non-agreement would be manifestly worse in the face of the new setback and crisis scenario of globalisation.

The second factor is the re-politicisation of the negotiations by the actors at play. Given this scenario of globalisation crisis, international trade negotiations transcend their regulatory role and, both in discourse and in practice, become a political tool for the defence of open markets, multilateral trade rules, and the values and institutions of the international liberal order. The negotiations are thus a sample of the Europe's pretensions – perhaps not so much of MERCOSUR – to establish itself as a "normative actor" against the current US policy and promote or lead new coalitions in favour of the liberal order and globalisation. However, in that effort they cannot ignore the limits that, on the one hand, impose the structure of their economies and the actors and national political dynamics that, beyond ideological fluctuations, continue to condition their defensive and offensive interests in the negotiations.

In that context it should be noted that the momentum given by both parties to the trade talks since 2016 responded to two factors: on the one hand, the renewed political rapprochement coming from the liberal-conservative turn in South America and the European globalist turn after the electoral victory of Emmanuel Macron in France and the re-election of Angela Merkel in Germany; on the other hand, the fears raised by events such as Brexit, the rise of the far right in the member states, rampant protectionism in the US, and the decline of mega-regional negotiations. Given these facts, both parties placed the EU–MERCOSUR agreement within a markedly political discourse in defence of the values and institutions of the international liberal order, and in response to their contestation by extreme nationalism and the far right.

In MERCOSUR this rapprochement responded to the turn to the right of most of its member states, initiated at the end of 2015 with the electoral victory of Mauricio Macri in Argentina and, later, in August 2016, with the arrival of Michel Temer after the dismissal of Dilma Rousseff in Brazil. The marked presidentialism that characterises MERCOSUR has been a relevant factor, since the new liberal-conservative governments adopted foreign policies favourable to globalisation and "open regionalism", supposedly "de-ideologised" and "pragmatic", based on the promotion of the private sector and foreign direct investment (FDI), aligned with the liberal order and the dominant consensus in the multilateral system, and, in their own rhetoric, eager to "return to the world" and "embrace globalisation". This turn meant, in particular, the return to a "commercial" MERCOSUR far from the social and political approach of "post-liberal regionalism" of the previous cycle of progressive governments.

After 2016 faced with the ups and downs of Brexit and the election of Donald Trump, the EU institutions reacted with a more vigorous position in defence of globalisation and the international liberal order. In May 2017 the Commission approved its important *Reflection Paper on Harnessing Globalization*, which in the face of rampant nationalism advocates for a globalisation governed by balanced rules and by effective multilateralism. In June of that same year the new European Consensus on Development (Council of the European Union 2017) was approved, committing the EU to the global development goals of the United Nations' 2030 Agenda. The EU and other actors, such as China, have held those positions at the G20 meetings trying to contain the US, especially in climate change and the governance of globalisation. On the eve of the G20 summit in Hamburg the EU announced an FTA with Japan, just outlined, but that launched a powerful political signal against US positions. The discourse that has justified the Comprehensive Economy and Trade Agreement with Canada (CETA), the agreements with Japan and Singapore, and the EU–MERCOSUR negotiation is also the expression of a marked "re-politicisation" of trade talks against the nationalist and protectionist threat. Although the difficulties of the negotiating agenda did not make possible its conclusion in December 2017, as initially anticipated, that expectation indicated a greater willingness of the parties to make concessions, and to reach an agreement, even if it were more modest regarding the optimum of liberalisation requested under the more technocratic standards of the European Commission or the WTO (Flôres 2013; Peña 2014).

In this process of re-politicisation it is important to highlight the role of some governments as agency factors. The last phase of the negotiation has been marked by the Argentinian leadership in the MERCOSUR side. Macri's arrival to presidency meant intense diplomatic activity, with visits to Europe in July 2016 and again in February 2017, where he met with the French president, the German chancellor and the Spanish prime minister. This momentum contributed to the agreement achieved by the foreign ministers of MERCOSUR concerning a common negotiation strategy for negotiations with the EU on 9 March 2017.

Brazil, on the other hand, has given up its leadership of the previous stages. The foreign policy of Jair Bolsonaro's government, in particular, has been dominated by ambiguity, if not by tensions and contradictions between the most ideological and reactionary sectors (the "crusaders"), openly anti-globalist; the most neo-liberal, and the most pragmatic, represented respectively by Foreign Minister Arãujo, the Minister of Economy Guedes, and the Vice Presidency of General Mourao (Rodrigues 2919; Frenkel 2019), as well as among different economic interests, particularly among the great industrialists in São Paulo and the agro-exporters. His government had spoken at different times in favour of the "flexibilisation" of MERCOSUR to make possible bilateral agreements (Stratfor 2019; Caballero 2019; Rozemberg and Gayá 2019). He also advocated a preferential bilateral relationship with the US, including commercial concessions, at the expense of MERCOSUR (Sanahuja 2019: 121), although he finally did not want to detach himself from negotiations with the EU. For both Argentina and the EU, the EU–MERCOSUR Agreement was, therefore, a tool to keep Brazil "anchored" in MERCOSUR and other multilateral frameworks, such as the Paris Agreement on climate change, and contain its drift towards positions contrary to multilateralism and closer to the US.

In the EU the final phase has been marked, again, by France's objections to the final phase of the negotiation, with the contradictory position of President Macron, whose globalist discourse is increasingly burdened by the internal opposition to liberalisation and free trade – either in the traditional view of the agricultural sector, the nationalist view of the far right or the more populist version of the "yellow vests", and for a visible resistance to making concessions in trade negotiations with third parties. Macron's warning letter to the Commission informing that France was "very attentive" to the agricultural negotiation motivated the response of the Commissioner of Commerce, Cecilia Malmström, who assured him that the agreement could be reached before the end of the Commission's mandate, but "not at any price" (Euroactiv 2019). Also in the final phase a key push came from Spain, which faced up the last-minute objections of France and other countries with a collective letter of support for the agreement addressed to the president of the Commission, Jean-Claude Juncker, also signed by the prime ministers of Germany, Holland, Sweden, Portugal, the Czech Republic and Lithuania (De Miguel 2019).

Political timing, determined by the internal political calendars of some actors at play, has also played a relevant role in explaining the final agreement. Whether in terms of "window of opportunity" or deadlines, the end of the EC's mandate in October 2019 and the elections in Argentina that same month set an immediate horizon to close the negotiation. The perception that after that period more nationalist and reluctant actors in both parties could be involved generated the conviction that it was the last opportunity – "It is now or never" – after almost twenty years of negotiation.

All these factors explain the concessions that both parties have made in their offensive and defensive interests to make the agreement possible. At the time of writing these pages the final text has not yet been made public, and it is available only in the generic "agreement of principle" reached on 28 June and some sections of the final document disseminated by the European Commission (2019) and the Ministry of Foreign Affairs of Uruguay (2019). It is premature, therefore, to assemble a detailed analysis of its content, but from the available information it should be noted that the EU has achieved significant advantages in industrial and service matters, and MERCOSUR manages, in return, to improve its access to the European market for its agricultural exports. A differentiated tariff reduction schedule has been established in recognition of existing asymmetries, both for industrial goods and for agricultural goods. MERCOSUR will liberalise 91 per cent of imports from the EU over a period of ten years, and fifteen years in more sensitive areas such as automotive, chemical and pharma. The EU will liberalise 92 per cent in ten years, and 95 per cent in fifteen years. In the industrial sector MERCOSUR will liberalise 90 per cent of the tariff items in fifteen years, and the EU 100 per cent in ten years. Specifically MERCOSUR will eliminate tariffs for all the EU's auto parts that will be taxed in a linear manner over a period of ten years (60 per cent) and fifteen years (30 per cent). This same tariff-reduction calendar will apply to finished vehicles, with a seven-year grace period, offset by an annual quota of 50,000 units from the European block, with a 50 per cent tariff preference. For its part the European bloc will liberalise 92 per cent of its imports in a period of ten years. Other sensitive sectors such as footwear and textiles will have a period of fifteen years to adapt to the levels of competitiveness of European companies. The accumulation of rules of origin is agreed.

Other relevant concessions are located in agriculture, an area of tension that permeated the entire history of the negotiations between both groups. Mercosur will liberalise 95 per cent of EU agri-food imports, and the EU will liberalise 82 per cent, with the rest subject to partial liberalisation commitments, with tariff quotas for the most sensitive products. This includes 99,000 tons of beef, with an EU entry fee of 7.5 per cent, except for the "Hilton quota", which will enter without tariffs: 180,000 tons of poultry meat, and 25,000 of pig meat. Products such as sugar, ethanol, rice and honey will be subject to quotas without tariffs, but to export quotas. Mercosur grants better access to high-quality EU food products such as chocolate, cheese, fruit, soft drinks and olive oil. Wine will have also special treatment. The EU maintained the right to agricultural subsidies for reasons of public interest, and achieved recognition of GIs, although a "grandfather clause" is maintained for certain Mercosur products with traditional names.

Mercosur also made concessions in services, an area where both parties will have full reciprocal access; in public procurement, granting national treatment to European companies, and in intellectual property and patents

(Frenkel and Ghiotto 2019). In the realm of trade defence, in attention to the risk of sensitive sectors damaged by rapid liberalisation, both parties recognise a safeguard clause applicable for two years during the first eighteen years of the agreement. Finally, the agreement does not include provisions to deal with investor–state disputes (Zelicovich 2019).

It is important to highlight the inclusion of a chapter on sustainable development and the mutual commitment to ILO treaties and others in environmental matters, and that neither party will reduce environmental or labour standards to attract foreign investment. In sanitary and phytosanitary matters, the most demanding European standards and the precautionary principle are assumed, which the EU applies, for example, in its own restrictions on genetically modified organisms, in a more demanding formulation than in the agreements with Chile or Mexico (Grieger 2019: 11). The sustainability study for this agreement, according to the EU, will be one of the most advanced (European Commission 2018). These elements appear only in the new generation of trade agreements, which seek to make openness compatible with the environment and labour rights, in the face of growing social contestation about their effects.

Environment, sustainable development and the Amazon crisis

The announcement that the negotiations had concluded generated an immediate wave of protests from EU's agricultural and livestock sectors, and from countries that will have to face most of the costs related to liberalisation, particularly in France. In France the Macron government has publicly declared that it will carry out a comprehensive evaluation of the content of the agreement before deciding its ratification (Ayuso 2019) and has reminded Brazil that in any case it will be linked to Brazil's observance of environmental norms and Brazil's membership of the Paris Agreement on Climate Change (EFE Agency 2019). In MERCOSUR unions and other organisations have warned about risks to national industry and services. European agricultural organisations and some governments, regional and national, have questioned that the underlying logic of the agreement is "cows by cars", demanding the reopening and modification of its clauses, something that is not possible, as the EC quickly recalled (El Mundo 2019). Ecologists and Greens in the EP have insisted on the risks of deforestation in the Amazon and on the different standards applied in the EU and in MERCOSUR regarding the use of agrochemicals. However, these protests, logical and predictable, evoked the broader debate about the necessity for both the EU and MERCOSUR of active policies to promote productive transformation and increase competitiveness, within the framework of international commitments on sustainable development and the 2030 agenda, which would surely be needed with or without agreement, since free trade is not a substitute for development policy.

The political and diplomatic crisis caused by the increase in Amazon rainforest fires between July and August 2019 demonstrates the importance of the environmental and sustainable development aspects of the Agreement, to such an extent that it conditions its ratification. The environmental crisis turned into a political one mostly due to a discursive move made by President Macron. In remarks made prior to the G7 Leaders' Summit in Biarritz on 26 August Macron depicted the Amazon fires as an "international crisis" that should be addressed by the summit (Oliveira 2019; Delfs and Fouquet 2019). Thus, on the one hand, he tried to ease the risk of failure of a meeting that was predicted to be conflictive and with few results in the face of the trade "war" between the US and China. And, on the other hand, it pretended to place France and President Macron in a position of moral and political leadership in the eyes of other countries and public opinion. Bolsonaro's nationalist rhetoric reinforced this position, as he responded by labelling Macron's remarks as "colonialist" (Sanahuja and Rodríguez, 2019).

The EU–MERCOSUR Agreement has played a central role in this controversy: Macron explicitly accused Bolsonaro of "lying" about the environmental commitments that were made at the Osaka G20 Summit where the Agreement was announced, adding that "under these conditions, France will oppose the agreement with Mercosur" (La Vanguardia 2019). Macron's stance was supported by Ireland and by the President of the Council, Donald Tusk, but not by other member states or by the EC, which in a very nuanced way have argued that the EU–MERCOSUR Agreement is actually the most adequate instrument to ensure the fulfilment of these commitments, and that therefore its ratification is even more necessary. In fact the confrontation between Macron and Bolsonaro did not prevent the signing of the Agreement between Mercosur and EFTA on 23 August 2019. This was the corollary of the Agreement with the EU, in so far as the EFTA countries are fully integrated into the EU internal market.

Actually, the environmental crisis and the rejection of Bolsonaro, being a "noble cause" have been the best excuses for France to oppose an Agreement that has not been fully accepted due to internal dissent. For Bolsonaro this crisis provided a new opportunity to showcase nationalistic rhetoric and polarisation discourses based on the "cultural wars" underpinning his presidency, and which also reflects the tension that exists within his government, in which the commitment to MERCOSUR is not guaranteed (Schiponi 2019). In fact, in his response to Macron, Bolsonaro put back on the agenda the possibility of choosing a free trade agreement with the United States.

Obstacles to the ratification of the agreement

Obstacles to the ratification also appeared across the Atlantic. In late 2019 respective presidential elections led to the victory of Alberto Fernandez in Argentina and Luis Lacalle Pou in Uruguay, causing new tensions between Argentina and Brazil (Stuenkel 2019; Frenkel 2020) also related to the relationship with the EU.

Bolsonaro, for example, went so far as to propose the unilateral reduction of MERCOSUR's common external tariff on sensitive products in intraregional trade, such as cars. This led to opposition from industrial organisations in Brazil and the withdrawal of the proposal. Finally, Argentina and Brazil decided to postpone the liberalisation of the sector scheduled for 2021, making it coincide with the schedule of tariff cuts set up in the EU–MERCOSUR Agreement. This means that the compensated and managed trade regime for vehicles and auto parts between the two countries will be extended to 2029 (Maduro et al. 2020: 19–20).

In Argentina the new minister for productive development, Matías Kulfas, began a round of discussions with industrialists on the possible impact of the Agreement on the country's productive structure. Some officials of the new Argentinian government expressed their concern about ratification, but President Alberto Fernandez has not rejected it and has maintained the stance that the agreement should be reviewed on the basis of a new impact study commissioned by the Economic Commission for Latin America and the Caribbean (ECLAC), which would consider the views of the Argentinian government, and would be submitted to parliament (La Nación 2020).

The arrival of the health emergency of the Covid-19 pandemic redirected the attention of both blocs in managing the crisis and its impacts. Argentina, which was also facing a difficult negotiation on external debt, proposed to withdraw from the trade negotiations between MERCOSUR and South Korea, but warned that this would not affect the agreement with the EU. This situation rekindled the political debate around decision 32/00 of the Common Market Council of MERCOSUR, which prevents a partner of the bloc from unilaterally negotiating extra-regional FTAs.

In the EU, in December 2019, the Austrian parliament voted against the agreement followed by the parliament of the Netherlands in February 2020. Meanwhile, Belgium, Ireland and Poland, members of the "agricultural-livestock coalition", announced that they would not ratify the agreement. In August 2020 Chancellor Merkel, after meeting with Greta Thunberg and other environmental leaders, declared that she had "serious doubts" about the Agreement, showing a change in Germany's stance, until then favourable. In September the French government confirmed its rejection, endorsed by the independent report of a commission chaired by Stefan Ambec, convened a year earlier by Macron during the Amazon fire crisis (Gouvernement de la France 2020). On 6 October 2020 the European Parliament's plenary session approved an amendment to a general report on trade stating that the EU–MERCOSUR Agreement could not be ratified "in its current state". In addition it demanded effective environmental protection measures consistent with the Paris Agreement on Climate Change. Shortly after, the new EU trade commissioner, Valdis Dombrovskis, acknowledged before this chamber that the EU was divided, and, alluding to the Bolsonaro government, pointed out that an additional MERCOSUR commitment to the environment would be necessary to overcome these objections.

The key factor in these changes in the EU's stance is the environmental crisis caused by the Bolsonaro government and its support for Brazilian agriculture, its denial of climate change, its threats to withdraw from the Paris Agreement, and also its alignment with the US, while questioning MERCOSUR itself and, therefore, the agreement with the EU. Meanwhile, electoral support for Greens is growing in Europe and progress is being made in the opposite direction, through the European Green Deal (EGD) of 2019, and the Next Generation seven-year budget and the European Recovery Programme, approved in July 2020, as innovative post-pandemic sustainable development strategies.

Conclusions and perspectives

This chapter has analysed twenty years of negotiations between the EU and MERCOSUR, examining how they has been affected, as causal factors, by changes in the international political economy, both in terms of structure and agency. The proposal for an EU–MERCOSUR Association agreement was an expression of the "regionalised globalisation" and the inter-regionalist strategies that both parties affirmed in the 1990s. However, the deep differences in the economic structure and the international insertion patterns of each group defined an agenda of offensive and defensive interests in which the non-agreement represented a less onerous choice, at least until 2016. In addition to those factors of structure, this chapter also analysed the agency factors that marked most of those two decades, such as the political-ideological misalignment of governments and leaders coming from a more progressive MERCOSUR, and a largely liberal-conservative-minded EU.

Although some of these factors are still at play, since 2016 the international political economy has undergone profound changes that explain, in the first place, that the negotiation has been concluded. Firstly, the relative importance of the agreement has varied. In the 1990s the EU was the first trading partner of MERCOSUR, with the US in second place, and Asia occupied a marginal position. Now China is MERCOSUR's first partner, with the EU in second place and the US ranks third. At the same time the EU remains as the first source of FDI for MERCOSUR, but China is making rapid progress in this area.

In addition international political economy is in the midst of the crisis of globalisation and the increasing contestation of multilateralism and regionalism by the US and by other nationalist and far-right forces and actors on the rise, which anticipates serious risks of trade war, the closing of markets and global economic recession. This scenario, very different from the one present only a few years before, has encouraged the "defensive convergence" of the EU and MERCOSUR in order to guarantee reciprocal access to their markets, which together cover 780 million people. The great paradox of the EU–MERCOSUR negotiations is that they were born under the influence of globalisation, as an instrument that should contribute to its diffusion, and it is precisely the fears raised by the crisis of globalisation that in the end, have made it feasible. In this context the political calendars of some of the parties marked a new deadline that encouraged its signature: on the one hand, the end of the mandate of the European institutions, with the elections to the European Parliament of May 2019, and the termination of the Juncker Commission term in October 2019; on the other hand, the elections in Argentina of the same month. It fed the perception of both parties that it was the last window of opportunity. Finally, some explanatory keys are found in the negotiation process itself, in which significant concessions have been made by both sides.

Secondly, this scenario has encouraged a visible re-politicisation of international trade talks, which now have important normative, political and geopolitical implications: the EU–MERCOSUR negotiation is seen as a strategy of defence of the international liberal order, beyond its commercial significance, and its culmination, as an opportunity to become normative actors in the face of tendencies towards increasing protectionism and economic nationalism. The greater political rapprochement of the EU and MERCOSUR governments, after the liberal-conservative turn that has been observed in South America since 2015, has contributed to this process of repoliticisation, mainly driven by the EU. The particular leaderships of the Commission and some governments such as those of Argentina and Spain have also been relevant within the political-normative discourse that reigned over the final phase of the negotiations.

However, the fate of the agreement and its entry into force will depend on its process of ratification, which will be complex and difficult. It should not be ruled out that the agreement could be stuck in any of the incumbent parliaments. It will require ratification in the parliaments of the four

MERCOSUR countries and the twenty-seven member states – in Belgium the vote of the regional chambers is also required, in addition to the EP and the Council, because, according to EU law, it is considered a "mixed agreement" encompassing matters related both to EU and member states' own competences.[1] The Commission has supported "splitting" the Agreement, i.e., the provisional application of the part of the agreement that affects EU exclusive competences in its commercial pillar, since it requires approval only by qualified majority in the Council and a majority vote in the EP, in addition to the four members of the MERCOSUR.

However, given the political evolution in several countries and the growing influence of Green parties, and also anti-free trade nationalist and far-right forces, particularly in the EU, it seems that this legal shortcut is not feasible either. Furthermore, this avoids the necessary debate on the fundamental reasons why the EU–MERCOSUR Agreement is relevant for the development strategies and international relations of both regions, beyond its obvious commercial interest.

It is important to remember that this agreement is not just about free trade. It has always had a deep geopolitical significance. When negotiations were launched in 1994 the aim was to provide a joint response to the hegemonic project of the FTA of the Americas (FTAA). When Argentina's presidency of MERCOSUR and Spain's presidency of the Council relaunched negotiations in 2010 it was a matter of responding, among other reasons, to the risk of reprimarisation associated with the increasing importance of commodities in exports to China. This reason is still relevant, but now the agreement is also reinsurance against the rampant economic nationalism and the fragmentation of the international trade system. Moreover, it is a tool that can contribute to the strategic autonomy of both regions in the face of competition between the US and China, which aims to place both Latin America and the EU in a position of strategic subordination. We must remember that, beyond their commercial core, MERCOSUR and the EU are also political projects, and an agreement between the two regions cannot be seen, in a reductionist way, just in terms of free trade.

Secondly, the agreement can also be a common forum for policy dialogue, regulatory convergence and productive transformation for the change of the economic model and the reconstruction of the social contract. For MERCOSUR, long transitory periods – up to fifteen years in some cases – provide options for that transformation with active long-term policies to overcome reprimarisation and growing dependency on China. The EU itself is no longer the same entity that started negotiations two decades ago, and it aims to be even more different by 2030. It is an EU that wants to promote an ecological transition that pretends to be, at the same time, a new strategy for development and industrial politics, a mark of its "soft power", and a renewed and mobilising narrative of the European construction.

It is true that there are inconsistencies between the EU–MERCOSUR Agreement and the EGD, and it does not quite fit, "in its current state", with this EU green renaissance. This requires integrating the Agreement into the external dimension of the EGD, as a space for political dialogue, reinforcing its environmental obligations within a common reform and regulatory convergence agenda for the "green" transition of both parties. Within this framework there are actors who appeal to legitimate environmental arguments for protectionist purposes. But the fact that there is covert protectionism does not mean that environmental objections to the Agreement are not valid. The objections raised by the Ambec report are worthy of attention: the causal link between MERCOSUR exports and deforestation; the risk of weakening environmental and health standards in those exports to the European market; and the absence of robust legal instruments to address climate change. These have been important reasons to understand why European citizens refuse to associate the EU with a Brazil governed by Bolsonaro. The EU–MERCOSUR agreement includes novel tools in environmental matters that set it apart from other previous agreements, but perhaps this is not enough. One possibility would be to add an "environmental clause" on the model of the human rights clause that already exists, linking, in a reciprocal manner, the validity of the agreement to the observance of international standards and, in particular, the Paris Agreement (Sanahuja 2020). In conclusion it is not a question of abandoning the EU–MERCOSUR Agreement, or of reopening a negotiation that has been complex and difficult. The idea is to strengthen it with more effective instruments, responding to the demands of citizens and their requirements for coherence with sustainable development and the 2030 agenda.

References

All websites last visited 30 September 2021.

Agencia EFE (2019). *Francia le enumera a Brasil sus condiciones para aprobar el Acuerdo Mercosur UE, EFE.* www.efe.com/efe/america/economia/francia-le-enumera-a-brasil-sus-condiciones-para-aprobar-el-acuerdo-mercosur-ue/20000011-4033136.

Arenal, C. (1997). "Los acuerdos de cooperación entre la UE y América Latina (1971–1997): evolución, balance y perspectivas", *Revista Española de Desarrollo y Cooperación* 1, 111–39.

Ayuso, S. (2019). "Francia encarga a expertos independientes analizar el Acuerdo UE-Mercosur", *El País*, 29 July. https://elpais.com/internacional/2019/07/29/actualidad/1564413789_546973.html.

Bianco, C. (2018). "Historia de una entrega: las negociaciones para un tratado de libre comercio entre Mercosur y la UE", *Revista Voces en el Fénix* 8 (69), 122–5.

Bizzozero, L. (2001). "El acuerdo marco interregional UE–Mercosur: dificultades y perspectivas de una asociación estratégica", in Sierra, G. (ed.), *Los rostros del Mercosur. Un difícil camino de lo comercial a lo social*, pp. 373–90. Buenos Aires: Consejo Latinoamericano de Ciencias Sociales (CLACSO).

Bizzozero, L. (2006). "Negociaciones Mercosur–UE. Articulación del espacio Euro-Latinoamericano/caribeño y gobernanza mundial", *Cuadernos de Integración Europea* 5, 5–27. Madrid: Fundació General de la Universitat de Valencia. https://intranet.eulacfoundation.org/es/system/files/NEGOCIACIONES%20MERCOSUR-UE%20ARTICULACI%C3%93N%20DEL%20ESPACIO%20EURO-LATINOAMERICANO.pdf/

Bouzas, R. (2004). "Las negociaciones UE–Mercosur. Entre la lentitud y la indefenición", *Revista Nueva Sociedad* 190 (March–April), 125–35.

Caballero, S. (2019). "Reformas para el Mercosur: ¿Solución o nuevos problemas?", 9 April. *Análisis Carolina*, 5.

Cienfuegos, M. (2002). "Las negociaciones para la ejecución del Acuerdo Marco Interregional de Cooperación entre la Comunidad Europea, el Mercosur y sus respectivos Estados miembros", *Revista Española de Derecho Comunitario (REDC)* 13, 723–74. https://nuso.org/articulo/las-negociaciones-union-europea-mercosur-entre-la-lentitud-y-la-indefinicion/.

Cienfuegos, M. (2016). "La anhelada asociación euromercosureña tras quince años de negociaciones", *Revista CIDOB d'Afers Internacionals* 112, 225–53. www.cidob.org/es/articulos/revista_cidob_d_afers_internacionals/112/la_anhelada_asociacion_euromercosurena_tras_quince_anos_de_negociaciones.

Coleman, W. and Underhill, G. R. D. (eds) (1998). *Regionalism and Global Economic Integration*. London: Routledge.

Comisión Europea (1994). *Hacia un fortalecimiento de la política de la UE respecto de Mercosur*. Brussels: COM (94) 428 final, 19 October.

Comisión Europea (1995). *UE–América Latina. Actualidad y Perspectivas del Fortalecimiento de la Asociación. 1996–2000*. Brussels: COM (95) 495 final, 23 October.

Comisión Europea (1998). *Mercosur–EU: Effects on Agriculture/* Brussels: DG-VI AI D.

Comisión Europea (1999). *Comunicación de la Comisión al Consejo, al Parlamento Europeo y al Comité Económico y Social, sobre una nueva Asociación UE-América Latina en los albores del siglo XXI*. Brussels: COM (1999) 105 final, March.

Comisión Europea (2018). *Sustainability Impact Assessment in Support of Association Agreement Negotiations between the EU and Mercosur, Inception Report*. Brussels: European Commission. https://trade.ec.europa.eu/doclib/docs/2018/march/tradoc_156631.pdf.

Confederación Sindical de Trabajadores/as de las Américas (2018). *CCSCS y CES: Carta a los negociadores del acuerdo UE–Mercosur*. http://csa-csi.org/NormalMultiItem.asp?pageid=12272.

Consejo Industrial del MERCOSUR (2018). *Negociaciones MERCOSUR Unión Europea*. www.ciu.com.uy/innovaportal/file/85860/1/declaracion-consejo-industrial-del-mercosur.-negociaciones-union-europea.pdf.

Cox, R. W. (1981). "Social forces, states and world orders: beyond international relations theory", *Millennium. Journal of International Studies* 10 (2), 126–55.
Delfs, A. and Fouquet, H. (2019). "Macron rips up agenda for his G-7 in a fit of climate fury", *Bloomberg*, 23 August. www.bloomberg.com/news/articles/2019-08-23/merkel-opposes-macron-threat-to-block-mercosur-deal-over-amazon.
De Miguel, B. (2019). "España dio el último acelerón al acuerdo con Mercosur", *El País*, 28 June.
Díaz Barrado, C. and Fernández Liesa, C. (eds) (2000). *Iberoamérica ante los procesos de integración. Actas de las XVIII Jornadas de la Asociación Española de Profesores de Derecho Internacional Público y Relaciones Internacionales, (23-25 de septiembre de 1999)*. Madrid, BOE/AEPDIRI.
Dieter, H. (2014). *The Return of Geopolitics: Trade Policy in the Era of TTIP and TPP*, Berlin: Friedrich Ebert Stiftung.
Domínguez, R. (2015a). *EU Foreign Policy Towards Latin America*. London: Palgrave Macmillan.
Domínguez, R. (2015b). *The Modernization of the EU–Mexico Global Agreement*. Brussels: European Parliament, Study EP/EXPO/B/AFET/2014/14.
Durand, M., Giordano, P. and Valladão, A. (eds) (2000). *Towards an Agreement Between Mercosur and Europe*. Paris: Presse de Sciences Politiques.
El Mundo (2019). "El acuerdo con Mercosur no se puede reabrir ni mejorar". www.elmundo.es/economia/macroeconomia/2019/07/12/5d274973fc6c83be348b4679.html.
El País (2018). *Macri no logra en Francia destrabar el acuerdo del Mercosur y la UE*. https://elpais.com/internacional/2018/01/26/actualidad/1516999989_078169.html.
Estevaordal, A. and Krivonos, E. (2000). *Negotiating Market Access between the European Union and Mercosur: Issues and Prospects*. Instituto para la Integración de América Latina y el Caribe (INTAL), Banco Interamericano de Desarrollo, Occasional paper No. 7, December. Euroactiv (2019). "Malmström: Mercosur trade deal within reach but not at any price". www.euractiv.com/section/economy-jobs/news/malmstrom-mercosur-deal-possible-this-mandate-but-not-at-any-price/. Accessed 30 August 2021.
European Commission (2017). *Documento de reflexión sobre el encauzamiento de la globalización*. Brussels: Comisión Europea, 10 May. https://eur-lex.europa.eu/legal-content/ES/TXT/PDF/?uri=CELEX:52017DC0240&from=PL.
European Commission (2017). "European Union, trade in goods with Mercosur 5", *Directorate General for Trade, Units A4/G2*, 3 May. http://trade.ec.europa.eu/doclib/docs/2006/september/tradoc_113488.pdf).
European Parliament (1999). "El proceso de asociación interregional de la UE con el Mercosur y Chile y su impacto en el sector agroalimentario de la UE". Luxemburgo, Dirección de Estudios del Parlamento Europeo, October, document 131 (ES).
Falk, R. and Unmüßig, B. (2014). *The Great Revenge of the North? TTIP and the Rest of the World*, Berlin: Heinrich-Böll-Stiftung.
Ferbelmayr, G., Heyd, B. and Lehwald, S. (2013). *Transatlantic Trade and Investment Partnership (TTIP): Who Benefits from a Free Trade Deal? Vol. I. The Macroeconomic Effects*. Gütersloh: Bertelsmann Stiftung, Global Economics Dynamics (GED) Project.
Ferbelmayr, G., Kohler, W., Aichele, R., Klee, G. and Yalcin, E. (2014). *Mögliche Auswirkungen der Transatlantischen Handels- und Investitionspartnerschaft (TTIP) auf Entwicklungs- und Schwellenländer*. Munich: IFO Institut. www.econstor.eu/bitstream/10419/167427/1/ifo-Forschungsberichte-67.pdf.

Flôres, R. G. Jr (2013). "In search of a feasible EU–Mercosul free trade agreement", CEPS Working Document No. 378. Brussels: CEPS.
Francois, J. (2014). *Reducing Transatlantic Barriers to Trade and Investment. An Economic Assessment*, Final Report. London: Centre for Economic Policy Research (CEPR). www.italaw.com/sites/default/files/archive/Reducing%20Trans-Atlantic%20 Barriers%20to%20Trade%20and%20Investment.pdf.
Frenkel, A. (2019). "Un cruzado en la cancillería brasileña: Ernesto Araújo y la política exterior bolsonarista", *Nueva Sociedad*, edición digital, February. http://nuso.org/articulo/araujo-brasilderecha-cancilleria-bolsonaro/
Frenkel, A (2020). "El Mercosur ante la COVID-19: de la disputa comercial a la amenaza sanitaria", *Análisis Carolina 40/2020*. Madrid: Fundación Carolina. www.fundacioncarolina.es/wp-content/uploads/2020/06/AC-40.-2020.pdf.
Frenkel, A. and Ghiotto, L. (2019). "Los perdedores de siempre / Apuntes sobre el acuerdo entre la Unión Europea y el Mercosur", *Nueva Sociedad*. https://nuso.org/articulo/ue-mercosur-europa-ganadores-perdedores-integracion/.
Freytag, A., Draper, P. and Fricke, S. (2014). *The Impact of the TTIP: Economic Effects on Transatlantic Partners, Third Countries and the Global Trade Order*. Vol. 1. Berlin: Konrad Adenauer Stiftung.
Gill, S. and Law, D. (1988). *The Global Political Economy*. Baltimore: The Johns Hopkins University Press.
Gómez Arana, A. (2014). "Explaining the renewed push for a European Union association agreement with Mercosur", *Revista Española de Relaciones Internacionales* 6, 136–58.
Gómez Arana A. (2017). *The European Union's Policy Towards Mercosur. Responsive Not Strategic*. Manchester: Manchester University Press. https://library.oapen.org/bitstream/id/5bc3e64b-856f-4821-8d57-a68852bb08f6/626404.pdf.
Gouvernement de la France (2020). *Remise du rapport de la commission d'évaluation du projet d'accord UE–Mercosur*, Communiqué, 18 September. www.gouvernement.fr/partage/11745-remise-du-rapport-de-la-commission-d-evaluation-du-projet-d-accord-ue-mercosur.
Grieger, G. (2019). "The trade pillar of the EU–Mercosur Association Agreement", *Briefing, International Agreements in Progress*. Brussels: European Parliament, PE 640.138, August.
Grugel, J. (2002). *Spain, the European Unión and Latin America: Governance and Identity in the Making of the New Inter-Regionalism*. Madrid, Real Instituto Elcano, November. Available at www.realinstitutoelcano.org/.
Grugel, J. and Hout, W. (eds) (1999). *Regionalism across the North–South Divide. State Strategies and Globalization*. London: Routledge.
Hänggi, H. (2000). *Interregionalism: Empirical and Theoretical Perspectives*. Paper prepared for the Workshop "Dollars, Democracy and Trade. External Influence on Economic Integration in the Americas", Los Angeles, CA.
Hänggi, H., Roloff, R. and Rüland, J. (eds) (2006). *Interregionalism and International Relations*, London: Routledge.
Hettne, B. and Söderbaum, F. (2005). "Civilian power or soft imperialism: the EU as a global actor and the role of interregionalism", *European Foreign Affairs Review* 10 (4), 535–52. https://kluwerlawonline.com/journalarticle/European+Foreign+Affairs+Review/10.4/EERR2005036.
Inama, S. (2018). *The Generalized Scheme of Preferences Regulation (No 978/2012). European Implementation Assessment*. Brussels: European Parliament, PE 627–134,

November. www.europarl.europa.eu/thinktank/en/document.html?reference= EPRS_STU(2018)627134.
Instituto para la Integración de América Latina y el Caribe (INTAL) (2011). *Informe MERCOSUR N° 16*. Buenos Aires, November. https://publications.iadb.org/publications/spanish/document/Informe-MERCOSUR-No-17-(2011-2012).pdf.
Instituto para la Integración de América Latina y el Caribe (INTAL) (2014). *Informe MERCOSUR N° 19*. Buenos Aires, November. https://publications.iadb.org/en/informe-mercosur-no-19-2013-2014-segundo-semestre-2013-primer-semestre-2014.
Juncker, J.-C. (2016). *Towards a Better Europe, a Europe that Protects, Empowers and Defends. State of the Union Speech*. Strasbourg: European Parliament, 14 November. https://ec.europa.eu/commission/presscorner/detail/en/SPEECH_16_3043.
Kleimann, D. and Kübek, G. (2018). "The signing, provisional application, and conclusion of trade and investment agreements in the EU: the case of CETA and Opinion 2/15", *Legal Issues of Economic Integration* 45 (1), 13–46. https://kluwerlawonline.com/journalarticle/Legal+Issues+of+Economic+Integration/45.1/LEIE2018002.
Konold, D. (2010). "Farm interests as bargaining chips: France in the EU–Mercosur free trade negotiations", *Journal of Public Policy* 30 (3), 321–43. doi:10.1017/S0143814X10000139.
La Nación (2020). "El plan de Alberto Fernández para el acuerdo entre el Mercosur y la Unión Europea", 10 March. www.lanacion.com.ar/economia/industria-el-plan-alberto-fernandez-acuerdo-ue-nid2341934/.
La Vanguardia (2019). "Macron acusa a Bolsonaro de mentir y no apoyará el acuerdo EU–Mercosur", 23 August. https://www.lavanguardia.com/internacional/20190823/464214543423/macron-acusa-bolsonaro-mentir-no-apoyara-acuerdo-union-europea-mercosur-irlanda-francia.html.
Lebrija, A. and Sberro, S (eds) (2002). *México–UE. El Acuerdo de Asociación económica, concertación política y cooperación*. Mexico: Instituto de Estudios de la Integración Europea / ITAM / Porrúa.
Maduro, L., Da Motta Veiga, P. and Polonía Rios, S. (2020). "Impactos normativos/regulatórios no Mercosul", in Rozemberg, R. (ed.), *Acordo Mercosul–União Europeia*. Buenos Aires: Instituto para la Integración de América Latina y el Caribe (INTAL) del Banco Interamericano de Desarrollo (BID).
Makuc, A., Duhalde, G. and Rozemberg, R. (2015). *La negociación Mercosur–UE a veinte años de Acuerdo Marco de Cooperación: ¿Quo Vadis?* Buenos Aires: Instituto para la Integración de América Latina y el Caribe (INTAL), Banco Interamericano de Desarrollo (BID), Nota técnica no. IDB-TN-841. www.unsam.edu.ar/escuelas/politica/ideas/documentos/Comercio%20e%20Integraci%C3%B3n%20Regional/Negociacion%20Mercosur%20UE.pdf.
Manrique, M. and Lerch, M. (2015). *The TTIP's Potential Impact on Developing Countries: A Review of Existing Literature and Selected Issues*. Brussels: European Parliament, DG EXPO/B/PolDep/Note 2015–84. www.europarl.europa.eu/thinktank/sv/document.html?reference=EXPO_IDA(2015)549035.
Messerlin, P. (2013). "The Mercosur–EU preferential trade agreement: a view from Europe", CEPS Working Document No. 377. https://core.ac.uk/download/pdf/10594579.pdf.
Obaya, M., Baruj G. and Porta, F (2017). "Modernización de la industria automotriz", in *Los futuros del Mercosur: nuevos rumbos de la integración regional*. Buenos Aires: Instituto para la Integración de América Latina y el Caribe (INTAL), Banco Interamericano de Desarrollo. http://dx.doi.org/10.18235/0000637.

Oliveira, J. (2019). "Macron tilda de 'crisis internacional' los incendios de la Amazonia y quiere que se aborden en el G-7", *El País*, 23 August. https://elpais.com/internacional/2019/08/22/actualidad/1566501636_486466.html.
Parlamento Europeo (1999). *El proceso de asociación interregional de la UE con el Mercosur y Chile y su impacto en el sector agroalimentario de la UE.* Luxembourg: Dirección de Estudios del Parlamento Europeo, October, document 131 (ES). www.europarl.europa.eu/thinktank/en/document.html?reference=IPOL-AGRI_ET%281999%29288141.
Peña, F. (2010). "¿Es factible que en la Cumbre de Madrid se relancen las negociaciones UE–Mercosur?", *Análisis del Real Instituto Elcano (ARI)* 66. Madrid: Real Instituto Elcano. https://intranet.eulacfoundation.org/es/system/files/Es%20factible%20que%20en%20la%20Cumbre%20de%20Madrid%20se%20relancen%20las%20negociaciones%20UE-Mercosur.pdf .
Peña, F. (2014). "Fragmentación en las negociaciones comerciales. Los mega-acuerdos interregionales y su potencial impacto en la gobernanza global", *Carta mensual*, March. www.biblioteca.fundacionicbc.edu.ar/index.php/FRAGMENTACION_EN_LAS_NEGOCIACIONES_COMERCIALES:_Los_mega-acuerdos_interregionales_y_su_potencial_impacto_en_la_gobernanza_global.
Puccio, L. (2016). "A guide to EU procedures for the conclusion of international trade agreements", Briefing, European Parliament Research Service, October. www.europarl.europa.eu/thinktank/en/document.html?reference=EPRS_BRI(2016)593489.
Rodrigues, G. M. A. (2019). "¿El Trump del trópico? Política exterior de ultraderecha en Brasil", *Análisis Carolina*, 6, 15 April.
Rosales, O., Herreros, S., Frohmann, A. and García-Millán, T. (2013). *Las negociaciones megarregionales: hacia una nueva gobernanza del comercio mundial.* Santiago de Chile: CEPAL, LC/L.3710. www.cepal.org/es/publicaciones/35911-negociaciones-megarregionales-nueva-gobernanza-comercio-mundial.
Rozemberg, R. and Gayá, R. (2019). *Mercosur en tiempos de cambio. Implicaciones para la negociación con la Unión Europea*, Documentos de Trabajo 9. Madrid, Fundación Carolina.
Sanahuja, J. A. (2000a). "Trade, politics, and democratization: the 1997 Global Agreement between the European Union and Mexico", *Journal of Interamerican Studies and World Affair*, 42 (2), 35–62.
Sanahuja, J. A. (2000b). "Asimetrías económicas y concertación política en las relaciones UE–América Latina: un examen de los problemas comerciales", in Díaz Barrado, C. and Fernández Liesa, C (eds), *Iberoamérica ante los procesos de integración. Actas de las XVIII Jornadas de la Asociación Española de Profesores de Derecho Internacional Público y Relaciones Internacionales* (23–25 de septiembre de 1999), pp. 283–98. Madrid: BOE/AEPDIRI.
Sanahuja, J. A. (2007a). "Regionalismo e integración en América Latina: balance y perspectivas", *Pensamiento Iberoamericano* 0, pp. 73–104.
Sanahuja, J. A. (2007b). "Regiones en construcción, interregionalismo en revisión. La UE y el apoyo al regionalismo y la integración latinoamericana", in Freres, C., Gratius, S., Mallo, T., Pellicer, A. and Sanahuja, J. A. (eds), *¿sirve el diálogo político entre la Unión Europea y América Latina?*, pp. 1–42. Madrid: Fundación Carolina, documento de trabajo No. 15.
Sanahuja, J. A. (2011). "Las relaciones entre la UE y América Latina y el Caribe tras la Cumbre de Madrid: el fin de un ciclo político y la necesidad de una nueva estrategia", in Malamud, C., Isbell, P., Steinberg, F. and Tejedor, C. (eds), pp. 23–43. *Anuario Iberoamericano 2010*, Madrid: Real Instituto Elcano / EFE.

Sanahuja, J. A. (2012). "Spain: Double track Europeanization, and the search for bilateralism", in Ruano, L. (ed.), *The Europeanization of National Foreign Policies Towards Latin America*, pp. 36–61. London: Routledge.

Sanahuja, J. A. (2015). *The EU and CELAC: Reinvigorating a Strategic Partnership*. Hamburg: EU–LAC Foundation.

Sanahuja, J. A. (2017a). "Beyond the Pacific-Atlantic divide: Latin American regionalism before a new cycle", in Briceño, J. and Morales, I. (eds), *Post-Hegemonic Regionalism in the Americas. Towards a Pacific–Atlantic Divide?*, pp. 99–124. London: Routledge.

Sanahuja, J. A. (2017b). "Posglobalización y ascenso de la extrema derecha: crisis de hegemonía y riesgos sistémicos", in Mesa, M. (ed.), *Seguridad internacional y democracia: guerras, militarización y fronteras. Anuario 2016–17*, pp. 35–71. Madrid: CEIPAZ.

Sanahuja, J. A. (2018). "La estrategia global y de seguridad de la Unión Europea: narrativas securitarias, legitimidad e identidad de un actor en crisis", ICEI Working Papers DT 01/18.

Sanahuja, J. A. (2020). "Acuerdo Mercosur–UE: por una cláusula ambiental vinculante", *Latinoamérica21*, 14 October. https://latinoamerica21.com/es/acuerdo-mercosur-ue-por-una-clausula-ambiental-vinculante/.

Sanahuja, J. A. and Comini, N. (2018). "Las nuevas derechas latinoamericanas frente a una globalización en crisis", *Nueva Sociedad* 275 (May–June), 32–46.

Sanahuja, J. A. and Rodríguez, J. D. (2019). "Veinte años de negociaciones Unión Europea–Mercosur: Del interregionalismo a la crisis de la globalización", Documentos de Trabajo No. 13 (2ª época). Madrid: Fundación Carolina.

Santander, S. (2002). 'EU–MERCOSUR interregionalism: facing up to the South American crisis and the emerging free trade area of the Americas', *European Foreign Affairs Review* 7, 491–505. https://kluwerlawonline.com/journalarticle/European+Foreign+Affairs+Review/7.4/EERR2002007.

Schiponi, A. (2019). "Brazil: Jair Bolsonaro pushes culture war over economic reform", *Financial Times*, 25 August. www.ft.com/content/f470734e-c41a-11e9-a8e9-296ca66511c9.

Schmieg, E. (2015). *TTIP – Opportunities and Risks for Developing Countries*. Bonn: Stiftung Wissenschaft und Politik (SWP). www.swp-berlin.org/publications/products/zeitschriftenschau/2014zs01engl_scm.pdf.

Stratfor (2019). "Brazil's next president is looking to shake up Mercosur", 30 November. https://worldview.stratfor.com/article/brazils-next-president-looking-shake-mercosur.

Stuenkel, O. (2019). "The trouble ahead for Argentina–Brazil ties", *Americas Quarterly*, 28 October. www.americasquarterly.org/article/the-trouble-ahead-for-argentina-brazil-ties/.

The Economist (2015). "Game of Zones", 21 May. www.economist.com/news/finance-and-economics/21646772-regional-trade-deals-arent-good-global-ones-they-are-still.

University of Manchester (2009). *Trade SIA of the Association Agreement under Negotiation between the European Community and MERCOSUR* – Final Reports, March.

Zelicovich, J. (2019). "El acuerdo Mercosur–Unión Europea en su recta final", 9 July, *Análisis Carolina* 13.

Note

1 For a detailed examination of this issue, highly complex from a legal perspective, see, among others, Puccio 2016 and Kleimann and Kübek 2018.

7

Inter-regionalism beyond the executives: contemporary dynamics of EU–LAC inter-parliamentary relations

Bruno Theodoro Luciano

Introduction

Inter-regional relations between the European Union and Latin America and the Caribbean (EU–LAC) have not been identified only within the diplomatic and intergovernmental spheres. In fact a prominent inter-parliamentary dialogue between the regions has been promoted since the 1970s, years before the first EU–LAC Executive Summits (Sanahuja 1999; Stavridis and Ajenjo 2010; Müller et al. 2017). The fact that the continents have historically shared the same language, political traditions and culture due to colonialism facilitated the political approximation of both sides, including at the inter-parliamentary level. Alongside this common political and cultural background, in 2006 the Euro-Latin American Parliamentary Assembly (Eurolat) was formalised as the parliamentary dimension of EU-LAC bi-regional Strategic Association (1999). Composed of 150 members, seventy-five representatives from Europe (members of the European Parliament) and seventy-five from Latin America (members of Latin American national and regional parliaments), Eurolat has been framed as the most comprehensive mechanism of inter-parliamentary dialogue between the continents, fundamental to provide the opportunity for parliamentary elites from the two region to discuss the most urgent political issues within a pluralist and international environment (Stavridis and Ajenjo 2010; Luciano 2017; Müller et al. 2017).

Given the importance of relations among parliamentarians from the two sides of the Atlantic, this chapters aims to shed some light on the past and current developments of EU–LAC inter-parliamentary relations, something still neglected by the academic literature on EU–LAC inter-regionalism. By unveiling recent debates and topics of the Eurolat agenda since its establishment in 2006, this chapter intends to highlight how EU–LAC relations at the parliamentary level have evolved over the past decades. Important emphasis is given not just to the development of the institutional settings of this relationship but also to the political or ideological aspects of it, which explain how parliamentarians and political parties of the two regions have dialogued and clashed over key political, economic and social issues over the past years. In this sense this chapter relies on Eurolat's official documents available online and the literature on the topic as well as semi-structured interviews conducted with parliamentarians, diplomats and officials of both sides in Brussels (2017) and Montevideo (2018).

The chapter is organised as follows. Firstly, some reflections on the rise of parliamentarians in international affairs and an overview on the history of EU–LAC inter-parliamentary relations are introduced, followed by an analysis of the format and characteristics adopted by Eurolat since its formalisation in 2006. Secondly, an assessment on the key topics on the parliamentary agenda is provided, with particular focus on the areas of human rights, migration, fight against corruption and climate change. Lastly, this chapter reflects on the most recent political debates observed within Eurolat, giving strong prominence to the parliamentary discussions regarding the trade deals between both regions and the humanitarian situation in Venezuela.

This chapter argues that, on the one hand, there is a marginalisation of parliamentarians from both continents when it comes to their involvement in trade negotiations. On the other hand, it unveils that, while the Venezuelan crisis has put the EU–LAC intergovernmental dialogue into a deadlock due to its consensual nature, parliamentarians of both continents via Eurolat have been able to debate and promote several political opinions – albeit often divergent – on the crisis recently affecting this country. Furthermore, the fact that Eurolat enables the political representation of parliamentarians from both the Venezuelan government and the opposition might also underpin the invaluable contribution of the parliamentary relations towards the promotion of a peaceful and plural dialogue between the parties.

The emergence of parliamentarians in international affairs and its effects on EU–LAC inter-parliamentary relations

The expansion of globalisation and democratisation at the global scale has led to an increase in the involvement of non-executive actors in international relations. Traditionally in the hands of diplomatic agents from nation-states and international organisations, international affairs have also become an area of interest for multiple non-state actors, such as advocacy groups, civil-society movements, trade unions and individuals. Furthermore, other state agents beyond national governments have increasingly given attention to international politics. This is the particular case of the involvement of parliamentarians in global and regional affairs (Puig 2004; Cofelice 2012; IPU and UN 2012). In contrast to the "unitary" or "national" preferences set out by diplomatic actors when representing their countries, parliamentarians tend to align themselves not only with national interests but also with the interest of subnational regions, ideology/political parties and social groups that they represent in parliament (Malamud and Stavridis 2011). In this sense parliamentary diplomacy has detached itself from the traditional diplomacy, considering that parliamentarians start acting as "moral tribunes", responsible for defending principles such as human rights and freedom at the international level; providing their own inputs in election monitoring; promoting the socialisation of parliamentarians from different regions across the globe; and supporting the peaceful resolution of global conflicts (Stavridis and Ajenjo 2010). With that regards, Jancic (2014: 6) pointed out that "Parliamentary engagement in international affairs is chiefly threefold and consists of influencing foreign policy domestically, conducting parliamentary diplomacy and establishing parliamentary bodies of international organisations".

This increasing engagement of parliamentarians in international relations has been especially seen in Europe and Latin America, which has also impacted EU–Latin America overall relations. In particular the creation of supranational or regional parliaments in both continents is one of the most significant responses to the insertion of parliamentary channels within the regional integration projects established over the past decades. Although the creation and subsequent empowerment of the European Parliament at the EU level is the most striking manifestation of the parliamentarisation of regional integration (Kreppel 2002), several regional initiatives in Latin America have also developed parliamentary institutions within their organisation framework (Malamud and Sousa 2007; Mariano et al. 2017). For instance the Latin American Parliament (Parlatino), the Central American Parliament (Parlacen), the Andean Parliament (Parlandino) and the MERCOSUR Parliament (Parlasur) are all examples of parliaments established in the basis of a regional vocation (Erthal 2006). Whilst Parlatino has been created as an independent international parliamentary forum, the others have been configured as parliamentary dimensions of the Central American Integration System (SICA), Andean Community (CAN) and the Southern Common Market (MERCOSUR), respectively.

This plethora of international parliamentary institutions constituted in Europe and Latin American has also affected EU–Latin America inter-regionalism. Hence "The parliamentary dimension of EU–Latin America relations has been built on pre-existing subregional structures which also reflect the respective degree of regional integration achieved to date in Latin America" (Stelios and Ajenjo 2010: 10). For instance EU–LAC inter-parliamentary dialogue predated intergovernmental inter-regionalism. Müller et al. (2017) highlight that:

> The EU's strategic partnership with Latin America and the Caribbean has always had a parliamentary dimension – regular meetings between members of national and regional parliaments from both regions. Between 1974 and 2005, 17 EU–LA Interparliamentary Conferences took place, one every two years, with members of the EP and the Latin American Parliament (Parlamento Latinoamericano, Parlatino). (Müller et al. 2017: 56)

In the context of political approximation between the EU and Latin America of the 1990s and especially the beginnings of the 2000s, demands from parliamentarians of both continents to institutionalise their relationship via the establishment of an inter-parliamentary assembly emerged. This would not only formalise the regular parliamentary meetings convened since the 1970s, but it would also allow stronger channels to influence the EU–LAC Strategic Partnership set out in 1999. In this sense in November 2001 members of the European Parliament presented for the first time a proposal to establish a Euro-Latin American Parliamentary Assembly (Eurolat). This initiative matured only in 2005, when European and Latin American parliamentarians gathered in Lima and jointly demanded EU–LAC member states create the Eurolat. In May 2006, within the fourth EU–LAC summit, member states acknowledged the parliamentary proposal to set out Eurolat. Therefore, over the following months, parliamentarians and parliamentary officials from both regions organised several working groups in order to draft Eurolat's Constitutive Act and its first rules of procedure. In November 2006, inter-parliamentary technical efforts succeeded, when Eurolat finally had its inaugural session in Brussels. Thereby, since 2007, regular ordinary and extraordinary plenary and committees meetings have been held in Europe and Latin America.[1]

Some key features from the previous inter-parliamentary meetings would also be identified in the initial years of Eurolat. Firstly, the EP's institutional experience and resources have asymmetrically shaped the constitution and the organisation of Eurolat. Although symmetry is one of the principles propagated within EU–LAC summits and Eurolat's sessions, the fact that the European side has been more homogeneous in terms of its composition and is equipped with more financial and personnel resources than the Latin American counterpart has influenced the institutional pendulum of Eurolat in its first meetings. Thus the organisation of the plenary and committee meetings has mostly relied on the leadership of the EP's staff. This imbalance is also reproduced in terms of the topics of the parliamentary agenda. For instance one may also observe that the inter-parliamentary meetings have regularly voiced stronger opinions on political, social and economic challenges in Latin America than on about issues faced by Europeans. Thereby, on many occasions, such as recently seen with the crisis in Venezuela, Latin Americans have adopted a more defensive posture than parliamentarians from Europe (Luciano 2017).

Moreover, given Europe's historical and immediate interests in the region, besides the language and cultural affinities, MEPs from Spain and Portugal have been the main actors from the European parliamentary side. This might suggest that parliamentarians from other countries might not be as interested in engaging with relations with Latin America, which brings additional challenges to the sustainability of this inter-parliamentary co-operation in cases that few European countries actually see it as a priority area.

Whilst the next section will provide more details on the structure and the agenda of Eurolat over the past years, it is also important to highlight that Eurolat is important evidence of the increasing parliamentarisation of international and inter-regional affairs, as it has institutionalised a long-standing parliamentary relationship between the regions (Stavridis and Ajenjo 2010). Although the actual impact of EU–LAC inter-parliamentary co-operation is limited with regards to shaping the decisions taken at EU–LAC Summits, Eurolat has a key role in "preparing the terrain" for the executives of both regions, promoting "the processes of convergence on issues on the agenda and of diffusion of best practices of regional governance" (Müller et al. 2017: 57). Eurolat, in association with other bodies such as the EU–LAC Foundation (2010) and channels such as civil society, business, academic meetings, has been key when it comes to the democratisation of inter-regional relations, providing democratic credentials and legitimacy to the overall EU–CELAC Strategic Partnership. This role was bolstered in the 2018 EU–CELAC Ministerial Summit, when ministers of the region "commend the valuable contribution of the EURO–LAT Parliamentary Assembly, the Academic and Knowledge Week, and the meetings of the Civil Society as well as the Business fora" (EU–CELAC 2018: 10).

Eurolat's inter-parliamentary agenda

Since its creation Eurolat has been the key parliamentary channel between Europe and Latin America. Its composition of 150 parliamentarians, seventy-five from Europe and Latin America each, represents the principle of symmetry desired for the relationship between both continents. However, whilst the European component has been homogeneously represented by directly elected MEPs appointed for the EP's delegation to the Eurolat Assembly, the Latin American side has been characterised by the heterogeneity of its composition, inasmuch as its members come from either regional and national parliaments of the region, elected or indirectly appointed for their parliamentary mandates.

When it comes to its internal organisation, prominence is given to the role of Eurolat's bureau, led by one European and one Latin American co-president, as well as to the deliberative work of the thematic commissions. On the one hand, the Executive Bureau – composed of the co-presidents and fourteen vice-presidents – has been the political motor of Eurolat. Besides being the key political actors involved in formatting Eurolat's parliamentary agenda, the co-presidents represent Eurolat during the EU–CELAC high-level summits. By delivering their message to high-level representatives of EU–LAC countries, Eurolat's co-presidents have the unique opportunity to voice to the members of the executives their positions on several issues of the bi-regional agenda, either supporting specific intergovernmental initiatives in place or demanding additional actions on topics which, according to the parliamentarians, deserve greater attention from the member states of both regions. For instance, in the last EU–CELAC Summit, held in June 2015, both co-Presidents of Eurolat shared with representatives of member states their concerns about many issues in both regions, in particular human rights, regional integration and sustainable development (Eurolat 2015a; Eurolat 2015b).

On the other hand, when it comes to the discussions on key parliamentary topics and the specialised works, prominence is given to the performance of the thematic committees. Currently, Eurolat organises its deliberative activities into four committees: Political Affairs Security and Human Rights; Economic, Financial and Commercial Affairs; Social Affairs, Youth and Children, Human Exchanges, Education and Culture; and Sustainable Development, the Environment, Energy Policy, Research, Innovation and Technology. In fact most of Eurolat's resolutions originate from the work of the committees, where they are firstly introduced and deeply discussed by the committee's members before being submitted for a final vote at the plenary sessions. In this sense, as with national parliaments, the resolutions' (co) rapporteurs are key actors within Eurolat's deliberative process as they are responsible for presenting a first assessment on the content of the resolution to their peers both at the specialised committee as well as at the plenary, which will ultimately approve or reject the resolution on the basis of the committee's outcomes.

Moreover, Eurolat has set out over time a number of temporary working groups, which aimed to address relevant topics for parliamentarians, transcending the regular activities of the committees. In the past particular attention was given to the topic of migration, by the creation of a working group on "EU–LAC migration issues" (Stavridis and Ajenjo 2010). Among other activities, this working group allowed the exchange of views between parliamentarians and officials of international and national agencies on the challenges and benefits of migration within and between the continents (Eurolat 2016). Most recently, Eurolat has set out a working group on Organised Violence, Security and Terrorism, demonstrating that security issues have gained relevance in the parliamentary works.

In addition members of Eurolat also have the opportunity to develop transnational ideological networks. Inspired by the political organisation of the EP, Eurolat's agenda is also open to the organisation of meetings between political groups represented in Europe and Latin America. For instance, since Eurolat's constitution, important connections have been set out between the EP's group of Socialists and Democrats with analogue centre-left parties and parliamentarians in Latin America (Socialists and Democrats 2017; Luciano 2017). More recently the dialogue between the EP's European United Left and left-wing parties in Latin America has gained strength as meetings between these ideologically linked parliamentarians have been inserted in the latest Eurolat programmes (Eurolat 2018b). As will be highlighted in the next section, key current political issues, such as the situation in Venezuela, have been mostly discussed along ideological lines, given that left-wing parties in Europe and Latin America have shared a common approach on this particular case.

The formal and informal meetings in the framework of Eurolat have led to important socialisation effects when it comes to the information exchange among its members. According to one of the EP's officials consulted, Eurolat has contributed to fostering mutual learning among parliamentarians from both continents. Although significant differences exist in terms of the parliamentarian and presidential traditions observed in each region (Malamud and Sousa 2007) and due to the fact that the EP has historically gained stronger competences and resources (Kreppel 2002), they have not hindered the regular exchange of experiences about the parliamentary practices and the challenges faced by parliaments and parliamentarians in Latin America and Europe.

In addition one may observe that the preparatory meetings of the Latin American component are the only opportunity for parliamentarians from LAC to gather and co-ordinate common regional positions before engaging with their European counterparts. In contrast to the European component, which is solely composed of the members of the EP, who are members of the EP's delegation to relations with Latin America, members of Latin American regional and national parliaments who compose Eurolat do not possess a common arena to exchange ideas and information apart from the formal meetings organised within Eurolat. Therefore the meetings of the Latin America component, often organised on the first day of Eurolat's agenda, are crucial to allowing parliamentarians to articulate their own "regional" positions on many fundamental issues of the region (Luciano 2017).

None the less, Eurolat's performance has faced important challenges during its development due to some institutional and political configurations in Latin America and Europe. Firstly, although some officials have recognised the high quality and experience of some members of Eurolat from both the EU and LAC, the volatile presence of parliamentarians in the meetings and the frequent changes in parliamentary composition, especially in the Latin American component, has negatively impacted the regularity and consistency of inter-parliamentary activities. Moreover, as with the past EU–LAC inter-parliamentary meetings, the most active European members of Eurolat are still from Latin countries, in particular Portugal and Spain (31 per cent of MEPs at Eurolat and half of the European members of the Bureau – including its co-President – are either Spanish or Portuguese).[2] On the one hand, it means that these countries are very interested in deepening their historical ties with Latin America. On the other hand, it shows how members of other European member states have not given higher relevance to relations with Latin America, instead giving priority to relations with other countries or regions of the globe, such as the US, China and the Middle East.

Secondly, one can observe a mismatch between the agendas prioritised by the Europeans and Latin Americans at Eurolat. Whilst the European component is very interested in debating the existing conflicts and problems in Latin America – such as the situation in Venezuela, but also US–Cuba relations and the peace negotiations with paramilitary groups in Colombia – representatives from Latin American tend to have a more reluctant position on these issues. In fact, due to the history of external interventions in the region, representatives of Latin America tend to be more cautious on issuing asserting positions about events that involve specific countries, often referring to the principle of non-interference in domestic affairs. On the other hand, the Latin American component has pushed for including in Eurolat's agenda the issue of the sovereignty over the Falklands/Malvinas islands, which appeared for the first time in one of Eurolat's reports (Parlasur 2018). In addition, when it comes to the comparison between the EU–LAC inter-parliamentary and intergovernmental agendas, previous study has shown that, whilst Eurolat aims to cover most of the topics addressed at the EU–CELAC forums, it has also made some room for new issues, especially social ones, not included in the intergovernmental dialogue, showing the interest of parliamentary actors in broadening the inter-regional agenda (Luciano 2017).

Thirdly, the drivers of the political behaviour of the Latin American and the European components are quite diverse. Due to its own institutional development over time, the EP has internally configured alongside political-ideological rather than national cleavages (Hix et al. 2006). Thus the European political groups have played a key role in EP's voting and decision-making processes in time. Meanwhile, Latin American regional parliaments have not developed substantial transnational ideological linkages since their constitutions. Although one can observe embryonic exceptions, such as the Progressive Group (centre-left) at the MERCOSUR Parliament, Latin American parliamentarians at Eurolat still behave according to regional or national cleavages rather than political or ideological ones (EP official, interview with the author; Luciano 2017).

Considering the past years of inter-parliamentary activities, Eurolat's political agenda has been marked by a strong emphasis in discussing issues such as protection of democracy, human rights, migration, sustainable development, climate change, corruption and drug trafficking. For instance members of Eurolat recently expressed their support to the promotion of key principles within EU–LAC relations: "We urge our governments to continue pursuing these aims by means of the agreement, whilst always upholding the general principles of human dignity: human rights, ILO standards, gender equality, corporate social responsibility, etc." (Eurolat 2018a: 1).

When it comes to human rights and democracy, members of Eurolat have voiced their strong concern with the state of democracy in both continents. The message of Eurolat's co-presidents in 2018 is very illustrative in this sense:

> The EuroLat Assembly considers that advances have generally been made in the exercise of democracy, but it is still deeply concerned about the emergence of dangerous actions and conditions which are harmful to democratic governance and the rule of law in some Strategic Partnership countries. Consequently, it urges the relevant governments and international, regional and sub-regional organisations to work together with a view to protecting the core features of democratic coexistence, placing emphasis on strengthening the rule of law and stepping up freedom, human rights and integration as the best possible avenues towards holistic and sustainable development conceived with the common good in mind. (Eurolat 2018a: 4)

In terms of sustainable development and climate change, members of Eurolat have voiced their desire to see more engagement from the governments from both continents on tackling this urgent issue. For instance Eurolat's co-presidents have stated that they expect a deeper commitment from both Europe and Latin America to the fight against climate change, given that both regions are not exempt from the negative impacts derived from climate change, such as natural disasters (El País 2015). As stressed by the message of the co-presidents, "The 2015 Paris Agreement signed by 195 countries as part of the UN Framework Convention on combating climate change

Inter-regionalism beyond the executives 163

now needs our support more than ever" (Eurolat 2018a: 3). Along these lines members of Eurolat issued a resolution on the implementation of the 2030 Sustainable Development agenda, emphasising that priority should be given to implementing the sustainable development goals at the local and regional levels (Eurolat 2018c).

Good governance and combatting corruption are also frequent topics on Eurolat's agenda. In 2018 Eurolat's plenary approved a resolution entitled "Justice and combating impunity", which – given the instable scenario of democracy in Latin America and Europe – highlighted the relevance of multiple actors such as judicial courts, media, and civil society, in fighting corruption and ensuring public transparency in both continents (Eurolat 2018d). According to the view of members of Eurolat, "The Bi-regional Partnership has to improve its mechanisms and practices to combat corruption, imposing sanctions on individuals and countries committing serious corruption offences" (Eurolat 2018a: 3).

As one can infer from the establishment of a working group on the topic, migration has been another recurrent issue within Eurolat's agenda. Besides acknowledging key instruments approved at the UN level on migration, and voicing the importance of combatting human trafficking, the latest Eurolat's message gave some emphasis on the need of setting out new ways of engaging with this key matter. "Migration management requires the adoption of innovative policies to regulate migration – a social reality – within the supranational sphere whilst ensuring at all times that human rights are upheld in full" (Eurolat 2018a: 2).

Finally, another key concern shared by parliamentarians from Europe and Latin America at Eurolat is drug trafficking, a topic often referred to within Eurolat's presidential messages and resolutions. Once more, parliamentarians from both continents have demanded from national governments new solutions to this issue:

> The EuroLat Parliamentary Assembly calls on the international community, and on the EU–CELAC countries and the UN in particular, to come up with new solutions to the problems of drug trafficking and organised crime. Among those new solutions, the EuroLat Assembly supports the creation of a Latin American Criminal Court for the prosecution of those accused of offences relating to drugs trafficking and organised crime, etc. (Eurolat 2018a: 3)

In sum, since its formalisation in 2006, Eurolat has constituted itself as the key vehicle of inter-parliamentary co-operation and parliamentary diplomacy within EU–LAC relations. Although some institutional and political challenges remain clear, parliamentarians from both continents have regularly met and exchanged information and views on key political, economic and social issues relevant from both sides. Ultimately, parliamentary agents have aimed to reach common positions on these topics in order to demand action from regional organisations and national governments in Europe and Latin America.

Eurolat and the recent trade and political challenges in Latin America and Europe

Taking into account the main configurations and challenges of Eurolat, this section focuses on two key topics of the contemporary EU–LAC agenda – the negotiation of association or trade agreements between the regions and the political situation in Venezuela – highlighting how parliamentarians via Eurolat have addressed these issues over the past inter-parliamentary meetings. This section argues that, whilst trade has been one area in which parliamentarians from both sides have remained marginalised and under-informed actors, the political crisis in Venezuela has configured as one of the topics prioritised by parliamentarians within Eurolat's political discussions.

On the one hand, trade – a key issue for the EU–LAC overall relations – has historically been overlooked when it comes to inter-parliamentary relations. Although "the EUROLAT Plenary Sessions Declarations and other documents have concentrated on economic and trade issues" (Stavridis and Ajenjo 2010: 16), one can regularly observe within the declarations a broader and unspecific support for ongoing trade negotiations between the EU and Latin American countries or regional blocs. This is mostly due to the marginal roles of the EP and Latin American regional and national parliaments in the negotiating process of trade deals, but also due to the lack of transparency with regard to the terms of the inter-regional negotiations. It is worth mentioning that, especially since the entry into force of the Lisbon Treaty, the EP has been regularly informed of progress and has acquired more access to negotiated texts. Besides, within the Civil Society Dialogue parliamentarians may also contribute to the negotiations. None the less, although the EP has more competences than Latin American regional parliaments, when it comes to trade policies the EP continues to push for further means to access the information on trade deals conducted by the European Commission (Mariano and Luciano 2018). For instance, one of the items of the 2018 Eurolat message about the EU–MERCOSUR negotiations illustrates how parliamentarians have overall supported the agreement under negotiation and expect that it results in a balanced outcome, without detailing their own positions about the terms of the agreement under negotiation by the two biggest trade blocs in Europe and Latin America:

> Over the past few months negotiations between the EU and Mercosur with a view to concluding an association agreement have entered a decisive phase.

We take the view that it is vital for the EU and Latin America to reach a comprehensive and balanced agreement that takes account of both sides' interests and places the necessary emphasis on their relations as regards politics, economics and trade, as well as in other areas, and we very much hope the agreement will be concluded as soon as possible, with the best possible terms for the parties. (Eurolat 2018a: 2)

On the other hand, this vague support means that, despite the existence of strong opponents of FTAs in both regions, the majority of members of Eurolat support the signing of trade agreements between the regions, but, on the other hand, it also implies that they have been unable to discuss in detail the nature and content of these agreements, mainly due to the lack of access to information on the deals under negotiation. None the less, this second perspective seems more evident when analysing the call of parliamentarians for more transparent negotiations between EU and LAC countries. Thus the last Eurolat declaration emphasised how parliamentarians from both sides of the Atlantic argued that more transparency was needed for the negotiation of agreements between the EU and Latin American regional blocs or countries in order both to include a broader participation of civil-society actors and to facilitate the future ratification of these agreements:

We take the view that those negotiations must be as transparent as possible and involve civil society, as well as the relevant sections of society, to the greatest possible extent. When it comes to the implementation of the agreements, this will pave the way for broader acceptance and a wider social consensus. (Eurolat 2018a: 1)

Meanwhile the situation in Venezuela has been one of the most discussed topics in Eurolat's meetings over the past years. Both in committees and plenary meetings, parliamentarians from the two continents have positioned themselves on the current crisis in Venezuela, leading to a significant polarisation in the Eurolat Chamber. For instance, as stated by one of the EP's press releases, the 2018 meeting of Eurolat once again gave special attention to the developments in Venezuela: "The humanitarian crisis resulting from the massive emigration of more than two million Venezuelan citizens and the next elections in Brazil following the ruling of the Brazilian Supreme Court were central to the political discussions between deputies, held in Vienna during the Austrian Presidency of the Council of the European Union" (European Parliament 2018: 1). Besides approving reports on diverse topics, the eleventh plenary sessions have seen an intense political debate on Venezuela.

Nevertheless, the case of Venezuela also highlights the political challenges of Eurolat, considering the plural representation of political ideologies at the chamber and the limits to the establishment of consensual positions in this parliamentary arena. Although Eurolat's plenary sessions have been dealing with the crisis in Venezuela for the past years, no specific political declaration has been issued so far on this crisis, demonstrating how polarised the chamber is on how to engage with the Venezuelan government and what to propose in order to solve this crisis. Whilst right-wings members of Eurolat have pushed for the suspension of Venezuela from regional and international organisations as well as for harsh sanctions, left-wing parties have been defending a mediated dialogue between the government and the opposition of Venezuela.

Even Eurolat's co-presidency at some point was unable to reach a common position on Venezuela. For instance, in 2015 the European and Latin American co-presidents of Eurolat, given the deep polarisation of the chamber, decided to deliver separate messages to the EU–CELAC High-Level Summit. Whilst the European co-president Jáuregui Atondo stated in his message the urgency to release political prisoners and to hold free elections in the country (Eurolat 2015a), the Latin America co-president Vásquez Búcaro adopted a softer tone on the Venezuelan government, by referring to the principle of non-intervention in domestic affairs of the country (Eurolat 2015b). None the less, given the deterioration of the situation of Venezuela and political changes in the Latin America component, an approximation within the co-presidency has been observed more recently. Thereby in 2017, the co-presidents of Eurolat issued a joint declaration demanding the respect for the rule of law in Venezuela (European Parliament 2017).

In contrast to the EU–LAC inter-governmental agenda, which has been suspended since there is no consensus on the issue of Venezuela, Eurolat meetings have been regularly organised, and representatives of both regions have called for a political solution to the instability in the country, which has recently led to the biggest humanitarian crisis ever seen in the region, having up to 2018 displaced more than three million people across the continent (AP News 2018). Indeed the deadlock of EU–CELAC Summits is something acknowledged by Eurolat in a message to the Foreign Ministers of Latin America and Europe:

> The postponement of the third CELAC–EU Summit – initially planned for October 2017 in San Salvador – in response to a request from a number of Latin American countries and given the political situation in Venezuela, has effectively put on hold the bi-regional dialogue that had been conducted at the very highest level since the first summit of Latin American, Caribbean and European Union Heads of State and Government was held in Rio de Janeiro on 28 and 29 June 1999. We urge the governments to solve the political problems that have led to this suspension, with a view to returning as soon as possible to the regular schedule of summits between Latin American, Caribbean and

European Union Heads of State and Government, which drive forward and direct the activities and programmes of the Strategic Partnership. (Eurolat 2018a: 1)

Hence, not only have parliamentarians extensively debated over the situation in Venezuela but they have also demanded that member states move beyond the political deadlock of EU–CELAC summits in order to restore the bi-regional agenda, which has stalled since the worsening of the crisis in Venezuela. As consensus is a driving force of the high-level Summits, the return of EU–CELAC meetings would be possible only if the countries find common ground to engage with the current Venezuelan government.

In the most recent context of the Covid-19 pandemic, members of Eurolat have continued to show their concern with the humanitarian crisis in Venezuela, calling for the return of the EU–LAC intergovernmental dialogue in order to enable the promotion of bi-regional health co-operation: "The Co- Presidents of the EuroLat Assembly have therefore called for a Meeting of EU–LAC Heads of State and Government to be convened to establish enhanced cooperation to tackle COVID-19" (Eurolat 2020: 1–2).

In sum, this section has demonstrated how members of Eurolat have performed in two crucial issues of EU–LAC agenda: negotiations of inter-regional trade agreements and the humanitarian crisis in Venezuela. On the one hand, members of Eurolat have been marginalised from the inter-regional trade talks, being unable to access information on the terms being negotiated by the governments of both regions. As a result the parliamentary declarations have provided only a broad and generic support to the ongoing negotiations between the EU and the blocs and countries of Latin America. On the other hand, the issue of Venezuela has seen more parliamentary than intergovernmental activism over the past years. Since the EU–CELAC Summits have entered deadlock, Eurolat has been the key inter-regional political forum where political actors from both regions can voice their concerns about the humanitarian conditions in Venezuela as well as propose solutions to overcome the political and economic instability of the country. Although a consensual position has not been found in the chamber – unlike EU–CELAC intergovernmental dialogue – this has not prevented members of Eurolat from discussing the issue and condemning the human rights situation in the country and promoting dialogue between the opposing forces in Venezuela, which has not ceased in the context of the Covid-19 pandemic.

Conclusions

This chapter has addressed EU–LAC inter-parliamentary relations, a dimension still overlooked within the literature on EU–LAC relations. Whilst significant attention has been given to the intergovernmental dialogue between the EU and Latin American countries and regional blocs, less relevance was given to the role of parliamentary actors within this relationship. Considering that the last decades have witnessed the emergence of parliamentary diplomacy at the global level and the establishment of regional or supranational parliaments in Europe and Latin America, more importance must be given to understanding the current and future role of these parliamentary assemblies in the development of international and inter-regional relations.

After introducing the historical relations between parliamentarians of both continents and the more recent institutional framework established by Eurolat, focus was given to how parliamentarians have addressed two of the most pressing issues of EU–LAC agenda: the negotiations of trade agreements between the regions and the humanitarian crisis in Venezuela. Whilst this chapter demonstrated that the former is still a neglected issue within the inter-parliamentary relations due to the marginal (but growing) role of national and supranational parliaments in trade policies, the latter has been vastly discussed by parliamentarians at Eurolat. In contrast to the recent deadlock of EU–CELAC summits, Eurolat has regularly convened and its members have intensely voiced their positions on the situation in Venezuela.

Taking into account the challenges brought about by the (re)emergence of populism, nationalism and the crisis of multilateralism, democratic crises such as the one recently observed in Venezuela might be seen more frequently in both Latin America and Europe. This means that not only diplomatic and governmental actors, but also parliamentary agents, must be prepared to foster peaceful and multidimensional co-operation even in junctures of isolation and introspection. Considering the historical ties which have bonded Europe and Latin America, and how respect for human rights, democracy, and social justice has been grounded in the societies across both continents, EU–LAC inter-regionalism, in both its governmental and its parliamentary dimensions, will be instrumental to the defence of these shared principles inside and outside the two regions.

References

All websites last visited 30 September 2021.

AP News (2018). "UN says there are 3 million Venezuelan refugees and migrants", 8 November. www.apnews.com/78ed216285544fb68587c05997eac322. Accessed 22 February 2019.

Cofelice, A. (2012). "International parliamentary institutions: some preliminary findings and setting a research agenda', UNU-CRIS Working Papers W-2012/3.

https://cris.unu.edu/international-parliamentary-institutions-some-preliminary-findings-and-setting-research-agenda.
El País (2015). "Europa y Latinoamérica, unidas frente al cambio climático", 3 December. https://elpais.com/elpais/2015/12/03/opinion/1449168109_285929.html.
Erthal, J. (2006). "Democracia e parlamentos regionais: Parlacen, Parlandino e Parlasul", *Observador On-line* 1 (9) (November).
EU–CELAC (2018). *Building Bridges and Strengthening Our Partnership to Face Global Challenges*, Declaration, 2nd EU–CELAC Ministerial Meeting, Brussels, 16–17 July.
Eurolat (2014). *Road Map 2006–2014* (European Parliament, Latin America Unit), September. www.europarl.europa.eu/intcoop/eurolat/key_documents/roadmap/september2014_en.pdf.
Eurolat (2015a). *Message of the European Component of Eurolat to the 2nd EU–CELAC Summit*, Brussels.
Eurolat (2015b). *Message of the Latin American Component of Eurolat to the 2nd EU–CELAC Summit*, Brussels.
Eurolat (2016). "Draft agenda – working group on migration in relations between the European Union, Latin America and the Caribbean, meeting, Tuesday 20 September 2016", EUAL_OJ(2016)0920_2. www.europarl.europa.eu/intcoop/eurolat/working_group_migration/meetings/20_09_2016_montevideo/draft_agenda_en.pdf.
Eurolat (2018a). *Message of the Co-Presidents of the Euro–Latin American Parliamentary Assembly to the EU and CELAC Foreign Ministers*, Brussels, 16 and 17 July. www.europarl.europa.eu/intcoop/eurolat/key_documents/messages/celac2018/1158907EN.pdf.
Eurolat (2018b). "Draft programme", Eleventh Ordinary Plenary Session, 17–20 September, Imperial Palace (Hofburg), Vienna, Austria. www.europarl.europa.eu/intcoop/eurolat/assembly/plenary_sessions/vienna_2018/programme/1154987EN.pdf.
Eurolat (2018c). "Resolution: effectively implementing the 2030 Agenda for Sustainable Development at the local level", Thursday, 20 September – Vienna, AP102.458v05–00.
Eurolat (2018d). "Resolution: justice and combating impunity based on the report by the Committee on Political Affairs, Security and Human Rights", Thursday, 20 September – Vienna, AP102.358v04–00.
Eurolat (2020). "Communiqué from the European Parliament Copresident to the Euro–Latin American Parliamentary Assembly on his participation in the international donors' conference in solidarity with Venezuelan refugees and migrants in the context of Covid-19", 26 May.
European Parliament (2017). "Venezuela: EuroLat co-presidents demand respect for the rule of law", Press Release, 22 September. www.europarl.europa.eu/news/en/press-room/20170920IPR84307/venezuela-eurolat-co-presidents-demand-respect-for-the-rule-of-law.
European Parliament (2018). "Humanitarian emergency in Venezuela was central debate of the EuroLat plenary", Press Release, 14 September. www.europarl.europa.eu/news/en/press-room/20180914IPR13511/humanitarian-emergency-in-venezuela-was-central-debate-of-the-eurolat-plenary.
Gratius, S. (2013). "Europe and Latin America: in need of a new paradigm", Fride working paper 116.
Hix, S., Noury, A. and Roland, G. (2006). "Dimensions of politics in the European Parliament', *American Journal of Political Science* 50 (2), 494–511. www.jstor.org/

stable/3694286?refreqid=excelsior%3A59585e8f7cd5430257f3589142061d40& seq=1#metadata_info_tab_contents.
Inter-Parliamentary Union and United Nations Development Programme (2012), *Global Parliamentary Report: The Changing Nature of Parliamentary Representation*. United Nations Publications. https://constitutionnet.org/vl/item/global-parliamentary-report-changing-nature-parliamentary-representation-undp-inter.
Jancic, D. (2014). "Multilayered international parliamentarism: the case of EU–Brazil relations", LSE Law, Society and Economy Working Paper 17. London: LSE.
Kreppel, A. (2002). *The European Parliament and Supranational Party System: A Study in Institutional Development*. Cambridge: Cambridge University Press.
Lazarou, E. and Luciano, B. T. (2015). "10 anos de relações do Brasil com uma Europa alargada", in Dane, F., Lazarou E. and Luciano, B. T. *A União Europeia alargada em tempos de novos desafios*. Konrad Adenauer on.
Luciano, B. T. (2015). "Democratizando a integração: eleições diretas para os parlamentos Europeu e do Mercosul", *Brazilian Journal of International Relations* 4 (2), 385–406.
Luciano, B. T. (2017). "Inter-parliamentary European Union-Latin American Caribbean (EU–LAC) relations and the increasing political convergence among Latin American regional parliaments (2006–15)", *Parliaments, Estates and Representation* 37 (3), 318–34. https://doi.org/10.1080/02606755.2017.1336326.
Malamud, A. and Sousa, L. (2007). "Regional parliaments in Europe and Latin America: between empowerment and irrelevance', in Hoffmann, A. and van der Vleuten, A. (eds), *Closing or Widening the Gap? Legitimacy and Democracy in Regional International Organizations*, pp. 85–102. Farnham: Ashgate.
Malamud, A. and Stavridis, S. (2011). "Parliaments and parliamentarians as international actors", in Reinalda, B. (ed.), *The Ashgate Research Companion to Non-State Actors*, pp. 101–15. Farnham: Ashgate.
Mariano, B., Bressan, R. and Luciano, B. T. (2017). "A comparative assessment of regional parliaments in Latin America: Parlasur, Parlandino and Parlatino', *Revista Brasileira de Política Internacional* 60 (1), 1–18. www.scielo.br/j/rbpi/a/Hs5StbZL6M95mXqjZ7FCJWf/?lang=en.
Mariano, K. and Luciano, B. T. (2018). "The parliamentarization of EU trade policy: unveiling the European Parliament's involvement in EU–MERCOSUR trade negotiations', *European Politics and Society* 20 (5), 591–608. https://doi.org/10.1080/23745118.2018.1559792.
Morazán, P., Fiapp, J. A. Sanahuja and Ayllón, B. (2011). "A new European Union development cooperation policy with Latin America", Directorate-General for External Policies of the Union, EXPO/B/DEVE/FWC/2009–01/Lot5/18, 2011. https://op.europa.eu/en/publication-detail/-/publication/f05b922d-cbcc-4250-ab4f-79a65eac97dc.
Müller G., Wouters, J., Defraigne, J., Santander, S. and Raube, K. (2017), *The EU–Latin American Strategic Partnership: State of Play and Ways Forward*, European Parliament, Policy Department, Directorate-General for External Policies, EP/EXPO/B/AFET/FWC 2013–08/LOT 4/05.
Parlasul (2018). "Islas Malvinas son tema de debate en la EuroLat", *Agencia Parlasur*, 21 Set. www.parlamentomercosur.org/innovaportal/v/15821/1/parlasur/islas-malvinas-son-tema-de-debate-en-la-eurolat.html. Accessed 14 May 2019.
Puig, L. M. (2004). "International parliamentarianism: an introduction to its history", *Parliaments, Estates and Representation* 24 (1), 13–62. https://doi.org/10.1080/02606755.2004.9522185.

Sanahuja, J. A. (1999). "25 años de cooperación interparlamentaria entre la Unión Europea y América Latina", European Parliament, POLI 107 ES.
Sanahuja, J. A. (2014). "Enfoques diferenciados y marcos comunes en el regionalismo latinoamericano: Alcance y perspectivas de UNASUR y CELAC", *Pensamiento propio 39*.
Sanahuja, J. A. (2015). "La UE y CELAC: revitalización de una relación estratégica", *EU–LAC Foundation*, Relaciones birregionales / Serie de los foros de Reflexión, Hamburg.
Saraiva, M. (2015). "Brasil, América Latina e a União Europeia diante de novas agendas globais", in Dane, F. Lazarou, E. and Luciano, B. T., *A União Europeia alargada em tempos de novos desafios*. Konrad Adenauer Foundation.
Socialists and Democrats (2017). "Progressives in the EU and Latin America move forward towards the EU–CELAC summit", Press Release. www.socialistsanddemocrats.eu/newsroom/progressives-eu-and-latin-america-move-forward-towards-eu-celac-summit.
Stavridis, S. (2006). "Parliamentary diplomacy: any lessons for regional parliaments?", in Kölling, M. Stavridis, S. and Fernández Sola, N. (eds), *The International Relations of the Regions: Subnational Actors, Para-diplomacy and Multi-level governance*. Zaragoza.
Stavridis, S. and Ajenjo, N. (2010). "EU–Latin American parliamentary relations: some preliminary comments on the EUROLAT', *Jean Monnet / Robert Schuman Paper Series* 10 (3), April.

Notes

1 A list of the meetings organised and declarations issued in the context of Eurolat from 2001 to 2014 can be found at Eurolat (2014).
2 Data retrieved from EP's and Eurolat's websites, available at www.europarl.europa.eu/intcoop/eurolat/presidency_and_bureau/members_en.htm, www.europarl.europa.eu/delegations/en/dlat/members (accessed 12 February 2019).

8

The impact of European political dialogue upon Chilean and Mexican domestic policies

Francis Espinoza-Figueroa

Introduction

In international complex scenarios of multilateralism, it is necessary to study bilateral agreements beyond economic implications, especially for those global actors that utilise a power which is not "deposited" necessarily in its material capabilities for exerting physical strength, still it is to be found in its ability to structure or organise (to shape) knowledge. The EU, as a global actor (Bretherton and Vogler 2006; Orbie 2009), has a significant impact upon non-European countries.

The increase of mega-regional agreements, such as the Pacific Alliance, US–Central America treaty, TTP11, affects the traditional way the EU has been establishing its affairs with Latin American continent. European relationships with external countries have mainly focused on trade, aid and technical assistance. The Union had extended ties with some Latin American countries, even though, before the 1970s, the EU did not consider foreign policy to Latin America very important. These dealings started as a consequence of European intervention in Central America in the 1980s. After this the EU inaugurated new institutionalised relationships with Latin America (LAC) through sub-regional and regional groups.

The EU decided to move its relations with Latin America towards some forms of "associated status" with Chile and Mexico. Through this particular condition as a European partnership, both Latin American countries are very active actors in horizontal programmes (social and co-operation programmes) in each country. These involvements increased close links between the EU and LAC and strengthened European influences in developing domestic policies in Chile and Mexico.

Within the framework of European foreign affairs, the political dialogue component has constituted a differentiating element that the EU maintains at bi-regional stages. The political dialogue has approached with LAC diverse topics such as political stability, the consolidation of the rule of law, respect for human rights, regional integration, fight against drugs and related crimes, and the trafficking of arms and people, among other things.

> A significant *lacuna* in discussion of the EU external relations is any serious consideration of these from a non-European perspective. (Moxon-Browne 2015: 276)

Therefore I argue that there is a need to define the role and limits of multilateralism (Álvarez 2000), taking into account different perceptions of the process beyond Latin American or European "eyes".

The chapter divides into three sections which study the European political dialogue from different perspective: (1) historical ties, (2) mechanisms of exerting "soft power" and (3) effects of the Union's political dialogue upon Chilean and Mexican domestic policies. From a theoretical perspective I discuss the EU as an influential actor exerting soft power.

The beginning of the political dialogue between the EU and Latin America

This first part draws a historical analysis of the political dialogue between the EU and LAC, emphasising the establishment of diverse agreements and trade relations considering the importance of the political dialogue within third- and fourth-generations treaties with Chile and Mexico.

There are many "conjectures" about why the EU decided to move its external spectrum towards LAC. From an idealist approach an altruistic perspective of the European Community was involved in diplomatic solutions of peace within the continent to stabilise the San José Process. Considering a realist view, a geopolitical and strategic decision allowed the EU to extend its frontiers beyond Europe for motives of military security and economic stability, showing socialist countries that the EC could be effective and efficient exerting a soft power (Zabludovsky and Gómez Lora 2005).

The institutional ties between the EU and Latin America and the Caribbean (LAC) were born in 1974 through different mechanisms such as bi-regional relations, specifically in political dialogue. Hazel Smith (2002) suggests that formal agreements were few and limited in their scope, "based around fairly narrowly defined economic objectives and none of the included political concerns. EC economic policy towards Latin America was also weak and incoherent" (2002: 212).

Sanahuja (quoted by Smith 2002) argues that there was an essential inequality between political commitments of the Union and the economic content of bi-regional relations, because the EU used to offer a classic model of "aid not trade". However, Hazel Smith (2002) emphasises that "the

Union has sought to sustain and expand *trade* links, but the core of the relationship is based on *development cooperation*" (2002: 212). In contrast Sanahuja (quoted by Smith 2002) insists that the relationship between the parties is characterised by developing regional strategies, which benefited European people more than Latin American ones.

From a critical approach, Bianculli (2016) points out the difference between the EU and the US strategies. The diverse tactics impact actors and their decisions at domestic and regional levels, "increasing procedural and governance demands taken as the standardization and harmonization of norms and rules" (Bianculli 2016: 160). Focusing on a constructivist approach, Bianculli (2016) argues that LAC has to be obliged to speak as the EU converses:

> The EU offers Latin America a model for development and consolidation through cooperation and trade (De Lombaerde and Schulz 2009), but also by forcing Latin American countries to speak with one voice, which certainly contrasts with the "divide and rule" strategy of the US. (Bianculli 2016: 160)

Bindi (2012) points out that the interest of the EU in LAC emerged as part of the commitment of Spain and Portugal within the integration process: "As a consequence, negotiations with Spain and Portugal stalled, and those two countries did not become members until January 1, 1986. With their membership, the EEC became more interested and involved in Latin America." (2012: 21). In contrast, Gómez Arana (2017) argues that Spain and Portugal never have enough power to play an important role in considering LAC as a remarkable candidate to establish any agreement.

Christopher Hill and Michael Smith (2005) suggest that EU–Latin America affairs have been determined by an influential degree that implies a particular category, a network of preferential relationships between the EU and non-European countries, a "Pyramid of privilege" (Smith 2003). The Union incorporated colonies and overseas territories of the member states into a close network of relationships. European ties with third countries have focused on trade, aid and technical assistance. That is what Thomas Diez (2005) calls "a spirit of partnership", a set of instruments that construct zones of dialogues, exchange and co-operation that guarantee peace, stability and prosperity and focus on cultural and human affairs.

Zabludovsky and Gómez Lora (2005) suggest a historical and different reason why the EU was interested in Latin America. They argue that after the fall of the Berlin Wall the EU decided to enlarge its "frontiers" eastward for motives of military security and economic stability. That sought to send a call to former socialist countries that would be part of the Union sooner or later.

> The other member countries shared a belief in the strategic importance of eastward enlargement, but the more Atlanticist countries – The United Kingdom,

Spain and Portugal – feared that this could entail a loss of their relative influence in the EU. Hence the United Kingdom promoted its interest in maintaining a preferential relationship between the EU and the United States, and sought to strengthen the Atlantic alliance. Spain and Portugal, in the same measure, sought to establish a similar agenda with Latin America. (Zabludovsky and Gómez Lora 2005: 8)

The EU decided to move its relations with Latin America towards "associated status", specifically with Chile and Mexico. The "associated status" symbolises, as Hazel Smith (2002) argues, a "marriage" of economic and political objectives, which combines "appropriate instruments in a way that could accommodate policy requirements towards the differing socioeconomic and political status of the different groups of states" (2002: 212).

A very useful approach was, for example, the "Parlatino – European Parliament Conferences", meetings that produced a crucial convergence of views and objectives between both regions in aspects such as pacific resolution of conflicts, and the transition and consolidation of democracy (Sanahuja quoted by Smith 2002: 185). Systematically the EU started its relations with Latin America as a consequence of its intervention in Central America in the 1980s:

> In subsequent years, relations were established or further developed with sub-groups in the region. The San José dialogue (with Costa Rica, Guatemala, Honduras, Nicaragua, and Panama) was particularly important as European foreign ministers decided to send a strong signal to the United States (which was at the time involved in several Central American countries) by attending in full the first meeting in San José de Costa Rica, in September 1984. (Bindi 2012: 21)

After this process the EU inaugurated new institutionalised relationships with Latin America through sub-regional and regional groups.

The Andean Community was the first Latin American group that established official relations with the EU in the form of a Framework Agreement on Cooperation. This group, which was initially named the Andean Pact and formed by Bolivia, Colombia, Ecuador, Peru, and Venezuela, started its relations with the European Community (EC) in 1983. The relations between the EC and the Andean Community focused on commercial issues and development of cooperation, they disconnected at first; but reactivated in the 1990s. In 1993, both Parties signed a second and more extensive Framework Agreement on Cooperation, which entered into force in 1998. The Central America Group, formed by Costa Rica, El Salvador, Guatemala, Honduras, Nicaragua, and Panama, signed a Cooperation Agreement with EC in 1985. This agreement resulted from a foreign policy engagement that the EU established with the Central American States to respond to the Central American conflict in the 1980s. Later, both parties, The EU and

Central America, signed in 1993 a Framework Cooperation Agreement, with a Joint Committee of high-level officials and a Sub-Committee for Cooperation to control the agreement, plan and implement the ministerial sessions. This agreement also provided an extension of political cooperation, because the early 1990s largely achieved the original aim of San José Dialogue, and restored the peace in the Region. The focus of cooperation between the EU and the Central America Group is on diverse issues such as regional integration, democracy and human rights. Besides, this dialogue includes rural development, disaster prevention and reconstruction.

During the second half of the 1980s, the former Rio Group,[1] joined originally by Argentina, Brazil, Colombia, Mexico, Panama, Uruguay, and Venezuela, started its relations with the EC as a way to strength the peace process in Central America and to help stabilise the San Jose Process. This agreement provided for regular annual meetings of the foreign ministers, considering, primarily, political issues.

Torrent and Polanco (2016) say that during the 1990s the EC (on its own or jointly with its member states) started a "car race" to negotiate bilateral agreements with all the countries and regions around the world. Therefore there was no surprise when the EU established formal ties with Latin America. Thus there were no concrete reasons to explain why the EU could not have included Latin America in this new wave of agreements. Nevertheless, the EC considered that the Andean Community and Central America "were not yet ready" for institutional relations, due to their violent internal conflicts.

Besides, Latin America, the Caribbean and the EU embarked in 1999 on the road to a "bi-regional strategic partnership". It was an ambitious project that sought to create a large free trade area between the two regions through the so-called partnership agreements with the various sub-regional groups, on the Latin American and Caribbean side and with the EU as counterpart (2015).[2]

The proposed strategic partnership did not achieve its objectives only with the trade dimension. Its primary purpose was to set up a sustainable socio-economic model to eradicate poverty, promoting development within both regions. An increasingly fluid political dialogue and co-operation focused on the political and social target and the intensification of commercial relationships. The conviction of that model was expressed as part of a joint action and commitment, which represented an effective added value in resolving issues within the bi-regional and global agenda. A sustainable socio-economic model implied the targeting of the goal of cohesion and social inclusion in both regions. At the same time the EU affirmed the desire for greater co-ordination in multilateral forums, where the global agenda is managed. The main purpose was to safeguard and promote common principles and values in the two regions, such as democracy, the rule of law and human rights, and to advance in an environment conducive to the sustainable development.

In October 1994 the EU decided to reformulate policy towards Latin America. It offered a nuanced approach, focusing on marrying economic and political objectives with adequate instruments and methods. That allowed accommodating policy requirements to balance various socio-economic and political statuses of many states in Latin America.

According to Smith (2003) the policy involved a tripartite approach, relating to the three historical times in the EU–Latin America relations. This policy focuses on aid and co-operation to achieve more sophisticated types of agreements, called "third" or "fourth" generation. In contrast Ahumada (2019, quoting Blanc Altemir 2005) argues that the EU's strategy with LAC was to weaken and counterweight the US's FTAA strategy. Therefore, in order "To achieve that goal, the EU initiated a wave of bi- and multi-lateral agreements with key markets in the region, including Mexico (2000), Chile (2002), Central America (2003), and the Andean Community of Nations (2003). There was also its failed attempt to reach an accord with the Mercosur" (2019: 176).

The EU decided to move its relations with Latin America towards associated status. This character of 'associated status' placed those two countries (Mexico and Chile) and to this group (MERCOSUR) in this 'pyramid of privilege', which "had been reserved for those states that either for historical reasons (the ex-colonial states of Lomé) or political reasons (the near abroad of East and Southern Europe) had been considered a foreign policy priory" (Smith 2002: 213).

> the concept of the "Partnership and Cooperation Agreement" (PCA) was born – designed to intensify trade relations, promote economic cooperation, assist and consolidate moves towards market economies and also allow for an element of political dialogue. (Smith 2002: 237)

Chile and Mexico share some characteristics that increase their tiny relationship with the EU. For example, they established agreements called third and fourth generations (Chile and Mexico, respectively) to develop social and co-operation programmes in each country, being considered European partnerships. Both Latin American countries participated actively in regional programmes, which increased the narrow links between the EU and Latin America, and they strengthened European influences in developing domestic policies (Espinoza-Figueroa 2013).

MERCOSUR also constituted an essential partnership with the EU, because it was capable of joining the two strongest Latin American economies – Brazil and Argentina – "in a functioning and rapidly accelerating project of economic integration. Like Mexico and Chile, MERCOSUR has an active linkage policy with its neighbours – formalizing association agreements with Chile and Bolivia in 1996" (Smith 2002: 213). Finally, in 2019, MERCOSUR signed a historical Strategic Association Agreement with the Union.

The European political dialogue

Levi Coral (2007) argues that the political dialogue means a mechanism that the European Union implemented within the agreements signed with Latin America at the regional, sub-regional and bilateral levels. That instrument helped the EU to deepen its ties with Latin America to improve its foreign policy, and reflected some aspects that were not considered in the specific agreement of a commercial nature or those related to co-operation.

Torrent (2005) believes that political dialogue's content is affected, in practice, by lack of enforceability and excess of statements, and by lack of knowledge about powers and mechanisms that make possible the implementation of agreements. Contrarily, for Freres et al. (2006) the European political dialogue is an effective and differentiating mechanism of the conventional management scheme of bilateral relations, which is always susceptible to improvement.

According to Freres et al. (2006), political dialogue overlaps one of the three pillars, including economic and development co-operation. Within the framework of its foreign affairs, that component constitutes a differentiating element that the EU maintains at bi-regional stages. The political dialogue with the LAC has approached diverse topics such as political stability, the consolidation of the rule of law, respect for human rights, regional integration, the fight against drugs and related crimes, and the trafficking of arms and people, among other things.

Levi Coral (2007) argues that the European Political Dialogue operates under different instances and channels such as inter-parliamentary dialogue; the group-to-group dialogues of a regional character (EU–Rio Group) and sub-regional relationships (Central America, MERCOSUR and Andean Community); inter-regional summits of heads of state and government; and bilateral relations with states that have signed third- and fourth-generation association agreements (Chile 2002 and Mexico 2000).

The European political dialogue included dialogues at different levels such as heads of state and governments, ministerial civil servants, senior officials and inter-parliamentary individuals. Nevertheless its use has been limited despite enormous potential that it could have had to deal with particular aspects of external affairs, considering the degree of influence of the two states in the region (Sanahuja 2004: 91).

The political dialogue in Chile and Mexico implied institutional adjustments, setting of standards, language use and specific policies, focusing on "the independent power of norms to influence actors' behaviour" (Diez 2005: 616). It was influencing some influential areas such as higher education, science and technology and social and productive areas.

If one analyses the institutional adjustments, it is possible to observe the creation of institutions as FOCUS EUROLATINO[3] in Chile and the Observatory of Effects in Mexico (Espinoza-Figueroa 2013). FOCUS EUROLATINO was formed as an innovative instrument to generate dialogues between the EU and Latin America to understand regional and bi-regional problems. The Observatory of Effects in Mexico focuses on examining the impacts of investment and trade relationships on the environment and the labour, social, economic and cultural rights, especially in disadvantaged regions and society sectors. Therefore those projects have extended and intensified co-operative activities in areas of common interests based on the reciprocity principle.

Chile developed diverse kinds of projects focused on the decentralisation and governance implementation. For example one could consider two projects materialised in this area: the "Governance and decentralisation integrated programme" and "Basic programme of support to the implementation of the association agreement". Similarly, Mexico implemented projects related with consolidation of the rule of law and institutional support in two areas of intervention: reform of the judicial system, and some action in terms of human rights.

An excellent example of the impact of norms in terms of "normative discourse" was about the concept of "social cohesion". That helped to analyse poverty, inequality and social exclusion in Chilean public policies during democratic governments (after the 1990s). The new co-operation strategy between the EU and Mexico 2007–13 focused on three priority areas: social cohesion and underpinning other dialogues about domestic policies; economy and competitiveness; and education and culture. Besides both Chile and Mexico included poverty, rural and indigenous areas, and gender topics in their public agendas through some projects such as the "Global programme to overcome urban poverty" (ACTUA II) and "Environment recovery and socio–productive development in rural and indigenous areas of the IX region of Araucanía 'Living Land', and 'Integrated and sustainable social development in Chiapas" in Chile and Mexico, respectively.

In sum in the EU "social cohesion" is defined as an objective in the social policy agenda. This term "and the processes derived from this is an essentially political issue, given that the State must be the main protagonist and the construction of citizenship should be one of its most important pillars" (Barros Lazaeta 2005: 8). The agreement issues were incorporated into the public agendas of Chilean and Mexican governments (Espinoza-Figueroa 2013) as part of developing "specific policies". Both countries aligned their political interests and governing projects with European topics.

The political dialogue impacting upon domestic policies in Chile and Mexico

The EU develops different manners of external affairs. Since the Second World War the Union has transformed into an important actor on the international stage (Smith 2001). European relationships with third countries have played different roles around the world, considering European constitutive and historical nature, types of global ties and mechanisms that the EU has used to establish strategic alliances in the international arena.

This third section analyses the ties between the EU, Chile and Mexico, specifically: how the EU influenced the development of domestic policies (by the nature of its relationships since 1997), and their effects in the constitution of identity processes. Therefore it is possible to observe European effects or "influential zones" when Chile and Mexico adopted different European models as part of regulation processes within the agreements.

If one uses an empirical perspective, political and social effects occurred due to a unique relationship between the EU, Chile and Mexico. These influences allowed propagation and expansion of specific European norms, regarding models, values, ideas, opinions, concepts etc.

The higher education area

From the 2000s until the present day the development of specific rapid changes has been observable in a significant number of Latin American HE institutions due to an intervening variable within the process, a sort of external influence. This phenomenon can be described as the manifestation of new ideas circulating throughout Latin American HE, especially in Chile and Mexico. At the outset these ideas have transmuted methods and tools applicable for transforming Chilean and Mexican HE. Such ideas were not coming, as they usually did, from the US: instead they were arriving from the EU as part of a more significant phenomenon occurring in Europe, in the form of the Bologna Process and its executive instrument, the Tuning Project.

The Bologna Process was a well-known endeavour born in 1999 when forty-six European countries launched a vast project to create a European Higher Education Area, rebuilding their systems to reach a significant convergence in standard procedures, mechanisms, methods and reference points. Besides, the Tuning Project was an initiative launched by a group of European universities in the summer of 2000 to take up the Bologna Process as a challenge. This pilot project was called "Tuning educational structures in Europe" and constitutes the practical materialisation of the Bologna Process. It addresses several of the Bologna action lines to adopt a system based on two cycles and establish a credit system. Thus, I give the name "European Model" to the Bologna Process and the Tuning Project (2013), called by Adelman "the most far-reaching and ambitious reform of higher education ever undertaken" (2009: 2).

Structural changes happened throughout the process of implementing the Bologna Process in Chilean and Mexican HE. These impacted public policies, curriculum and study programmes in Chilean and Mexican universities. In practical terms the effects of the Bologna Process on Chilean HE can be seen as strengthening the role of state and HE institutions. Concretely this phenomenon was characterised by the presence of significant changes specifically in three fields of HE: (1) the implementation of institutional adjustments within the planning of institutional policies, (2) the development of specific public policies and (3) the use of "Bologna Language" in institutional and official documents, in speeches and in expressing the opinions of experts and academic authorities (Espinoza-Figueroa 2013).

Chile and Mexico

Since 2005 I have studied the progress of European concepts flowing throughout the field of Latin American HE, as part of the Bologna Process and the Tuning Project. This phenomenon was manifested in procedures, methods and tools that contributed to the transformation of Chilean HE (Espinoza-Figueroa 2013). The effects of the Bologna Process on Chilean HE can be detected in the consolidation of the Chilean state's role and HE institutions.

Chilean universities worked on teaching and learning, structuring curricula, and public policies focused on diffusing and implementing the Bologna Process through the Tuning Latin America Project (2004). Besides this new actors within HE institutions and governments, such as the Council of Rectors (Vice-Chancellors) of Chilean Universities (CRUCH), have played a significant role in diffusing and managing European influences. Even though these changes represent pragmatic effects, they were oriented to transform HE continually into renovating knowledge. These transformations implied the construction of a conceptual building more complex and more concentrated than hitherto. This process also involved adopting new approaches and teaching forms focused on lifelong learning. The Bologna Process encouraged universities to implement programmes that allow mobility and flexibility in a global world and guarantee the quality of studies.

The most significant impact observed is in the structural base of the educational models of Chilean universities. That occurred through implementing the Transferable Credit System at both graduate and postgraduate levels. Most state universities refer in their documentation to the historical process in which the European Higher Education Area is formed. The European effects are evident in educational projects and models of the vast majority of HE institutions (Espinoza-Figueroa 2013; 2021). Other impacts were noticed in international accreditation mechanisms. Chilean universities used European agencies to define and implement their quality-assurance processes (Espinoza-Figueroa 2021).

Nowadays the European model is impacting upon internationalisation processes within Chilean university and public policies. This phenomenon is characterised by a more institutionalised flow of academic and student mobility and the internationalisation of research clusters. Here effects are seen as part of guiding principles, normative processes and curricular management (Espinoza-Figueroa 2021). This phenomenon can be observed in the description of its educational models associated with the Bologna Process, and the establishment of international agreements and projects such as Erasmus and Alban, and European postgraduate accreditations.

In terms of Chilean public policies, European ideas have had a significant impact on three main aspects: (1) the mechanism of allocating public financial resources (MECESUP, Programme for the Improvement of the Quality and Equity of Education in Chile); (2) a new culture of planning and assessing projects for HE; and (3), in an indirect way, the National Accreditation System which has come under European influence. If one considers university policies, European ideas have substantially impacted curricular architecture and the curricular re-engineering processes in traditional Chilean universities. The effect is also visible in constructing a National Academic Credit System (STC – Chile) and in developments of internationalisation and accreditation of Chilean HE institutions (Espinoza-Figueroa 2013; 2021).

The Consortium of Mexican Universities (CUMEX) and technological institutions were direct "recipients" of the process. However, the CUMEX acted as the head of the process, not only leading campaigns to promote Bologna but also suggesting "loudly" its implementation among its HE institutions. In parallel the National Association of Universities and Institutions of Higher Education co-ordinated workshops and conferences, disseminating amongst Mexican institutions the "state of the art" Bologna Process and their adaptation and implementation activities.

At public policies level the main actor was the Secretariat of State Education, which acted as a simple diffuser of the Bologna Process and the Tuning Project. Its instruments for circulating information were also the EULAC/ALCUE and the Tuning Latin America Project. One of the effects of European "guidance" was developing a new culture of planning and assessing HE projects. Another public policy implemented due to the impact of European ideas was the placing of the National Tuning Centre firmly within the Secretariat of State Education. Furthermore, it was possible to discern an indirect effect on HE's accreditation and evaluation process through the National Centre for the Evaluation of Higher Education. European ideas have had impact on three significant university policies: the internationalisation process of Mexican HE institutions; the design of curricular architecture and the implementation of the Tuning Methodology (Beneitone and Yarosh 2015; Espinoza-Figueroa 2018).

Some Mexican authorities argue that Mexican universities implemented the Tuning Project but "à l'Européenne". In Chile universities had begun the process of "negotiating" with their European partners before Tuning Latin America was fully articulated.

Actors in both countries played the roles of diffusers and co-ordinators of the Bologna Process. However, Bologna impacted Chile more strongly on both fronts, public and university policies. In contrast Mexico was affected only in the planning of institutional or university policies. Chile followed domestic policies determined by the Ministry of Education and the CRUCH to implement HE changes. In contrast Mexico preferred to concentrate on international policies. It has joined large agreements such as EULAC/ALCUE, using the Latin America Tuning Project as an umbrella to make changes. Mexican technological institutes and some public and private universities, taking into account welcome suggestions from the OECD, have made some sporadic efforts to follow the Bologna Process and the Tuning Project.

At this point one can recognise that in Chile and Mexico the Tuning Latin America Project was simply the vehicle of diffusion, the diffuser of the Bologna Process. However, the main argument is that one of the weightiest tools of formally instituting a political dialogue has been the Bologna Process with its intrinsic Tuning Project (Espinoza-Figueroa 2013).

The Bologna Process constituted a -setting of standards. Chile and Mexico followed European models to design their higher education. Thus Europe can be considered a model-maker or model-offerer impacting on Latin American HE from the "birth" of universities there, whilst Latin America is observed as a traditional model-taker. Therefore, the EU plays the role of a global teacher (Adelman 2009 170), i.e. the Union is spreading and exporting its model beyond the geographical boundaries of Europe.

Science and technology areas

Science and technology are central elements contributing to co-operation among countries beyond the EU. Scientific and technological collaboration between the EU, Chile and Mexico has become an essential aspect of sustainable economic and social development in both regions.

Chile and the EU share a common interest in facing several global and regional challenges. Science, research, innovation and technology are among the priorities of their relationships, and they are reflected in the signing of a scientific co-operation agreement in 2002.

The Agreement of Scientific and Technological Co-operation between Mexico and the EU derives from the Agreement of Economic Association, Political Agreement and Co-operation between the EC and its member states and the United Mexican states in 1997. In article 29 the treaty identified science and technology as an area of co-operation of particular interest, establishing at the time the possibility of formalising an agreement on the matter. Therefore science and technology co-operation feature the New Global Agreement between the EU and Mexico. The meeting showed how both sides are co-operating in areas of mutual benefit through academic and research exchanges.

The Global Agreement of 1997 governs the political, commercial and co-operation relations between the EU and Mexico. Since 2008 Mexico has been a strategic partner of the EU. The government of Mexico and the EU, through the Consejo Nacional de Ciencia y Tecnología (National Council for Science and Technology) and the EC respectively, formalised the Scientific and Technological Co-operation Agreement, which entered into force in 2005, was renewed in 2010 and had a validity of five years. After eight rounds of political dialogue, in 2020 Mexico and the EU concluded negotiations for the modernisation of the commercial pillar of the Agreement. The new agreement included political, economic and co-operation issues to strengthen the political dialogue, improve trade and investment and increase technical and scientific co-operation among both parties.

This co-operation agreement aims to stimulate, develop and facilitate co-operation activities between the EU and Mexico in areas of common interest where research and development activities in science and technology are carried out. The agreement focuses on mutual-benefit principles, reciprocal opportunities for participation in research and technological development activities, timely exchange of information, and the protection and equitable distribution of intellectual property.

Therefore it is possible to distinguish a "new process", a "network of excellence". The network of excellence implies scientific knowledge as part of European influences "and partnership in social, cultural and human affairs: developing human resources, promoting understanding between cultures and exchanges between civil societies" (Diez 2005: 630). For example the so-called "BILAT" projects, as an institutional platform, have promoted interaction between European and Latin American scientific communities and fundamentally facilitated access to calls for EU framework programmes.

European and Latin American scientists are working according to the terms of their respective agreements, focusing on durable integration of research groups' capabilities, constituting a critical mass of resources and knowledge to achieve leadership and transform virtual centres of excellence. Besides, 65 per cent of Chilean[4] and 26 per cent of Mexican[5] scholars and students have taken advantage of different scholarship programmes to study in European institutions.

Both Chile and Mexico have actively participated in Horizon 2020 to transform the future through research and innovation. Co-operation for research between the EU, Mexico and Chile under the Horizon 2020 programme has contributed to greater social cohesion, profitable opportunities and better quality of life in the continents (Espinoza-Figueroa 2018).

Nevertheless, Alejandra Kern (2018)[6] offers a critical perspective about the EU's co-operation in science and technology. She argues that development co-operation and scientific-technological assistance have run parallel in a minor scale or with no linkage channels in parallel. According to her, instruments and frameworks for European collaboration with Latin America and Caribbean countries have been a good example of this dissociation. With countries presenting higher scientific and technological development such as Argentina, Brazil, Chile and Mexico, the EU has established scientific and technological collaboration agreements, which have not had a programmatic articulation with other mutual aid instruments.

Thus co-operation for development and scientific-technological collaboration pursued different policy objectives. The first structured purpose was focused on a superior goal that sought particular interests of European "donor states": the development of Latin American recipients. The second aim was founded on all countries' interest in increasing their research and innovation capabilities, improving their international competitiveness. The common point is that both types of co-operation took place in the same context of asymmetries. The second objective did not intend to diminish the asymmetries and, consequently, an essential resource was left aside to promote developing countries' economic and social progress (Kern 2018; Sianes et al. 2018).

Productive and social areas

According to the report of NU-CEPAL (2015), this area of European influences signified an in-depth understanding for small- and medium-sized enterprises (SMEs). They meant structural change for development, innovation and value chains. For example, the VI Framework Programme contemplated encouraging SMEs to participate in research consortiums created to shape networks of excellence.

The effects were observed within economic development policy and policies for SMEs such as:

- the development of clusters, districts and the linkage to global value chains
- the governance of networks and processes of learning
- the importance of social capital for entrepreneurship and innovation
- the creation of firm, business incubators, scienentres and academic spin-offs
- evolutionary processes within the manufacturing sector and high-tech industries
- the role of the informal economy in developing and industrialised countries.

In policies for industrial development, European influences were seen in two fields: (1) innovation policies of business system: Chilean and Mexican entrepreneurs followed European and Italian industrial development models, i.e. industrial development associated with analysis and policy-making; (2) creation of projects that embody European types of industrial policy. In that sense, Latin American countries were opened up, learning and transferring knowledge from European models and experiences.

There are significant differences between Latin American and European perceptions about the political dialogue in social and productive areas, according to a study prepared by the Association of European Chambers of Commerce and Industry (EUROCHAMBRES)[7] with the financial support of the Services Consortium of the AL-INVEST programme.

Whilst more than half of Latin American representatives of SMEs evaluated working with the EU as "good or very good", most of their European partners assessed it as "regular, poor or very poor". Considering Latin American perceptions, people believe that the EU has been focused on "the larger economies and on trade issues, and that an aid-based and subsidiary mindset has prevailed" (ECLAC/AL-INVEST 2013: 14), whilst European partners have been very critical about "the institutional, top-down nature of those relations, which leaves little room for participation by the private sector and in particular by small firms" (2013: 14), which the EU has called "social dialogue".

The report "Impact Evaluation of SME Programs in Latin America and the Caribbean, the International Bank for Reconstruction and Development / The World Bank" (López Acevedo and Hong 2010)[8] recognises that Chile has developed significant improvements in a series of intermediate activities such as training, incorporation of new technology and organisational practices. Besides, Chilean SMEs present positive achievements in sales, labour productivity, wages and employment, this last to a lesser degree. Nevertheless, Chile has not structured a primary and robust system for evaluating effects of programmes.

According to the same study (2010), the case of Mexico is scarcely different. It invested significant public resources to support SMEs, but these were not well assessed. Although Mexico has offered a great range of SME programmes, the design has not proposed a coherent framework to adjust programmes more efficiently and strategically to avoid overlapping plans. Like Chile, Mexican SMEs have not enough valuable data for making decisions. The changeable Mexican system of programmes, always in evolution in terms of names, structures, closing and opening plans, represents a considerable challenge for making rigorous assessments of effects.

When Westphalian logic and its inconsistencies prevail, in the face of the emerging global governance scenarios, the responsibility for co-operation policies appears easily elusive by not having legal, political or administrative frameworks of a binding nature. Therefore, its impact remains highly contingent, and its legitimacy questioned. This situation occurs even in processes of institutionalised inter-regionalism, where development co-operation plays an important role, and responsibility for the instruments of the policy is assumed by formal regional organisations, as is the case with the collaboration between the EU, Chile and Mexico (Sianes et al. 2018).

The political and juridical-institutional imbalance occurs in the interaction between domestic and transnational levels. That affects crucial aspects of the policy, such as the transfer of sovereignty or the democratic legitimacy of decisions. Scartascini et al. (2011), studying the nature of Latin American public policies for a long time, believe that policies in the transnational sphere, not necessarily driven by the states, are interdependent, appearing from multiple centres without a hierarchy. Similarly, Stone (2008) considers that decision-making occurs in a dispersed manner due to the fragmentation of governance. Therefore there is a significant gap between benefactor's offer (the EU) as co-operation, and what the recipient does with that collaboration.

Conclusions

Formal relations between the EU and Latin America and the Caribbean started formally due to the EU intervention in Central America in the 1980s for contributing to the peace process through the San José progression (Smith 2002). After this, in the 1990s, the EU sought to move forward in its relations with Latin America, inaugurating new institutionalised relationships through sub-regional and regional groups to establish, as Hill and Smith (2005) suggest, a "new strategic partnership".

The EU moved its relations with Latin America towards some forms of "associated status" with Chile and Mexico, which established third- and fourth-generation agreements. Through this status they participated actively in social and co-operation programmes, increasing links between the EU and Latin America, and strengthened European influences in developing domestic policies in Chile and Mexico. The (association) agreements constituted a "gatekeeper", which allowed establishing contact zones or influence areas between the parties (the EU, Chile and Mexico).

The analysis described 'influenced zones' such as HE, science and technology, and productive and social areas. For example, in HE, the Chilean and Mexican universities changed their graduate and postgraduate programmes to work with or follow the Bologna Process. With respect to political dialogue, after the association agreement between EU, Chile and Mexico entered into force, some "ONG institutions" were constituted (or were created) to reproduce or diffuse the European political model: EUROLATINO in Chile and observatories of effects in Mexico.

In science and technology, Chile and Mexico incorporated European scientific programmes, and they developed their scientific knowledge in a European way. Additionally, this area has facilitated the development of scholarship programmes to Latin American postgraduate students. Intellectual knowledge is being acquired in European studies centres with European study programmes.

If one considers productive and social areas, European influences signified an in-depth understanding for SMEs. That impacted the business system's innovation policies and the creation of projects following European industrial policy types.

European influence allowed propagation and expansion of specific European norms regarding models, values, ideas, opinions and concepts in developing domestic policies in Chile and Mexico. That was observed by adopting European models in terms of the constitution of framework documents, creating institutions and generating projects.

In a still Westphalian world order, there is consensus about the need for co-operation, but not so much on how to do it (Barnett and Sikkink 2010). Specifically, co-operation requires us to articulate explicitly the technical aspects at the domestic level, with the institutional arrangements promoted from the new governance formulas of sovereignty, which implies the regulation of obligations acquired between the parties (Chayes and Handler Chayes 1995).

It is essential to reflect that the future of the European political dialogue is still part of the EU external relationships and agreements. Nowadays there is a very realistic world, determined by the commercial conflict between the US and China, the lack of progress with the Doha Round, numerous regional trade agreements and the compromises of diverse WTO-plus agreements. Therefore one can ask whether it is convenient for the EU to continue establishing treaties of the last generation and exercising a soft power to show itself as a pedagogic actor (Adelman 2009) within the international arena. The answer is that the "jungle" needs a gentle power such as the EU (Padoa-Schioppa 2001).

References

All websites last visited 30 September 2021.
Adelman, C. (2009). "The Bologna Process for the U.S. Eyes. Re-learning higher education in the age of convergence", Washington, DC: Institute for Higher Education Policy. https://files.eric.ed.gov/fulltext/ED504904.pdf.
Ahumada, J. M. (2019). *The Political Economy of Peripheral Growth. Chile in the Global Economy*. Geneva: Palgrave Macmillan.
Álvarez, J. E. (2000). "Multilateralism and its discontents". *EJIL* 11 (2), 393–411.
Barnett, M. and Sikkink, K. (2010). "From international relations to global society", in Reus-Smit, C. and Snidal, D. (eds). *The Oxford Handbooks of Political Science*, pp. 63–83. Oxford: Oxford University Press.
Barros Lazaeta, L. (2005). "Reflections about social cohesion". *Focus Eurolatino Journal* 6, Justice and Democracy Corporation.
Beneitone, P. and Yarosh, M. (2015). "Tuning impact in Latin America: is there implementation beyond design?", *Tuning Journal for Higher Education* 3 (1),187–216. http://www.tuningjournal.org/.
Bianculli, A. C. (2016), "Latin America", in Börzel, T. A. and Risse, T (eds), *The Oxford Handbook of Comparative Regionalism*, pp. 155–77. Oxford: Oxford University Press.
Bindi, F. (2012). "European foreign policy: a historical overview", in Bindi, F. and Angelescu, I. (eds). *The Foreign Policy of the European Union. Assessing Europe's Role in the World*, second edition. Washington, DC: The Brookings Institution.
Bindi, F. and Angelescu, I. (eds) (2012). *The Foreign Policy of the European Union. Assessing Europe's Role in the World*, second edition. Washington, DC: The Brookings Institution.
Blanc Altemir, A. (2005): "Los tres pilares del acuerdo de asociación Chile–Unión Europea: diálogo político, cooperación y comercio", Estudios Internacionales 38 (151), 73–116. doi:10.5354/0719-3769.2011.14393.
Börzel, T. A. and Risse, T. (2016). *The Oxford Handbook of Comparative Regionalism*. Oxford: Oxford University Press.

Bretherton, C. and Vogler, J. (2006). *The European Union as a Global Actor*, second edition. Abingdon: Routledge.

Chayes, A. and Handler Chayes, A. (1995). *The New Sovereignty: Compliance with International Regulatory Agreements*. Cambridge, MA, and London: Harvard University Press.

De Lombaerde, P. and Schulz, M (2009). *The EU and World Regionalism: The Makability of Regions in the 21st Century* (New Regionalisms Series). Farnham:Ashgate

Diez, T. (2005). "Constructing the self and changing others: reconsidering normative power Europe", *Millennium: Journal of International Studies* 33 (3), 613–36. https://doi.org/10.1177/03058298050330031701.

ECLAC/AL-INVEST (2013). *Building SME Competitiveness in the European Union and Latin America and the Caribbean. Policy Proposals by the Private Sector*. https://repositorio.cepal.org/bitstream/handle/11362/3093/1/S2013022_en.pdf.

Espinoza-Figueroa, F. (2013). *European Influence on the Development of Domestic Policies in Chile and Mexico: The Case of Higher Education*. PhD thesis, University of Birmingham. https://etheses.bham.ac.uk/id/eprint/3855/.

Espinoza-Figueroa, F. (2018). "Higher education (HE) in Chile as a strategy of international cooperation: analysis of American, European and Asian models". Project Fondecyt de Iniciación 2015–2018. No. 11150378.

Espinoza-Figueroa, F. (2021). "Modelos de internacionalización, una mirada comparativa de nuestros sistemas nacionales de acreditación", *Cuadernos de Investigación* 17. Comisión Nacional de Acreditación, CNA-Chile.

Espinoza-Figueroa, F. (2021). "The Tuning Project as a global actor. The EU impacts upon policies of Higher education", Freres, C., Gratius, S., Mallo, T., Pellicer, A. and Sanahuja, J. A. (eds) (2006). *¿Para qué sirve el diálogo político entre la Unión Europea y América Latina?* Madrid: Casa de América, FRIDE, Fundación Carolina, ICEI.

Gómez Arana, A. (2017). *The European Union's Policy towards Mercosur. Responsive Not Strategic*. Manchester: Manchester University Press.

Hill, C. and Smith, M. (2005): *International Relations and the European Union*. Oxford: Oxford University Press.

Kern, A. (2018). "Ciencia y tecnología, ¿una prioridad para la cooperación?" www.somosiberoamerica.org/tribunas/ciencia-y-tecnologia-cooperacion/.

Levi Coral, M. (2007). "El diálogo político como pilar de las relaciones entre la Unión Europea y América Latina: reflexiones sobre su desarrollo y contenido". Centro de Investigaciones y Proyectos Especiales, CIPE, Facultad de Finanzas, Gobierno y Relaciones Internacionales. Universidad Externado de Colombia. Oasis, No. 12, pp. 483–93.

López Acevedo, G. and Hong, W. T. (2010). *Impact Evaluation of SME Programs in Latin America and Caribbean*. The International Bank for Reconstruction and Development / The World Bank.

Moxon-Browne, E. (2015). "A two-way mirror. Latin American perceptions of European integration", in Winand, P., Benvenuti, A. and Guderzo, M. (eds), *The External Relations of the European Union*, pp. 275–90. P.I.E. Brussels: Peter Lang. .

NU-CEPAL (2015). "Reinforcing production cooperation and dialogue spaces: the role of SMEs". ECLAC. https://repositorio.cepal.org/bitstream/handle/11362/38243/1/S1500521_en.pdf.

Orbie, J. (2009). *Europe's Global Role. External Policies of the European Union*. Farnham: Ashgate.

Padoa-Schioppa, T. (2001). *Europe's Gentle Power*. Bologna: Il Mulino.

Richardson, J. (2001). *European Union: Power and Policy-making*, second edition. Abingdon: Routledge.
Sanahuja, J. A. (2004). "Un diálogo estructurado y plural", *Revista Nueva Sociedad* 189, 80–96.
Scartascini, C., Spiller, P., Stein, E. and Tommasi, M. (eds) (2011). *El juego político en América Latina ¿Cómo se deciden las políticas públicas?* Washington, DC: Banco Interamericano de Desarrollo.
Sianes, A., Santos Carillo, F. and Fernández Portillo, L. A. (2018). "Acordes y desacuerdos en la política de cooperación de la UE con América Central", *Revista CIDOB d'Afers Internacionals* 120 (December), 119–45.
Smith, H. (2002). *European Union Foreign Policy. What It Is and What It Does.* London: Pluto Press.
Smith, K. E. (2003). "The European Union as a distinctive actor in international relations", *The Brown Journal of World Affairs* 9 (2), 103–13. www.jstor.org/stable/24590469.
Smith, M. (2001). "The EU as an international actor", in Richardson, J. (ed.), *European Union: Power and Policy-making*, second edition. Abingdon: Routledge.
Stone, D. (2008). "Global public policy, transnational policy communities, and their networks", *Policy Studies Journal*, 36 (1), 19–38.
Torrent, R. (2005). *Las relaciones Unión Europea – América Latina en los últimos diez años: el resultado de la inexistencia de una política.* Barcelona: OBREAL–EULARO.
Torrent, R. and Polanco, R. (2016). "Análisis de la próxima modernización del pilar comercial del acuerdo global entre la Unión Europea y México". Comisión de Comercio Internacional del Parlamento Europeo. www.europarl.europa.eu/RegData/etudes/STUD/2016/534012/EXPO_STU(2016)534012_ES.pdf.
Winand, P., Benvenuti, A. and Guderzo, M. (eds) (2015). *The External Relations of the European Union.* P.I.E. Brussels: Peter Lang.
Zabludovsky K. J. and Gómez Lora, S. (2015). *The European Window: Challenges in the Negotiation of Mexico's Free Trade Agreement with the European Union.* Special Initiative on Trade and Integration. INTAL – ITD. Working Paper – SITI-09.

Notes

1 G-Rio originally constituted a long-lasting association of political discussion created on 18 December 1986 in Rio de Janeiro, Brazil. Its main objective was to create a better political relationship among Latin America and Caribbean countries. It was replaced by the Community of Latin American and Caribbean States (CELAC).
2 https://eprints.ucm.es/39070/1/Published%20version_ES.pdf.
3 Justice and Democracy Corporation.
4 www.nexstepchile.cl/guia-becas-chile-2020/.
5 http://publicaciones.anuies.mx/pdfs/revista/Revista125_S3A1ES.pdf.
6 www.somosiberoamerica.org/tribunas/ciencia-y-tecnologia-cooperacion/.
7 https://repositorio.cepal.org/bitstream/handle/11362/3093/1/S2013022_en.pdf.
8 http://documents.worldbank.org/curated/en/319161468337915156/pdf/526680ENGLISH010evaluation01PUBLIC1.pdf.

Conclusion: The more things change the more they stay the same?

María J. García and Arantza Gómez Arana

Mass protests on the streets of Bolivia, Ecuador, and even South America's most stable democracy, Chile, marked the end of the 2010s. Demonstrations were motivated in all cases by lack of progress in improving social conditions for the middle classes and large parts of the population. Argentina had just elected Alberto Fernández, a protégé of the Kirchners, as its new president, and negotiations were under way to renegotiate a loan with the IMF. Brazil's Jair Bolsonaro was losing popularity at the same time that the former President Lula da Silva was freed from jail, after the Brazilian Supreme Court determined that prison sentences in the "Jato Lavato" corruption case should commence only once the final decision on the case had been made (see Crabb 2019).

After years of sustained economic growth in Latin America, in part fuelled by Chinese demand for energy, minerals, raw materials and agricultural products, Latin America found itself, once again, gripped by financial and political instability. Despite a series of left-leaning governments taking power in the last decade, in the so-called "pink tide" (Spronk 2008), Latin American countries continue to display some of the highest rates of inequality anywhere in the world (Rojas 2017).

In Europe the "gilets jaunes" protesters in France started making the same demands of their government as the peoples of Latin America throughout 2019: more affordable costs of living, and demands for social justice after a decade of austerity policies in the aftermath of the 2008 financial crisis, are leading to increasingly fragmented political systems and even ungovernability (Boyer et al. 2020). On 10 November 2019 Spain held its fourth election in as many years. In the UK the result of the Brexit referendum of 2016 has been linked to social inequality (O'Reilly et al. 2016), and has completely divided the country, leading to a highly divided Parliament which struggled to reach agreement on how to navigate and negotiate the exit from the EU. On 12 December 2019 the UK returned to the polls, for the third time in three years. Boris Johnson's victory changed parliamentary arithmetic and led to the UK's departure from the EU on 31 January 2020, and to frantic negotiations for a trade and co-operation agreement with the EU that secured a post-Brexit relationship as of 1 January 2021.

These are not the only regions in the world beset by upheavals; however, the current situations serve as reminders of the many similarities that exist between Latin America and Europe. Latin American democratic and political formal institutions were inspired by those in Europe. Cultural ties and traditions, rooted in a shared historical religious faith with a social justice mission, underpin the social demands being made on both sides of the Atlantic. Despite their commitments to these values, both regions are increasingly struggling to deliver social improvements. The rise of economic competitors in Asia, not least the rise of China, the fallout of the financial crisis, which may have started in the US but spread to Europe and beyond as a result of the rise of global finance in the preceding decades, challenges narratives of continued progress and aspirations to ever-improving living conditions.

Over the last decades the EU and Latin America have grown closer together, in terms of challenges they face and their institutionalised links. Ironically, at the same time they have also become farther apart as a result of the economic challenges in both regions and exogenous global changes and pressures.

Institutionally, the dense network of institutional and political relations that have, since the 1980s, characterised the relationship between the EU,[1] as an entity, and Latin America continue. As the chapters by Susanne Gratius and Bruno Luciano suggest, these are flourishing at the formal level more so than in terms of substance as genuine fora to reach policy decisions. Susanne Gratius divides institutional dialogues into three categories: (1) a global governance based on inter-regional CELAC–EU and Brazil–EU dialogues; (2) a democratic conditionality-driven dialogue as part of the trade, co-operation and association agreements (Chile, Mexico, Colombia–Ecuador–Peru and Central America); and (3) a shared problem-focused sector dialogue on concrete issues (drugs, migration, social cohesion, environment etc.). Tracing the evolution of these dialogues over time, she concludes that EU attempts at inter-regional engagement through dialogues with CELAC, or region-to-region dialogues on key issues, have been stymied by the absence of monitoring of progress and follow-up, and by the heterogeneous interests of Latin American governments. By contrast, dialogue and co-operation relations enshrined in trade agreements facilitate monitoring through the annual joint committees established by the agreements. Roberto Dominguez's chapter demonstrates how the implementation of the co-operation pillar of the EU–Mexico Global Agreement of 2003 enabled the parties to move through the gridlock of global governance at the multilateral level (slowdown at WTO, election of President Trump), clearing a path for the successful negotiation of the modernisation of the global agreement. Nonetheless, on a series of crucial social issues, such as the situation of trade unionists in Colombia, even the stricter monitoring of a trade agreement, and the human rights roadmaps mandated by the European Parliament ahead of ratification, do not deliver immediate changes on the ground, but rather set the framework for greater external pressure on the issues (García's chapter).

Beyond government-level interactions, inter-parliamentary dialogues have also been firmly institutionalised within transatlantic relations. As with other high-level inter-regional dialogues, Eurolat has failed to reach agreements. Subsequent decisions and plans for action on key issues, such as the deteriorating social situation in Venezuela, have failed to materialise, given different views on the matter and Latin American states' opposition to intervention in domestic political affairs. None the less, Luciano's chapter highlights the positive value of inter-regional parliamentary dialogues, by allowing transcontinental co-operation amongst political party families, and creating a space where different points of view on controversial matters can be discussed, even if no agreement is reached and no action ensues.

Economically, however, and despite stronger ties with key economies through preferential trade agreements and solid trade and investment relations, the EU has been losing economic weight in Latin America. If in the 1990s the EU was the top trade partner for countries in MERCOSUR and Chile, and second (after the US) for Central America and Andean countries, in 2017 the EU was the second trade partner (after the US) for Central American and Caribbean countries only. It lost its position to China in the remaining markets, and was second trade partner to MERCOSUR after China, and third (after the US and China) to Mexico and Chile and the Andean Community (Grieger and Harte 2018: 6). This relative loss in significance comes despite increased trade flows resulting from the preferential trade agreements that the EU has established in the region, with Mexico and Chile at the turn of the millennium (2000 and 2003 respectively) and later on with Central America, Peru and Colombia (2012) and Ecuador (2017). A decline in European demand following the financial crisis (2008) and Eurocrisis, which peaked around 2012, dovetailed in time with increasing demand for primary products from China. Although the EU remains the top source of investment in Latin America (in part due to the historical accumulation of foreign direct investment stocks in the region) (EEAS 2018), and top provider of aid, the speed with which China became a key partner for Latin American states in the 2010s was dramatic, and reflects the broader geopolitical and geo-economic shifts occurring at the global level.

Chapters in this volume considering specific trade-agreement negotiations coincide in stressing the key role of the international trading environment and events in determining the start, timings and relative successes or failures in negotiations (Schade; García; Dominguez; Sanahuja and Rodríguez). The EU's initial focus on the negotiation of trade agreements with Latin American countries in the late 1990s to early 2000s responded largely to geo-economic competition with the US in the Western Hemisphere (García; see also Meissner 2018). Trade negotiations prospered with governments aligned with a liberalisation agenda (Schade), and languished where governments affected by the crises of 1998–2002 (Brazil, and especially Argentina) opted for neo-developmental policies (Sanahuja and Rodríguez). Alignment of approaches is important in trade negotiations, but, as this volume demonstrates, exogenous pressures can serve as critical enticement to overcome differences. Daniel Schade shows how the Ecuadorian government's opposition to an agreement with the EU was overcome once Ecuadorian exporters, particularly banana exporters, started to see their competitors in Colombia and Peru being able to export under more beneficial terms to the EU given their trade agreement. An even greater incentive was the EU's reform of its GSP, which would see Ecuadorian exporters losing the preferential access to the EU market they had enjoyed under GSP (Schade). María García's chapter emphasises the parallelism between Andean states' trade agreements with the US and EU, arising from the EU's desire to balance US economic advantages. Both powers' motivations to seek a bilateral trade negotiation route, after the dilution of the negotiation agenda at the WTO's Doha Round, are responses to developments in the international system.

In the 2010s the need to respond to a decade of gridlock at the WTO and other multilateral fora, resulting in an inability to co-operate via international institutions to address international policy problems (Hale and Held 2017), has encouraged the successful modernisation of the global agreement between the EU and Mexico (Dominguez) and the reactivation and conclusion of two decades of EU–MERCOSUR negotiations (Sanahuja and Rodríguez). These agreements are seen as a "counterbalance to a decade of global economic slowdown, contestation of the global liberal order and emergence of economic nationalism" in particular under President Trump's administration, including his initial threats to "tear up" NAFTA which led to its renegotiation (Dominguez). José Antonio Sanahuja and Jorge Rodríguez argue that, given the economic conditions in the countries concerned, and the diverging offensive and defensive interests of the parties in the EU–MERCOSUR agreement (Gómez Arana 2017), which account for the lengthy negotiations, the conclusion of negotiations of 2019 is hard to understand. Instead they explain this outcome as the result of a crisis of globalisation, highlighted in increased US protectionism during Donald Trump's presidency (January 2017 to January 2021), which "encouraged a 'defensive convergence' between the EU and Mercosur to ensure reciprocal access to their markets". They argue that the repoliticisation of trade negotiations, casting these as a defence of the liberal order, and a window of opportunity in terms of timing (the desire to complete negotiations ahead of a change of EC and Argentine elections in October 2019) were also key factors encouraging the parties to make sufficient concessions to each other to conclude the agreement.

This volume has shown how inter-regional relations have evolved over time, and how they have been mediated by exogenous factors, mainly US policies and economic crises, and more recently by the perceived crisis in globalisation. President Barack Obama's approach to trade policy, with his desire to engage in mega-regional agreements in the Pacific and Atlantic spaces in order to set the global trade rules, to bypass the WTO and stagnating Doha Round negotiations, and to counter Chinese economic power, helped to encourage MERCOSUR states to re-engage in negotiations with the EU (Gómez Arana 2017). Even more importantly, after the election of President Donald Trump in November 2016 the EU took on the baton of promotion of a liberal trade agenda and redoubled efforts to conclude ongoing trade negotiations with partners across the globe, in symbolic defiance of the US stance. The EU and MERCOSUR recast their agreement as mutual reinforcement in light of US policy and a defence of the liberal global order (Sanahuja and Rodríguez), and finally reached agreement for an association agreement in June 2019, after two decades of negotiations (European Commission 2019). The ratification process for this agreement is far from secure at the time of writing. France's President Macron insists on the need for MERCOSUR states, and in particular Brazil, to seriously commit to the Paris Agreement on climate change as a *sine qua non* for ratification of the agreement. Forest fires in the Amazonian region in 2019, and rumours that Brazilian President Jair Bolsonaro may have taken a lenient approach to these, led to a row in the media between the two presidents (Politico 2019). The focus on the climate agreement also enables President Macron to stymie the ratification of an agreement that has never been fully endorsed by the French government on account of farmers' concerns (Gómez Arana 2017). After two decades balancing domestic political and economic constraints, divergent economic interests, and responding to dramatic changes in the global trading environment, the EU–MERCOSUR Agreement is close to seeing the light of day, yet remains imperilled. After decades of closer institutional and political relations, and some successful projects, key transatlantic challenges like drugs trafficking, environmental and climate matters and development remain. Despite five trade agreements and the conclusion of the one with MERCOSUR, and a close economic relationship, of particular significance to Latin American states, the EU's relative importance in the region has been slowly decreasing since the Eurocrisis, reflecting broader power shifts internationally.

This tendency is likely to be amplified in the aftermath of the Covid-19 outbreak of 2020–21. Europe and Latin American states, like Brazil, have been amongst the worst-affected regions in terms of the spread of the disease, which has strained even the robust health systems of the EU. Government-imposed lockdowns have led to unprecedented contractions in economic growth. Major European investment and trade partners of Latin American states have suffered GDP losses estimated at 12.4 per cent for Spain, 10.3 per cent for the UK, 9.4 per cent for France, 5.6 per cent for Germany and 5.3 per cent for the Netherlands (Statista 2021). Latin American economies have also borne dramatic contractions of 7.7 per cent on average (with Peru experiencing –12.9 per cent GDP growth, Argentina –10.5 per cent, Ecuador –9 per cent, Colombia –7 per cent, Chile –6 per cent and Brazil –5.3 per cent) (CEPAL 2021). The tragic human costs of the Covid-19 health crisis unite Latin Americans and Europeans as never before, but the continents, beset by temporary cancellations of flights and travel bans to stem the spread of virus variants, feel farther apart than ever. Against this background, inter-regional institutional dialogues and co-operation have continued. At the twenty-fifth informal EU–Latin America ministerial meeting, the parties reiterated their willingness to co-operate internationally and to support the World Health Organisation in its endeavours to control the pandemic, as well as their commitments to the UN's sustainable development goals and to rebuilding economies in greener ways. They also stressed "that Covid-19 vaccines should be considered as a global public good that can only be provided through a multilateral approach" (EU–LAC 2020), and reiterated their commitment to the European approach to Covid co-operation through Team Europe. Team Europe "brings together the EU, its Member States and their diplomatic networks, and financial institutions such as the European Investment Bank (EIB)" and committed €2.4 billion to Latin America for Covid-19 emergency responses (EU–LAC 2020). A few weeks later the EU made headlines over its threats to ban the export of vaccines manufactured in the EU and its decision to register vaccine exports (Euractiv 2021), raising doubts about its commitments to supporting other countries in the fight against the virus, including those articulated at the meeting with Latin American states.

In the last years of the 2010s EU–Latin American co-operation for a united front in defence of the liberal order, exemplified in the conclusion of EU–MERCOSUR negotiations and motivated by the need to respond to Donald Trump's presidency, showed a renewed spirit of co-operation amongst two regions united by common values and goals. However, as in past decades, each side's complicated domestic political and economic situations, which the Covid-19 outbreak has exacerbated, threatens once again to relegate EU–Latin American relations in the hierarchy of foreign policy priorities.

References

All websites last visited 30 September 2021.

Boyer, P. C., Delemotte, T., Gauthier, G., Rollet, V. and Schmutz, B. (2020). "Les déterminants de la mobilisation des Gilets jaunes", *Revue économique* 71 (1), 109–38. www.jstor.org/stable/26895613.

CEPAL (2021). *Latin America and the Caribbean: Growth Projections for 2020 and 2021*. www.cepal.org/sites/default/files/pr/files/table_press_gdp_preliminaryoverview 2020-eng.pdf.

Crabb, J. (2019). "PRIMER: Operation Car Wash / Lava Jato", *International Financial Law Review*, 7 March.

EEAS (2018). *EU–LAC Relations*. https://eeas.europa.eu/sites/eeas/files/factsheet_ eu_lac.en__3.pdf.

Euractiv (2021). "EU's COVID-19 vaccine export ban risks global retaliation, warns pharma industry", 29 January. www.euractiv.com/section/coronavirus/news/eus-covid-19-vaccine-export-ban-risks-global-retaliation-warns-pharma-industry/.

European Commission (2019). "EU and Mercosur reach agreement on trade", Press Release, Brussels. http://trade.ec.europa.eu/doclib/press/index.cfm?id=2039.

EU–LAC Ministerial Meeting (2020). "Joint communiqué 25th EU–Latin America Informal Ministerial Meeting". Brussels, 14 December. https://eeas.europa.eu/headquarters/headquarters-homepage/90561/joint-communiqu%C3%A9-eu27-latin-america-and-caribbean-informal-ministerial-meeting_en.

García, M. (2015). "The European Union and Latin America: 'Transformative power Europe' versus the realities of economic interests", *Cambridge Review of International Affairs* 28 (4), 621–40.

Gómez Arana, A. (2017). "European Union policy-making towards Mercosur", in *the European Union's policy towards Mercosur. Responsive not Strategic*. Manchester: Manchester University Press.

Grieger, G. and Harte, R. (2018). "EU trade with Latin America and Caribbean. Overview and figures". European Parliament Research Service, PE 625.186.

Hale, T. and Held, D. (2017). *Beyond Gridlock*. Medford: Polity Press.

Meissner, K. L. (2018). *Commercial Realism and EU Trade Policy: Competing for Economic Power in Asia and the Americas*. Abingdon: Routledge.

O'Reilly, J., Froud, J., Johal, S., Williams, K., Warhurst, C., Morgan, G., Grey, C., Wood, G., Wright, M., Boyer, R. and Frerichs, S. (2016). "Brexit: understanding the socio-economic origins and consequences", *Socio-Economic Review* 14 (4), 807–54. https://doi.org/10.1093/ser/mww043.

Politico (2019). "Macron opposes Mercosur deal over Bolsonaro forest lie", 24 August. www.politico.eu/article/macron-opposes-mercosur-deal-over-bolsonaro-forest-lie/. www.jstor.org/stable/26895613.

Rojas, R. (2017). "The ebbing 'pink tide': an autopsy of left-wing regimes in Latin America", *New Labor Forum* 26 (2), 70–82.

Spronk, S. (2008). "Pink tide? Neoliberalism and its alternatives in Latin America", *Canadian Journal of Latin American and Caribbean Studies*, 33 (65), 173–86. https://doi.org/10.1080/08263663.2008.10816944.

Statista (2021). "Real gross domestic product growth rate forecasts in selected European countries from 2020 to 2021". www.statista.com/statistics/1102546/coronavirus-european-gdp-growth/.

Note

1 Prior to 1993, when the EU was legally created by the Treaty of Maastricht, the relationship was with the European Community.

Index

2030 Agenda 141, 146, 163, 169, 137

ACP 27, 46, 63
Africa 2, 8, 9, 17, 22, 46, 129
ALBA 15, 31, 59, 129
Andean Community 4, 27, 28–30, 33, 123, 124, 156, 175–178, 194
  Negotiations with EU 44–60, 66, 68–70
Argentina 2, 11, 12, 14–17, 43, 119, 120, 127, 130, 131, 134–136, 138, 142, 144, 145, 152, 176, 177, 185, 192, 195, 197
ASEAN 13, 18, 23, 50, 61
Asia 2, 12, 14, 19, 29, 41, 50, 63, 68, 69, 91, 120, 127, 128, 144, 193, 198
Association Agreement 30, 33, 36, 45, 118, 164, 178, 179, 188, 193, 196
  with Andean states 48, 50, 51, 54–56, 60
  with MERCOSUR 124–143
Atlantic Triangle 66

Belt and Road Initiative 14
Bolivia 13, 16, 31, 32, 40, 41, 124, 175, 178, 192
  Andean states-EU negotiations 47, 49–57, 59, 60, 66, 69
Bologna Process 180–183, 188, 189
Bolsonaro, Jair 1, 4, 8, 9, 16, 32, 121, 137, 141–143, 192, 196
Brazil 2–4, 8–11, 13–18, 24, 25, 27, 29–34, 39–41, 102, 119–121, 124–143, 146, 165, 174, 177, 185, 192, 193, 195–197
Amazon crisis 140
Brexit 1, 4, 7, 96, 97, 135–137, 192, 193
BRI 14, 21, 112
BRICs 2, 3, 9–17, 19, 20, 32, 129

Caribbean 13, 24–30, 35, 38–41, 46, 66, 105, 117, 118, 128, 142, 154, 157, 174, 176, 185, 187, 188, 194
CARICOM 27–29
CAP 125, 127
CELAC 12, 24, 16–31, 34, 36–41, 100, 105, 193
  Summits 158–161, 163–168
Central America 14, 24–29, 33, 36, 40, 41, 46, 50, 54–57, 68, 69, 100, 105, 118, 123, 124, 156, 172, 175–178, 188, 193, 194
Central American Common Market 4, 29
Chavez, Hugo 47
Chile 5, 12, 13, 15, 16, 19, 24, 25, 27–30, 32, 33, 34–36, 39, 40, 43, 62, 69, 82, 86, 90, 93, 100, 101, 105, 116, 118, 119, 123, 125, 126, 140, 148, 151, 172, 173, 175, 177–194, 197
China 12–21, 24–26, 29, 34, 35, 37–39, 41, 69, 94, 97, 102, 106, 117, 120, 127–129, 135, 137, 141, 144, 145, 161, 189, 193, 194

climate change 28, 32, 38, 39, 41, 103, 107, 137, 138, 140, 143, 146, 155, 162, 196
Colombia 40, 44, 100, 118, 124, 126, 161, 175, 176, 194, 195, 197
   FTA with EU 66–87
   labour unions 77–80
   negotiations of FTA 46–60
Contadora Group 26, 27
COREPER 50, 61
Correa, Rafael 50, 55
Costa Rica 13, 14, 175
Covid-19 24, 32, 97, 114, 142, 149, 167, 169, 197, 198
CPTTP 20, 99, 100
Cuba 11–13, 25–35, 37, 39, 59, 118, 161, 186

DAG 80, 81
DG RELEX 48, 49, 53
DG TRADE 45, 48, 53, 57, 58, 69
drugs 27, 28, 30, 31, 38, 106, 123, 162, 163, 173, 178, 193

Ecuador 13, 24, 25, 27, 28, 30, 33, 36, 40, 70, 82, 93, 118, 175, 192–195, 197
   Andean states-EU negotiations 44–47, 50–60, 66, 68, 69
EMIFCA 124
EUROLAT 28, 30, 35, 154, 155, 157–171, 194
European Commission 42, 45, 46, 51, 56, 58, 59, 61, 62, 69, 76, 81, 90, 93, 103–106, 108–110, 112–114, 118, 130, 137, 139, 140, 147, 148, 164, 196, 198
European Parliament 51, 77, 82, 87, 106, 111, 125, 143, 144. 156, 157, 175, 194

FDI 98, 103, 130, 136, 144
France 2, 28, 103, 125, 130, 133, 135, 136, 138, 140, 141, 143, 149, 150, 192, 197
FTAA 27, 39, 47, 63, 122, 126, 127, 145, 177

GATS 73
GATT 17, 99, 101, 123

Gerasimov Doctrine 11
Germany 2, 28, 103, 130, 133, 135, 136, 138, 197
Global Strategy 40, 41
GSP 27, 55, 56–60, 62, 63, 92, 93, 123, 131, 195
Guadalajara Summit 48, 66, 68, 69
Guaidó, Juan 31, 38

High Representative 104, 113, 118
higher education 31, 103, 179–183, 189, 190
Human Rights 11, 26, 28, 32, 33, 26, 51, 52, 54, 56, 72, 75, 81, 103–106, 110
   roadmap 57, 77–79

IADB 14, 37, 88, 89, 115, 150
ILO 79, 82, 85, 93, 140, 162
IMF 2, 3, 6, 10, 18, 23, 192
India 2, 3, 8, 10, 17, 18, 29, 35, 50, 61, 93, 129
intellectual property 17, 20, 67–71, 82, 83, 86, 99, 101, 108, 120, 124, 127, 130, 139, 185
inter-regionalism 4, 5, 18, 24–30, 34–35, 38–41, 44, 46, 52, 53, 60, 66, 70, 98, 100, 117, 119, 124–129, 131, 143–158, 168, 178, 187, 193, 194, 196, 197
   dialogues 31–32
   inter-parliamentary 158–164

Macron, Emmanuel 133, 136, 138, 140, 141, 143, 196
Maduro, Nicolás 13, 31, 38, 39
Mega-regional agreements 9, 18–2, 68, 98–100, 120, 121, 129, 132, 135, 136, 172, 196
MEPs 54, 158, 161
Merkel, Angela 136, 142
Modernised Global Agreement 2, 95–97, 106, 109–111
Mogherini 104, 112
Morales, Evo 47, 49, 50

NAFTA 69, 95, 99–101, 112, 122, 126, 135, 195

OAS 4, 14, 37, 38, 41
Obama, Barack 13, 15, 19, 21, 68, 99, 196
　Obama-Santos Plan 68
OECD 79, 183
　Colombian accession 83, 87
open regionalism 29, 30, 107, 119, 121, 127, 128

Pacific Alliance 8, 14, 29, 82, 120, 127, 172
Panama 13, 14, 26, 43, 93, 175, 176
pandemic 7, 16, 19, 24, 26, 32, 97, 142, 143, 167, 197
Paris Agreement 7, 21, 32, 138, 140, 143, 146, 196
Parlatino 30, 156, 157, 175
Peru 4, 5, 11–13, 19, 24–28, 30, 33–36, 40, 44, 118, 119, 124, 126, 175, 193–195, 197
　Andean states-EU negotiations 47–48, 50–60, 64–70
　FTA with EU 70–86
Portugal 7, 28, 29, 37, 138, 158, 161, 174, 175
procurement 67, 71, 74, 82, 108, 109, 110, 118, 125, 127, 129, 130, 134, 139

Rio Group 26, 27, 176, 178
Russia 2–4, 8–13, 26, 95, 122, 129

SICA 27, 28, 34, 156
SME 88, 106, 186–188
Spain 7, 28, 29, 37, 49, 54, 64, 103, 123, 130, 138, 144, 149, 152, 158, 161, 174, 175, 192, 197

Strategic Partnership 11, 12, 23–25, 30, 32, 42, 69, 94, 95, 102, 106, 110–113, 117, 121, 122, 124, 128, 152, 157, 158, 162, 167, 170, 176, 188

Taiwan 13, 14, 29
TPP 1, 19–21, 68, 99, 100, 120, 132, 135
Trade and Sustainable Development Chapter 79–82, 87, 110
TRIPS 72
Trump, Donald 1, 8, 9, 16, 19, 20, 25, 37, 39, 67, 96, 99, 117, 121, 135, 137, 195–197
TTIP 13, 18, 19, 68, 99, 100, 120, 132, 135

UNASUR 11, 27, 29, 127, 129

vaccine 7, 197, 198
Venezuela 4, 9, 11–13, 15, 16, 26, 30, 31, 47–50, 59, 124, 131, 155, 158, 161, 175, 176, 194
　Andean Community 37–39
　Eurolat 164–168

WTO 1, 16–19, 45, 46, 50, 53, 56, 69, 72, 82, 84–86, 102, 110, 120, 123–129, 131–133, 136, 137, 189
　Doha Round 16, 17, 19, 68, 71, 82, 96–98, 125, 128, 129, 195, 196

EU authorised representative for GPSR:
Easy Access System Europe, Mustamäe tee 50,
10621 Tallinn, Estonia
gpsr.requests@easproject.com